Exploring Ecolinguistics

Bloomsbury Advances in Ecolinguistics

Series Editors:

Arran Stibbe and Mariana Roccia

Advisory Board:

Nadine Andrews (Lancaster University, UK)
Maria Bortoluzzi (University of Udine, Italy)
Martin Döring (University of Hamburg, Germany)
Sue Edney (University of Bristol, UK)
Alwin Fill (University of Graz, Austria)
Diego Forte (University of Buenos Aires, Argentina)
Amir Ghorbanpour (Tarbiat Modares University, Iran)
Nataliia Goshylyk (Vasyl Stefanyk Precarpathian National University, Ukraine)
Huang Guowen (South China Agricultural University, China)
George Jacobs (Independent Scholar)
Kyoohoon Kim (Daegu University, South Korea)
Katerina Kosta (Oxford Brookes University, UK)
Mira Lieberman-Boyd (University of Sheffield, UK)
Keith Moser (Mississippi State University, USA)
Douglas Ponton (University of Catania, Italy)
Robert Poole (University of Alabama, USA)
Alison Sealey (University of Lancaster, UK)
Nina Venkataraman (National University of Singapore, Singapore)
Daniela Francesca Virdis (University of Cagliari, Italy)
Sune Vork Steffensen (University of Southern Denmark, Denmark)

Bloomsbury Advances in Ecolinguistics emerges at a time when businesses, universities, national governments and many other organizations are declaring an ecological emergency. With climate change and biodiversity loss diminishing the ability of the Earth to support life, business leaders, politicians and academics are asking how their work can contribute to efforts to preserve the ecosystems that life depends on.

This book series explores the role that linguistics can play in addressing the great challenges faced by humanity and countless other species. Although significant advances have been made in addressing social issues such as racism, sexism and social justice, linguistics has typically focused on oppression in human communities and overlooked other species and the wider ecosystems that support life. This is despite the disproportionate impact of ecological destruction on oppressed groups. In contrast, this book series treats language as an intrinsic part of both human societies and wider ecosystems. It explores the role that different areas of linguistic enquiry, such as discourse analysis, corpus linguistics, language diversity and cognitive linguistics, can play at a time of ecological emergency.

The titles explore themes such as the stories that underpin unequal and unsustainable industrial societies; language contact and how linguistic imperialism threatens the ecological wisdom embedded in endangered languages; the use of linguistic analysis in ecocriticism, ecopsychology and other ecological humanities and social sciences; and emerging theoretical frameworks such as Harmonious Discourse Analysis. The titles also look to cultures around the world for inspirational forms of language that can lead to new stories to live by. In this way, the series contributes to linguistic theory by placing language fully in its social and ecological context, and to practical action by describing the role that linguistics can play in addressing ecological issues.

Titles published in the series:

Corpus-Assisted Ecolinguistics, Robert Poole
Language and Ecology in Southern and Eastern Arabia, edited by Janet C.E. Watson, Jon C. Lovett and Roberta Morano
Storytelling and Ecology, Anthony Nanson
TESOL and Sustainability, edited by Jason Goulah and John Katunich

Exploring Ecolinguistics
Ecological Principles and Narrative Practices

Douglas Mark Ponton

BLOOMSBURY ACADEMIC
LONDON • NEW YORK • OXFORD • NEW DELHI • SYDNEY

BLOOMSBURY ACADEMIC
Bloomsbury Publishing Plc, 50 Bedford Square, London, WC1B 3DP, UK
Bloomsbury Publishing Inc, 1359 Broadway, New York, NY 10018, USA
Bloomsbury Publishing Ireland, 29 Earlsfort Terrace, Dublin 2, D02 AY28, Ireland

BLOOMSBURY, BLOOMSBURY ACADEMIC and the Diana logo are trademarks of
Bloomsbury Publishing Plc

First published in Great Britain 2024
Paperback edition published 2026

Copyright © Douglas Mark Ponton, 2024, 2026

Douglas Mark Ponton has asserted his right under the Copyright, Designs and Patents Act, 1988, to be identified as Author of this work.

For legal purposes the Acknowledgements on p. xiv constitute an extension of this copyright page.

Series design: Ben Anslow

All rights reserved. No part of this publication may be: i) reproduced or transmitted in any form, electronic or mechanical, including photocopying, recording or by means of any information storage or retrieval system without prior permission in writing from the publishers; or ii) used or reproduced in any way for the training, development or operation of artificial intelligence (AI) technologies, including generative AI technologies. The rights holders expressly reserve this publication from the text and data mining exception as per Article 4(3) of the Digital Single Market Directive (EU) 2019/790.

Bloomsbury Publishing Plc does not have any control over, or responsibility for, any third-party websites referred to or in this book. All internet addresses given in this book were correct at the time of going to press. The author and publisher regret any inconvenience caused if addresses have changed or sites have ceased to exist, but can accept no responsibility for any such changes.

A catalogue record for this book is available from the British Library.

Library of Congress Cataloging-in-Publication Data

Names: Ponton, Douglas Mark, author.
Title: Exploring ecolinguistics : ecological principles and narrative practices / Douglas Mark Ponton.
Description: London ; New York : Bloomsbury Academic, 2024. | Series: Bloomsbury advances in ecolinguistics | Includes bibliographical references and index. | Summary: "In a crucial moment for the global ecosystem, through the use of two case studies this book explores the role of language in mediating and determining our relationship with nature, and in shaping attitudes and social practices in environmental areas. Analysing the discourse of engaged ecological figures, it highlights what we can learn about the environmental visions that sustain their work, and maps out research pathways for informed ecological debate concerning both the planet and the discipline"– Provided by publisher.
Identifiers: LCCN 2023053569 (print) | LCCN 2023053570 (ebook) | ISBN 9781350281424 (hardback) | ISBN 9781350281462 (paperback) | ISBN 9781350281448 (epub) | ISBN 9781350281431 (ebook)
Subjects: LCSH: Ecolinguistics.
Classification: LCC P39.5 .P66 2024 (print) | LCC P39.5 (ebook) | DDC 306.44–dc23/eng/20240304
LC record available at https://lccn.loc.gov/2023053569
LC ebook record available at https://lccn.loc.gov/2023053570

ISBN: HB: 978-1-3502-8142-4
PB: 978-1-3502-8146-2
ePDF: 978-1-3502-8143-1
eBook: 978-1-3502-8144-8

Series: Bloomsbury Advances in Ecolinguistics

Typeset by Deanta Global Publishing Services, Chennai, India

For product safety related questions contact productsafety@bloomsbury.com.

To find out more about our authors and books visit www.bloomsbury.com and sign up for our newsletters.

Do different.
    (Norfolk motto)

Contents

List of Tables	x
Foreword	xi
Acknowledgements	xiv
1 Introduction	1
2 Ecolinguistics, Ecology and the Environment	15
3 Aspects of Ecolinguistic Methodology	43
4 Situated Narratives (1) High Ash Farm and the Countryside Hour	65
5 Situated Narratives (2) Priolo Saltpans	99
6 Conclusion	133
Notes	153
Appendix	163
Bibliography	164
Index	181

Tables

3.1	Stages of a narrative	46
3.2	Jean's treecreeper story	47
3.3	Turtle video, appraisal	56
4.1	Countryside diary	69
4.2	Countryside diary, narrative structure	71
4.3	Countryside Hour story one: 'Success/Failure'	78
4.4	'Success/Failure' narrative structure	78
4.5	Countryside Hour: Ant story (1)	80
4.6	Countryside Hour: Ant story (1), narrative	81
4.7	Countryside Hour: Ant story (1), evaluation	81
4.8	Countryside Hour: Ant story (2)	83
4.9	Countryside Hour: Ant story (2), evaluation	84
4.10	Countryside Hour: Ant story (2), narrative	86
4.11	Countryside Hour: Ant story (3)	87
4.12	Countryside Hour: Ant story (3), narrative	87
4.13	Countryside Hour: Ant story (3), evaluation	88
4.14	Carrion Crows and Pheasants story	90
4.15	Carrion Crow: Narrative structure	91
5.1	The Priolo-Melilli industrial pole	102
5.2	Enel promotion	106
5.3	Enel promotion, narrative structure	108
5.4	The flamingos and the drone	114
5.5	The flamingos and the drone	115
5.6	Cilea flamingo story	119
5.7	Cilea flamingo story: narrative structure	120
5.8	Glass half full	126
5.9	Glass half full: narrative structure	127
6.1	Global boiling headline and framing	134
6.2	In-group judgement evaluation	136
6.3	In-group affect evaluation	137
6.4	Out-group judgement evaluation	138
6.5	Boiling planet, religious terms	140

Foreword

Maria Bortoluzzi

Foreword for the book by Douglas Ponton *Exploring Ecolinguistics*, Bloomsbury Academic.

This book is a bridge between distant areas of the natural world and the human narratives that belong and contribute to them. Through the analysis of narratives 'in place', the volume gives voice to testimonials that resist and challenge the human-induced environmental crisis we are living through. In this book, Ponton gives evidence that, by changing our perspective and envisaging novel pathways, action on the environment can also bring change, initiate a healing process and establish a more balanced relationship in the lifescape.

Ponton has the keen vision of a discourse analyst who well knows and values the contexts he investigates through the voices and narratives that construe them. He considers advantages and contradictions in situated communication and offers the reader innovative perspectives on a variety of settings that become epitomes of an alternative vision, each markedly different and seemingly detached from the others. Crises and past errors become the field for reflection concerning innovative ways to comprehend and narrate the places we inhabit, belong to and contribute to shaping.

The voices summoned in the book (local and international media, local experts' and citizens' reactions and the two extended case studies that testify to resilience and change) are examined by Ponton to capture complexities and establish parallels across worlds: both in ecosystems and in communicative spheres. The two main places narrated in the book could hardly be further apart: High Ash Farm at Caistor St Edmund near Norwich (UK) and Priolo Saltpans Nature Reserve in Sicily (Italy). Ponton's sense of place transforms these case studies into exemplars of his own commitment to Ecolinguistics and deep-seated values of respect for ecosystems. He believes, and shows through his book, that '[t]he long-term aim [of Ecolinguistics] is to contribute to the raising of awareness of the role of language in mediating, controlling and potentially transforming these processes', to bring about more holistic and satisfying relations with nature and the 'more than human world' (Introduction). Ponton pursues this aim by linguistically exploring, analysing and interpreting a variety of discourses which construe these places for different publics; the activities taking place in them and through them, the human and non-human participants contributing to their degradation or well-being and negative and positive forces that contend their spaces and influence change. High Ash Farm and Priolo Saltpans become the protagonists of their own stories through events and participants, voices and counter-voices, in a polyphony of co-constructed meaning where human and non-human transform the ecosystems and themselves in the process.

Ponton focuses on the crucial and ever-present power of narrative to shape and influence our comprehension of the world we inhabit and, ultimately, our action in it. The author intertwines the investigation of narratives instantiated in a variety of written and oral texts in a continuum of complexity: we construe our reality, ourselves and others through the stories, memories and myths that we tell ourselves and so shape our world visions.

As well as across places, this book is also a bridge across disciplines since it draws on theories and analytical frameworks from Ecolinguistics, (positive) discourse analysis, pragmatics and studies on narrative. Its foundations rest on principles of ecosophy such as profound respect for all ecosystems and living beings, and it offers testimony of positive, constructive voices and actions which are alternatives to the ravaging influence of commodification and growthism. As already mentioned, among the many voices represented in this book, two become salient and identified with positive communication and action in the two case study environments of the volume.

One such voice is Chris Skinner's; he is a farmer, naturalist, radio broadcaster and owner of High Ash Farm in Norfolk. Ponton's reflection on Skinner's work and contribution is well in line with the overall aim of the book: Skinner provides 'models for the spread of this "kind of understanding" which, if shared by a critical mass of the population, could effect a real transformation in the kinds of "stories we live by" in modern societies, and hence help the emergence of a range of genuinely sustainable, ecologically-directed social practices' (Section 4.4.4). Through his analysis, Ponton demonstrates how Skinner's public discourse is influential in disseminating an ecological vision that promotes biodiversity and sustainable farming practices as well as respectful communication about the environment.

The second testimonial represents the seemingly impossible mission of recovery and naturalistic protection of an area menaced by the rampant and exploitative policies of a heavily polluting industrial plant nearby. Fabio Cilea is the director of the natural reserve of Priolo Saltpans in Sicily, home and shelter of migrating birds across the Mediterranean Sea and a natural treasure trove adjacent to important archeological sites that date back to Ancient Greece and beyond. Cilea calls the reserve 'an oasis among the smokestacks' (Section 5.1), discursively transforming the ravages of industrialization ('toxic community') into a place of natural beauty where human determination has helped the resilient natural world restore and maintain life in balance. Ponton's analysis of situated narratives shows that the miracle performed by environmentalists has been exploited by industrial stakeholders as part of a greenwashing strategy. He notes that this would better be termed 'pink-washing', since the most relevant local attraction (and flagship species) is the flamingo nesting and breeding in the area. As Ponton mentions, discourses about flamingos intertextually blend and are exploited as commodified corporate image discourses, by powerful stakeholders who need to distance themselves from their own problematic and far from environmentally sound practices.

Ponton looks into the narratives of Skinner and Cilea along with other interrelated opinions, reports, comments on those two situated contexts and gathers evidence of communication and action as 'instances of an inherent ecosophical wisdom' (Section 5.4) that subverts the negative status quo and initiates sustainable change.

Ponton assesses these two voices in the complexity and contradictions of present-day communication, the infosphere that informs our communicative worlds and influences our beliefs. Solutions are not ready-at-hand, perspectives are rendered complex by systemic interrelations and correlations among issues. The two testimonials speak, write and 'act out', embody their narratives within complex and contradictory settings where ecosystems that sustain life are generally valued less than economic gain and the fallacies of 'growthism'. Skinner's and Cilea's narratives are also caringly and carefully contextualized by Ponton through the work they carry out for the local and wider community: their voices become actions which are given individual and collective voices that spread 'ecosophical wisdom' both locally and in the infosphere at large. Words are actions by means of which individual narratives intertwine with community and global narratives, ideally generating biocentric individual and social behaviour.

Acknowledgements

Every effort has been made to trace copyright holders and to obtain their permission for the use of copyright material. However, if any have been inadvertently overlooked, the publishers will be pleased, if notified of any omissions, to make the necessary arrangement at the first opportunity.

The third party copyrighted material displayed in the pages of this book are done so on the basis of 'fair dealing for the purposes of criticism and review' or 'fair use for the purposes of teaching, criticism, scholarship or research' only in accordance with international copyright laws, and is not intended to infringe upon the ownership rights of the original owners.

1

Introduction

1.1 Outline of the book

This book's theme is the damage to ecosystems caused by industrial activity and the ways in which nature finds to thrive in spite of it, issues which appear to be coming to a head in our time. As a species, we have transformed the social landscape through the industrial, agricultural and technological revolutions and created a global village that connects people everywhere as producers and consumers in the structures of a capitalist system. In terms of many indicators of well-being, it is hard to argue with those who claim that we have never had it so good, though the downsides of industrial activity are also many. In this book, the focus is on our relations with the natural world,[1] aspects of contemporary human existence seen as marginal in mainstream social discourse, where the focus is on achieving constant economic growth, to expand continuously the reaches of a nation's productive activity.

Ecolinguistics, as we shall see more fully below, represents the attempts of linguists to share in ecological movements more generally. The long-term aim is to contribute to the raising of awareness of the role of language in mediating, controlling and potentially transforming these processes, to bring about more holistic and satisfying relations with the natural world.

In the book, two specific contexts feature prominently. The first is a farm in the UK, High Ash Farm at Caistor St Edmunds, a few miles south of Norwich. It is run by naturalist Chris Skinner, who has done a BBC local radio programme called the Countryside Hour for upwards of twenty years. In the programme, he mainly talks about things that have happened on the farm during the week, focusing on wildlife events like migratory birds arriving or leaving, badger cubs being born and so on. Skinner describes everything with infectious enthusiasm, from the lives of large predators like buzzards or goshawks to the hibernation of butterflies and the sex lives of ants. The programme is a window on the natural world, from the perspective of a practical farmer who is also a nature activist. All good things come to an end, and sadly the programme went off the air during preparation of this book, though the BBC still carries an extensive collection of recordings available in podcast form.

The second place is a nature reserve near my home in Sicily called Priolo Saltpans, a site that I have been visiting for research over the last ten years. It is situated at the southernmost point of a humongous industrial area, the Priolo-Gargallo petrochemical plant, which stretches from the northern fringes of Siracusa for about 30 kilometres, along the coast towards the city of Catania. More details at the appropriate point; for now, it is sufficient to say that the effects on local ecosystems are devastating and have been well documented. As anyone who has visited Sicily will know, it has splendid coastlines and a rich variety of habitats for Mediterranean flora and fauna. From an ecological perspective, it would be hard to imagine a greater act of ignorant vandalism than to situate a petrochemical plant in that precise spot which, apart from its outstanding natural beauty, was also an important archaeological site, part of 'Magna Grecia' in the days of Archimedes. Yet this was done by the Italian government in the 1950s. The site achieved national fame when, in 2015, communities of migrating flamingos chose to nest and breed at the site. This means that to visit the reserve when the flamingos are present is to view these gorgeous birds against a backdrop of smokestacks that rise across the marshes. The visitor is thus afforded a moving picture of both the enormity of the threat to nature posed by industrial pollution and the fragile beauty of living organisms that manage to find living spaces somehow amid all the mess.

In its way, the story told by High Ash Farm has much in common with that of Priolo-Gargallo. It also concerns the destruction of ecosystems by modern life and tentative paths towards their recovery, protection and eventual rebirth. The methods of modern agriculture, in the case of the farm, play the role of villain because of their deeply anti-ecological practices that homogenize nature, destroy supposedly unproductive ecosystems and spread toxic pesticides over swathes of the countryside.

In both case studies, the emphasis is on narrative, as I analyse how these places are talked about in interviews with the protagonists and in their spoken and written pronouncements concerning the sites. The way we talk about the natural world is central to Ecolinguistics, and a focus on narrative has proven to be a fruitful area for research.

The book is organized as follows: in the first part, I discuss Ecolinguistics and contextualize the book in a background of contemporary issues in social science research. Methodological tools that will be applied in later sections are presented. The two contexts are then described in depth. Linguistic analysis will explore aspects like the construction of eco-narratives, the role of speaker evaluation and other pragmatic features of discourse concerning the environment found in interviews with protagonists and, in the case of High Ash Farm, transcripts of Skinner's radio appearances. Some final comparative observations are made and conclusions drawn.

1.2 Introduction

In 2023, David Suzuki, host of CBC's environmental programme, 'The Nature of Things', announced his retirement from the show after almost forty years, saying:

> I'm in a position of sifting through a lifetime and saying, what have I learned from that that I can pass it on that's my job, and I say to every elder what have you learned from your life? You know I'd like to have retired companies' CEO's, retired economists come out of the woodworks for Christ's sake, and tell us the truth that this economic system is what is driving us into the ditch.[2]

This book assumes the truth of Suzuki's last assertion, but instead of focusing exclusively on such elite social actors, it explores the way ordinary people conceptualize nature through language, and how our understandings of the environment and the natural world affect the way we behave.

Much of what we consider modernity rests on ancient foundations, especially the realities ushered in by the industrial, technological and IT revolutions which today characterize life in Western countries. We have come so far down this particular road that the idea of living without the comforts of an advanced modern society appears unthinkable for many, but we have also reached a point where scientific consensus is calling for a major reassessment. Our current industrial–technical brand of capitalism is simply unsustainable in environmental terms, and in saying this, modern science raises the same concerns that have been voiced since the earliest days of the industrial revolution by Luddites, Romantic poets, Victorian novelists and modern authors, leading up to our own times with its eco warriors and protest movements. In their different ways, such voices have pointed out the negative aspects of the processes that have triumphantly established themselves in industrialized nations – human-driven environmental desolation and species loss, the disruption of traditional livelihoods, the loss of valuable know-how associated with trades, the creation of urban ghettoes and overall a sense of alienation that accompanies humans in modern cityscapes.

In our times, some of the loudest contrary voices against industrial capitalism and its environmental impact have come from poets and musicians. In the influential Anglo-American context, such protest songs have included 'Little Boxes', a hit for US folk-singer Malvina Reynolds in 1962; Joni Mitchell's 'Big Yellow Taxi' (1970), which warned 'you don't know what you've got 'til it's gone'; and Cat Stevens's 'Where Do the Children Play?' (1970), which includes the lines: 'you roll on roads over fresh green grass, for your lorryloads pumping petrol gas'. Fifty years down the road, the lorries are still running faster, further, more numerous and bigger than ever before. Overwhelmingly, environmental voices have not been listened to – not in the sense that they have been allowed to guide public policy, which has continued to encourage the spread of modern structures wherever possible.

The Covid global health crisis in 2019–20 enforced a brief period of reflection. In this interlude of self-isolation, many of the urgent environmental and quasi-philosophical questions that were already raging before global lockdown, thanks to the efforts of climate activists and the affordances of social media, sank into popular consciousness on a deeper level. Escaping for an hour or so from house arrest, people around the world discovered again the simple pleasures that awareness of nature can provide. During the crisis, some people began to question whether the capitalist project was good after all, or whether the sparks that lit the torch of the industrial revolution were kindling flames of eventual, inevitable self-destruction.[3]

In modern societies, the panacea for every social ill is economic activity that produces growth. In a 2013 article in the *Harvard Business Review*, Umair Haque coined the neologism 'growthism' for the current capitalist 'religion', whose central tenet is described thus:

> Growthism contends that growth is the point; the alpha and omega; the sole purpose of all human effort – and therefore, all human effort must be directed towards growth.[4]

Growth is proposed as a value, enshrined in the figures that report a nation's economic performance, which is usually interpreted by mass media as evidence that a certain country is doing better or worse than its rivals (Haque, ibid.). Politicians use the figures to argue either that their policies are working or, if they are in opposition, that their opponents' policies are not. Growthism involves all of us, since it is our passive acquiescence in consumer values that creates what economists call 'demand' for material goods and keeps the machine in a state of constant activity.

As Tawney reminds us, however:

> A reasonable estimate of economic organisation must allow for the fact that, unless industry is to be paralysed by recurrent revolts on the part of outraged human nature, it must satisfy criteria which are not purely economic. (Tawney 1961: 41)

Some things have value but no price. The destruction of habitats because of human industrial activity, continuous cementification and agricultural revolutions in modern times have all contributed to dramatic declines in the populations of birds and other fauna. Whatever the changes in human life might have been during the capitalist-industrial period, from the perspective of the natural world, these processes have been nothing short of disastrous. They have meant the erosion of habitats, escalating rates of species loss and unprecedented global warming. Many once common birds, including house sparrows, starlings and thrushes, as well as other more exotic species, have been added to the 'Red List', which includes species whose numbers have declined more than 50 per cent in twenty-five years. The reasons for the decline, in each case, are varied and hard to identify precisely; however, there can be little doubt that human activity is largely to blame. What would be the cost of eliminating the dawn chorus or of looking skyward in spring and seeing neither swallow nor swift returning from their annual journeys? These, and many other comparable questions, form the burden of Rachel Carson's classic *Silent Spring*, which explores the environmental damage wreaked by modern agricultural methods and especially pesticides:

> Who has decided – who has the *right* to decide – for the countless legions of people who were not consulted that the supreme value is a world without insects, even though it be also a sterile world ungraced by the curving wing of a bird in flight? The decision is that of the authoritarian temporarily entrusted with power; he has made it during a moment of inattention by millions to whom beauty and the ordered world of nature still have a meaning that is deep and imperative. (Carlson 1962: 127)

Carson here echoes Tawney's reflection that there are systems of value which go alongside economic ones, which need to be included in policy deliberations if a balanced outcome is to be achieved. Though significant development projects are occasionally stalled because their pathways coincide with the presence of some breeding butterflies, such occurrences are exceptions to the rule, which is that in a clash between commercial interests and those of the natural world, the former generally win out.[5]

To appreciate what has been excluded in Western societies by our enthusiastic embrace of Cartesian rationalism, we should reflect on the words of Isaiah Berlin, whose work re-emphasizes the importance of certain 'anti-Enlightenment' philosophers:

> Why study the chaotic amalgam of childish stories about the past, still less the passions and crimes of our dark beginnings, when reason can provide true and final answers to the problems which had puzzled our irrational ancestors? Valid knowledge is to be obtained only by the methods of the sciences, which Descartes and his followers contrasted with the unscientific hotchpotch of sense perception, rumour, myth, fable, travellers' tales, romances, poetry and idle speculation that in their view passed for history and worldly wisdom, but did not provide material amenable to scientific, that is, mathematical, treatment. (Berlin and Hardy 2013: 36)

This is not to say, of course, that such things as myth and fable, or poetry, were not still valued in successive ages. However, they were valued in a lesser category, as essentially superfluous embellishments, in no way comparable in importance to the rational empiricism of the natural sciences, and especially mathematics. With the beginnings of the industrial revolution, in late eighteenth-century Britain, came proof of the practical utility of scientific research, which was apparently engaged in a process of discovering truths about the basic mechanisms of nature, to manipulate it for the common good. What has followed, until our own day, has been the unstoppable spread of this victorious ideology, with the results that are evident to all.

The emergent field of Ecolinguistics views language as central in directing the way we think about nature, our environments and the natural world, and hence our relationships with these aspects of our lives. As one of the pioneers in the field, M. A. K. Halliday argues,

> There is a syndrome of grammatical features which conspire – in Martin's term – to construe reality in a certain way; and it is a way that is no longer good for our health as a species. (Halliday 2010: 164)

Halliday provides many examples of this, including the following:

> So we have problems with David Suzuki's formulation *all the kinds of things that forests do.* In English if I say of an inanimate object *what's it doing?* It means 'why is it there? – remove it!' So *what's that forest doing?* implies 'clear it!' rather than expecting an answer such as that it's holding water in store, it's cleaning and moistening the atmosphere, it's stopping flooding, it's stabilizing

> the soil, harbouring life forms and so on. The language makes it hard for us to take seriously the notion of inanimate nature as an active participant in events. (Halliday 2010: 165)

His point is that the origin of such systems of meaning is the assumption that human beings are situated at the centre of creation, that they are the only beings with the capacity to actually perform meaningful actions, while animals, birds, plants, mountains, rivers are less conscious entities driven by instincts or physical laws. As an example of this effect of grammar, he discusses pronouns, where conscious things are referred to as *he/she,* while non-conscious things are referred to as *it* (Halliday 2010: 166). The passage continues:

> More far-reaching, however, is the fundamental distinction made by the grammar of mental processes, where the Senser is always a conscious being: thus a clear line is drawn between entities that understand, hold opinions, have preferences, etc., and those that do not. Non-conscious entities can be a source of information, but they cannot project an idea (we can say *my watch says it's half past ten,* but not *my watch thinks it's half past ten*).[6]

One intriguing possibility for further research could be to explore indigenous languages, to see if there are peoples in the world whose perspectives are not so human-centric, that perhaps construe the natural world as endowed with significant agency (see Section 2.2). This would be to follow in the tracks of the American linguists Sapir and Whorf, whose well-known 'hypothesis' emerged in the context of work among the Hopi (O'Neill 2015).

Ecolinguistics thus assumes that how we speak about the natural world reflects underlying habits of thinking that, especially since the industrial revolution, have increasingly accentuated instrumental understandings. In 1785, Robert Burns could regret that 'Man's dominion' had broken 'Nature's social union', and speak with affection to a mouse, as to an 'Earth-born companion, and fellow mortal'. In his famous poem, he recognizes the creature's right to a home, to shelter from winter, to feed on the farmer's superfluity of grain. Burns' poem, however, is written against a dominant current of thought which was to stigmatize such beasts as 'pests', 'vermin', 'rodents' and to seek their wholesale elimination from industrial farming. Far from returning to any state of 'social union' with the natural world, first world societies are driving forward exploitative ideologies that are based on limited understandings of rich natural diversity and its basic contribution to human happiness and well-being. Ecolinguistics is thus engaged in the search for what Stibbe (2015) calls 'new stories to live by', to recover simpler, more wholesome ways both of relating to the natural world and relating to it.

1.3 The background to Ecolinguistics: George Orwell

Ecolinguistics is a recent branch of socially orientated linguistic studies that applies a wide range of analytical techniques to environmental topics. It is sometimes seen as little more than an extension of the already existing 'school' of critical discourse analysis (hereafter CDA) to ecological issues. CDA, which flourished mainly in British research in the 1980s and 1990s, is a politically engaged approach to linguistic research that explores the relationship between language and society. By highlighting the role of language in perpetuating abuses of power and social ills in general, it aims to bring about social change. For certain studies, it may be fine to situate Ecolinguistics under the CDA umbrella, but if this is all it is, it has little claim to be a separate discipline. Studies that critique the role of language in perpetuating environmental injustice simply figure alongside critical discourse studies of other social evils. There are two senses in which Ecolinguistics appears original and distinct: first, in the fact that it encourages a reflection back on language as an ecosystem, and second, in that it explores what Arran Stibbe calls:

> the role of language in the life-sustaining relationships of humans with other species and the physical environment. (Stibbe 2021: 84)

As we shall see, the scope of such a vision goes beyond a simple focus on the injustices of the capitalist system, taking Ecolinguists into the realms of philosophy and poetry, anthropology and similar areas.

First, however, some reflections on 'language as an ecosystem'. This is not such a new idea; rather, as Haugen (1998: 57) explains, it was once a frequent metaphor for languages:

> In writings of the nineteenth century, it was common to speak of the 'life of languages', because the biological model came easily to a generation that had newly discovered evolution. Languages were born and died, like living organisms.

For such a discussion, a useful starting point is Orwell's 1946 essay 'Politics and the English Language',[7] still relevant for what it also reveals about the origins of CDA. Orwell believed that the English language was in decline, a process driven by mental laziness that permitted ready-made phrases and clichés to dominate discourse, and for euphemism and vagueness to take the place of plain speaking in political circles.

As a committed socialist, Orwell's main concern, like that of the later CDA school, is with social justice rather than with the health, or otherwise, of the

English language. Thus, his main point in the following text is to show how an idea that is unacceptable to describe openly (killing off political opponents in Communist Russia) is rendered less offensive by obscurity and euphemism. Here, the speaker is an academic, a hypothetical apologist for the system:

> While freely conceding that the Soviet regime exhibits certain features which the humanitarian may be inclined to deplore, we must, I think, agree that a certain curtailment of the right to political opposition is an unavoidable concomitant of transitional periods, and that the rigors which the Russian people have been called upon to undergo have been amply justified in the sphere of concrete achievement.[8]

It is interesting, in passing, to observe Orwell's use of metaphors from the natural world, as he reflects on the language:

> A mass of Latin words falls upon the facts *like soft snow*, blurring the outline and covering up all the details.

> When there is a gap between one's real and one's declared aims, one turns as it were instinctively to long words and exhausted idioms, *like a cuttlefish spurting out ink.*[9]

Orwell suggests that language itself may be seen as an ecosystem, polluted and distorted by manipulative, sloppy thinking and downright mendacity. Orwell, indeed, did not develop the ecological connotations very far, beyond using such images, and elsewhere in the essay metaphors like 'natural growth', 'in a bad way' and 'decay' to suggest the organic nature of language. However, it is possible that he put his prescient finger on a relatively underexplored aspect of CDA, that is the effect of socio-political discourse on language itself. Normally, the critical analyst's concern is to oppose some social ill, and the role of language is critiqued insofar as its abuse contributes to the problem. As an example, consider this, from the work of Robert de Beaugrande (2004). It focuses on the euphemistic language used in modernity to describe worker dismissal:

> According to one recent survey of usages (Lutz 1997), workers get 'dehired', 'selected out', 'transitioned', 'surplussed', 'excessed', 'rightsized', 'uninstalled', or 'managed down'; or, they become the objects of 'workforce adjustments', 'headcount reductions', 'negative employee retention' or 'a volume related production schedule adjustment'. Another survey taken from the pages of the New York Times alone reported the workforce being 'downsized', 'rightsized', 'destaffed', 'degrown', 'disemployed', or subjected to 'personnel surplus reduction', 'resource reallocation', 'redundancy elimination', and 'workforce imbalance correction'.

In Orwell's terminology, these phrases allow us to name things without calling up mental pictures of them. What Beaugrande and Lutz (cited here) are doing in their studies is drawing attention to the duplicitous use of language in perpetuating a form of social injustice. What they are not doing is lamenting the pernicious effects of such terms on *language itself*; such a consideration is simply not raised, since it falls beyond the mandate that CDA sets for itself. However, it is easy to see that, according to an aesthetic theory of language such as Orwell's, it would be possible to view what is happening in these instances as a kind of 'de-generation'.

Orwell (ibid.) sets out some rules to guide a renewal of the English language:

Never use a metaphor, simile or other figure of speech which you are used to seeing in print.
Never use a long word where a short one will do.
If it is possible to cut a word out, always cut it out.
Never use the passive where you can use the active.
Never use a foreign phrase, a scientific word or a jargon word if you can think of an everyday English equivalent.
Break any of these rules sooner than say anything barbarous.

The problem with Orwell's recipe is that, in the end, like other prescriptivists, he objects to certain usages that are unpleasing to his own aesthetic tastes, which of course is a wholly subjective matter. He objects to what he calls 'pretentious diction', under which category are listed words I find inoffensive, such as *phenomenon, element, individual (as a noun), objective, categorical, effective, virtual, basis, primary, promote, constitute, exhibit, exploit, utilize, eliminate, liquidate,* as well as *epoch-making, epic, historic, unforgettable, triumphant, age-old, inevitable, inexorable, veritable* and so on. The aesthetic preferences of a single 'individual' – to use, immediately, one of the words Orwell objects to – have always been poor authorities in matters of lexical choice.

However, the notion that language is somehow 'decaying' is persuasive, especially in the social media age, which daily presents us with neologisms, abbreviations, cool terms and original phrases. Like prescriptivists in former times, it is fairly common to find instances of sloppy usage that grate on the ear, leading to the conviction that the language of Shakespeare and Samuel Johnson is indeed approaching a phase of terminal decline. Some years ago, for example, I noticed that the construction 'as far as X is concerned' appears to be slipping towards a new form that simply omits the 'is concerned' part, especially in American speech:

Bret Baier told Fox News viewers: 'I think this is a really dangerous period, as far as what is going to happen between now and January 20.'[10]

Once you notice a phenomenon[11] like this, it is not long before you find yourself listening to the radio with more attention as speakers use the construction, mentally applauding them if they remember to add 'is concerned', cursing them if they fall short. This would seem to be an example of Orwellian language decay, driven by laziness, by a declining attention span or some other reason.

Alternatively, the explanation could simply be that this is another instance of the principle of *usage*, which has always been the authentic driver of language change. In her book about linguistic change, Joan Bybee claims that linguistic structure emerges through language use, and compares language to shifting sand dunes (Bybee 2010: 1–2); language is not like buildings made from concrete or bricks, but something much more fluid.

This is an age-old debate.[12] One of the best-known of all prescriptivists is Henry Fowler, whose *Dictionary of Modern English Usage* (Fowler 2009) can be seen as an attempt to preserve language norms, enshrined in the classical culture of Victorian scholarship, against the multiple voices of modernity. David Crystal's introduction to a recent edition highlights the importance of these issues at that time, which saw poet laureate Robert Bridges and other academics found a 'Society for Pure English'. Crystal (Fowler/Crystal 2009: ix) quotes the founding tract of this society:

> The ideal of the society is that our language in its future development should be controlled by the forces and processes which have formed it in the past; that it should keep its English character, and that the new elements added to it should be in harmony with the old.

The project is a conservative one, which implicitly sees danger in innovation. This example shows how the tendency to look backwards towards a past when things were better linguistically did not begin with Orwell, but recurs throughout the history of a language.

Let us jump forward to 2023, and ask ourselves what these scholars – Orwell included – would make of the language of the netspeak generation. Here are some neologisms, idioms and abbreviations taken at random from the Urban Dictionary website. Many of them use clearly recognizable words (watermelon and sugar, for example), but I think the meanings will be obscure to those outside a specific demographic group:[13] *watermelon sugar, dogshot, sputnik, knockin', nuke the fridge, obnoxion, heels up, yak shaving* and so on. The site usefully provides not just definitions of these terms, but also instances of invented conversations, to show that they all occur in natural language, presumably among the young generation in specific social contexts:

> Star Wars didn't really **nuke the fridge** until Jar Binks was introduced.[14]

The dunes of usage shift under all these terms, some of which will disappear, and some will last; even the English language itself, when once it has outlasted the social conditions which produced and nourished it, may fall into disuse, replaced perhaps by Chinese, by Esperanto or by the tongue of alien invaders from space.

Attempts such as Orwell's to arrest these processes, to somehow keep alive the 'soul' of English, to maintain it or restore it to a hypothetical golden age, appear futile in the long run. More importantly, this is not where I would look for the kind of purification of the linguistic ecosystem with which our discussion began.

Two trends in Orwell's thinking in his essay can be distinguished; the first, that of aesthetic criticism, has already been discussed, and I have said why this may be unsatisfactory. The second is more convincing and regards the ethical/political sphere. His writing here reaches peaks of extraordinary clarity and conviction:

> In our time, political speech and writing are largely the defence of the indefensible. Things like the continuance of British rule in India, the Russian purges and deportations, the dropping of the atom bombs on Japan, can indeed be defended, but only by arguments which are too brutal for most people to face, and which do not square with the professed aims of political parties. Thus political language has to consist largely of euphemism, question-begging and sheer cloudy vagueness. Defenceless villages are bombarded from the air, the inhabitants driven out into the countryside, the cattle machine-gunned, the huts set on fire with incendiary bullets: this is called pacification. Millions of peasants are robbed of their farms and sent trudging along the roads with no more than they can carry: this is called transfer of population or rectification of frontiers. People are imprisoned for years without trial, or shot in the back of the neck or sent to die of scurvy in Arctic lumber camps: this is called elimination of unreliable elements. Such phraseology is needed if one wants to name things without calling up mental pictures of them.

It is easy to find other examples to add to Orwell's list. Perhaps the most notorious of all, from his own time, is the infamous phrase 'final solution', apparently first used by Goering in 1941 to characterize what later became known as the Holocaust, or the attempt to exterminate Europe's Jewish population.[15] Or, consider the phrase 'weapons of mass destruction', which became current in 2003 in the discourse of US president George Bush and British prime minister Tony Blair, who repeatedly advanced a claim, the falsehood of which was later convincingly demonstrated, that Iraqi dictator Saddam Hussein had stockpiled vast quantities of these things and was ready to deploy them. The phrase 'weapons of mass destruction' has a terrifying ring to it and was arguably used by Blair and Bush to garner consensus for war by generating fear in their populations. Yet all nations, including the UK and America, possess weapons of mass destruction, a phrase which could be seen as nothing more than a collective noun for bombs, rifles, machine guns, tanks, grenades, missiles, landmines, battleships, fighter planes and so on.[16]

Another phrase to ponder is 'collateral damage', coined in the 1990s to refer to unintended civilian deaths from military action. In a nuanced discussion, Deborah Cameron (1995) rejects Orwellian interpretations by pointing out that it is impossible to conceive of a truly neutral term, one that would simply describe what has happened without favouritism, sensationalism or ideological bias. However, there is no doubt that the phrase has the potential to conceal or minimize the fact that military action has killed not just enemy soldiers but innocent civilians, which serves the rhetorical ends of those who wage wars:

> This process is fairly effective for taking territory, albeit slow, expensive, and resulting in extensive *collateral damage*. (Vikram Mittal, *Forbes*, 31 July 2022)[17]

Russia's 2022 invasion of Ukraine offers another example of mendacious, Orwellian language use, as President Putin passed laws to ensure that the phrase 'special military operation' should be substituted in the media for any references to 'war' or 'invasion'.[18]

In making people aware of these linguistic practices in political language and highlighting the role of media in their dissemination, Orwell was a forerunner of CDA, one whose work was foundational for critical discourse studies. Regrettably, as these examples show, his work is still highly relevant in the age of social media.

If we try to connect the two aspects of Orwell's linguistic philosophy displayed in *Politics and the English Language*, the one aesthetic, the other critical, an interesting picture emerges. From the former perspective, it might appear that what Orwell desires most in a politician is a direct, plain form of speech that makes equivocation impossible. The politician is apparently to use no 'metaphor, simile or other figure of speech', no 'long words', no complex passive formulations, no 'foreign phrase [...] scientific word or [...] jargon word'. If asked to choose between Barack Obama and Donald Trump then, Orwell would probably select the latter. Obama's language is, for example, highly metaphorical, speaking of 'roads' and 'landscapes', of 'journeys' and 'paths' (Atwater 2007). His diction is rich in most of the features Orwell objects to, while that of Trump has notoriously been identified as comprehensible by nine- to eleven-year-old students (Kayam 2017). When he speaks of 'building a wall', he is not talking metaphorically but literally. Yet this well-known trope of Trump's discourse may illustrate the point here. If we are to pare language down to its simplest elements, what remains may be inadequate to express the complexity of our experience. For a politician, it would mean that, like Trump, they would be compelled to seek solutions that can be expressed in such language; to erase any sense that after all, the problem in question is complicated, in order to bypass the need for linguistic nuance and subtlety. In short, Orwell does not really establish what is, for him, the evident connection between linguistic sophistication and the practice of lying or – to use a more political expression that the writer of 1984 would have scorned – 'being economical with the truth'.

2

Ecolinguistics, Ecology and the Environment

2.1 First steps in Ecolinguistics

According to Zhou (2022), Ecolinguistics celebrated its fiftieth anniversary in 2022, the reference being to a paper from 1972 by Einar Haugen. However, as Zhou herself mentions, this paper is more concerned with the ecology of language than the language of ecology. The natural world is used as a metaphor for what occurs in the realm of a language, rather than vice versa, and his aim is to show that 'languages do have life, purpose, and form' (Haugen 2001 [1972]: 58).

A rough landmark for the appearance of more ecologically focused Ecolinguistics is a 1990 paper by the founder of Systemic Functional Linguistics, Michael Halliday. In this paper he tackles many current ecological issues, and places the human destruction of nature on an agenda for linguistic research.

It had long been argued, among critical linguists, that language and society exist in a mutually constitutive relationship, and this idea supports the notion that linguistics could have relevance in understanding ecological questions. In this view the social fabric and everything within it depends for its shape on the language underlying its creation, which in its turn is profoundly affected by the structures and human behaviour it gives rise to. As Halliday says (Halliday 2010):

> our 'reality' is not something ready-made and waiting to be meant – it has to be actively construed; and that language [has] evolved in the process of, and as the agency of, its construal.

He also focuses on the role of language in promoting an 'ideology of growth or growthism', echoing the theme already touched on above. In the following example, he takes a typical newspaper text regarding an economic report about aviation, and critiques the assumptions that underlie it:

> Its forecast, regarded as one of the most reliable indicators of aviation trends, says airlines will buy 9,935 jet aircraft of all types over the next 15 years at a cost of A$834 billion. It says airline traffic to, from and within the Pacific area will lead the growth with rates unmatched anywhere else in the world. The study says the rationale for a more optimistic outlook includes prolonged air travel expansion driven by continued growth in discretionary income and a decrease in the real cost of travel. *Sydney Morning Herald*, 12 March 1990 (Halliday, ibid..: 161)

Halliday comments:

> Everything here, and in countless other such texts repeated daily all round the world, contains a simple message: growth is good. Many is better than few, more is better than less, big is better than small, grow is better than shrink, up is better than down. Gross National Products must go up, standards of living must rise, productivity must increase.

The notion that humans are somehow hard-wired to think that 'growth is good' recalls conceptual metaphor theory, where Lakoff and Johnson (2003) argue that we conceive of 'up as good' thanks to bodily memories of infancy where the toddler attempts to stand, enthusiastically encouraged by parents and relatives. In like manner, manifestations of bodily growth tend to be celebrated during childhood. Thus, in Halliday's words, 'the motif of "bigger and better" is engraved into our consciousness' (ibid.: 165).

As well as the 'lexis of growth', Halliday critiques the grammar system in English, which encodes human-centric understandings that are less than perfectly ecological. For example, that non-conscious entities lack any capacity for thought or, in Halliday's terminology, that 'the Senser is always a conscious being' (ibid.: 166). We can say *my watch says it's half past ten*, but not *my watch thinks it's half past ten*. The ecological consequences of this are far-reaching:

> it imposes a strict discontinuity between ourselves and the rest of creation, with 'ourselves' including a select band of other creatures that are in some semantic contexts allowed in – the most typical of these being first our farm animals and now our highly destructive pets. And, of course, it totally excludes the concept of Gaia – of the earth itself as a conscious being. The grammar makes it hard for us to accept the planet earth as a living entity that not only breathes but feels and even thinks: that maintains its own body temperature despite massive changes in the heat that it receives from the sun, and that dies slowly but inevitably as each of the living species that compose it is destroyed.

2.2 Ecology, shallow and deep

Studies in the field that came to be known as Ecolinguistics followed up some of these insights (see, e.g., Fill 2001; Fill and Mühlhäusler 2001; Fill and Penz 2018; Stibbe 2012, 2014, 2015). To a degree, Halliday and other ecolinguists reflected the mood of the age, which already in the 1990s was alive to the need to remodel human thought and behaviour.

In his book on religion and environmental crisis Roger Gottlieb lists eight areas critically affected by unchecked industrial capitalism: *Global climate/atmospheric change, toxic wastes, loss of land, loss of species, loss of wilderness, devastation of indigenous peoples, human patterns and quantities of consumption* and *genetic engineering* (Gottlieb 2004: 5–6). The ecological movement itself is a reaction to all this, part of an awakening to the Anthropocenic effects of modern man on the biosphere (Ponton and Sokół 2022).

One of its early proponents, Norwegian philosopher Arne Naess, distinguished two forms of ecology, 'shallow' and 'deep':

1. The Shallow Ecology movement. Fight against pollution and resource depletion. Central objective: the health and affluence of people in the developed countries.
2. The Deep Ecology movement: Rejection of the man-in-environment image in favour of the relational, total-field image. Organisms as knots in the biospherical net or field of intrinsic relations. [. . .] The ecological field-worker acquires a deep-seated respect, or even veneration, for ways and forms of life. He reaches an understanding from within, a kind of understanding that others reserve for fellow men and for a narrow section of ways and forms of life. (Naess 1973: 95–6)

The former kind of ecology encompasses governmental measures to protect the quality of living in industrial nations, such as 'clean air' acts (in the UK 1956, in the United States 1963), 'clean water' acts (United States 1972, UK 1991) or a provision of Article 3 of the Treaty on European Union, which aims at a 'high level of protection and improvement of the quality of the environment'[1]. However, such environmental goals are basically self-serving and human-centric, motivated by the fact that affluent Westerners dislike living in a dirty, smelly environment. They recognize the necessity to rein in the worst excesses of free-market industrialism and accept loss of profitability as a necessary evil.

What is missing from this conception is any reference to the natural world, or suggestion that nature may have purposes of its own that do not centrally concern us. Naess's views situate humanity with the other animals in a 'biospherical net' where the latter are 'respected' or 'venerated'.

These positions are familiar among certain indigenous cultures, which have ancient traditions and origin stories that exist beyond the narratives of Judeo-Christianity and Greco-Roman rationalism that have dominated in the industrial West (Mead 1932; Stringer 1999; Praet 2014). The conflict between such cultures and the current mindset of globalized capital is apparent from numerous case studies such as this one, reported by Robinson et al. (2021: 4):

> The ongoing stewardship of restorative ideals over many generations is in stark contrast to the colonial ideals and mindsets that have pervaded since the colonization of Indigenous lands. The Maralinga Tjarutja people, for example, tell stories of sustaining themselves on the Ooldea soak for 60,000 years (Brockwell et al. 1989), whereas it took only 60 years from colonization for the precious water source in Australia's desert outback to be ruined by western practices.

In 'This Sacred Earth', Gottlieb reprints many testimonies to ecological sensibilities expressed in the traditional religious cosmologies and practices of, to list a few, Native American, Hindu, Aztec, Greek, Sumerian, Chinese, Hebrew, Arabic, Hawaiian, Thai, Indian, African, Native Australian, African and Malay groups of peoples. The stories reveal an extraordinary variety of cultural and religious aspects but have in common Naess's 'deep ecological' perspective, the respect and veneration for all forms of life and a sense of humans' belonging in a 'biospherical web'. For example, Gottlieb cites an earlier study Gottlieb cites Dudley (2004) concerning Hawaiian traditions. Dudley distinguishes between traditional knowledge and modes of experience of nature and those that prevail in the modern West:

> In the Western world, where the cleavage is most pronounced, animals are disdained as having senses but no reason; the plant world is recognized as alive, but in no way even aware; and the elements of the cosmos are treated as inert objects that follow mechanical laws. Hawaiians, on the other hand, view all these beings as sentient ancestral forms that interrelate with them as family. Therefore, they experience reality differently because of these views. (Dudley, ibid.)

The following animistic sentiments, also found in accounts from the other contexts mentioned, were clearly still powerfully present in Hawaii, at least until recent times:

> In ancient Hawai'i, humans, gods, and nature formed a consciously interacting and interrelating cosmic community. All the species of nature were thought to be sentient – capable of knowing, choosing, and acting. Through evolution, all were related as kin. Hawaiians lived in a community in which humans, gods, and nature cared for one another and watched over and protected one another as family. (Dudley, ibid.)

The profound sense of relatedness that unites all living beings, human and non-human, is manifest in the following anecdote:

> If one meets a Hawaiian fisherman loading his nets and gear into his truck, he never asks if the man is going fishing. He might ask if the man is going *holoholo* (out for a ride) or he might ask if he is going to the mountains. But if he asks if the man is going fishing, the man will remove his gear out of the truck, and that will be the end of fishing for the day. For the fish will 'hear' and know that the fisherman is coming, and they won't be there when he gets to the sea. (Gottlieb, ibid.: 111)

Dudley provides another striking illustration of the traditional Hawaiian mindset, claiming that for a Hawaiian there would be no difference in opening a door to a shed containing tin cans to opening one where an audience are listening to a lecture. There would be no sense of embarrassment in the latter situation, nor of inert contact in the former. For the Hawaiian, he says, there are no 'empty storerooms'. He writes: 'Confronting the world about them, they experience conscious beings at every turn' (Dudley ibid.: 114). Thus, the concept of 'natural world' is extended to objects considered inanimate in a Western worldview.[2]

Such attitudes may be found in anthropological work among primitive peoples, but they also occur in the literature of so-called developed countries. Stibbe (2007), for example, discusses the Japanese poetry form, *haiku*, which frequently focuses on animals or plants. As he says, the choice of such non-human subjects for a prestigious art form is an implicit tribute to their importance for writers and readers:

> By taking ordinary plants and animals, and giving them a prime position within a highly appreciated cultural art form, haiku give the message that they are important for themselves, with no need to recourse to abstractions such as the 'intrinsic value of nature' used in the discourse of deep ecology. (Stibbe 2007: 104)

Shallow ecology, then, may confirm habitual exploitative relations and practices, since it is based only on a superficial concern for the environment as far as it provides a backdrop to the only significant stage, that is that of human events. Deep ecology, by contrast, acknowledges the importance not just of animals but of the entire extra-human world.

2.3 Some recent studies in Ecolinguistics

Some recent ecological and ecolinguistic studies have tried to redress the disdain in which the natural world is typically held in the modern West. Ross (2019) considers the possibility that 'personhood' may be found outside the human world and considers the case of elephants. He provides samples of behaviour that support the notion that they could have 'conscious narrative selves' (Ross, ibid.: 15), though also recognizes the limitations of such conclusions.

In general, as he acknowledges, human investigations of attempts to teach animals recursive syntax have yielded 'dismal' results (Ross, ibid.: 8). Such studies have been limited by the anthropocentric nature of their assumptions about language, that is that chimps or parrots must learn to speak a human language, rather than the other way around. Some evidence confirms that communication with animals is possible but requires the human partner to make the effort to adapt to the animals' realities (see, e.g., the work of Konrad Lorenz, described in Lorenz and Wilson (2002)). There are occasional apparent breakthroughs, as in the case of Irene Pepperberg, who achieved conversational exchanges with her parrots Alex and Griffin.[3] Studies have also demonstrated that, though they may not be able to talk to humans, birds 'talk' to each other. Suzuki (2016), for instance, showed that the Japanese Great Tit uses a differentiated alarm call for two predator types, thus conveying a nuanced message. Thompson (2019) cites research showing that a variety of animals display human-like qualities: dolphins have individual names for each other, hyraxes speak different socially learned languages, octopi are playful and learn quickly from one another, fish use tools and so on. Whether they demonstrate human-like behaviour or not, there is thus recognition in some scientific circles that, as Kohn (2013) puts it, 'living beings are loci of selfhood'.

There are, as yet, few ecolinguistic studies that actively explore the relationship of man with animals and the natural world (Stibbe 2003, 2005, 2007; Milstein 2007, 2012; Mitchell 2012). As an example of such research, Milstein (2012) presents a critical analysis of an episode at a zoo, when a young gorilla bangs on a glass panel to attract the attention of a group of visiting children, producing a moment of 'equivalence, empathy and reaching across the divide' (Milstein 2012: 177).

Most ecolinguistic studies tend to critique our mistreatment of the natural world (Fill and Mühlhäusler 2001; Vasta 2005; Stibbe 2012, 2015; Fill and Penz 2018), for example in the meat industry (Fiddes 2004; Glenn 2004; Mitchell

2013; Stibbe 2015; Fairlie 2010, etc.). Even in a study such as that just mentioned by Milstein, which does foreground animals as thinking and feeling subjects, the author's main focus appears to be to critique both zoos as institutions and the guide, whose language euphemizes some realities, omits others, in order to convey an ideal image of human–gorilla relations which the unruly young ape disrupts.

One of Stibbe's books (2015) foregrounds, among other critical tools, the idea of 'erasure', introduced in a seminal study of representation of social actors by Van Leeuwen (1996). The notion accounts for the way that texts can suppress, background or exclude participants, play down their roles, effectively erasing them as significant agents in social situations. In the following example, from the context of safaris, Stibbe shows how the specific grammatical choice effectively 'erases' the individual animals involved:

> 'We saw giraffe, elephant, and lion', instead of 'We saw giraffes, elephants, and lions.' Using mass nouns instead of count nouns removes the individuality of the animals, with the ideological assumption that each animal is just a (replaceable) representative of a category. (Stibbe 2015: 24)

By referring to an animal in terms of the meat it is associated with (*pork, ham, veal, sausages, beef, chicken*) instead of with its species name, the individual animals are again erased. In meat industry discourse, they become 'livestock', a 'herd' or 'animal units', part of a 'swine enterprise', a 'pork production enterprise' and so on (Stibbe, ibid.: 41).

2.4 Ecolinguistics and metaphor

Recent Ecolinguistic studies have also devoted critical attention to environmental or ecological metaphors (e.g. Meisner and Takahashi 2013; Väliverronen 1998; Goatly 2006; Keulartz 2007; Larson 2011). Metaphor has emerged as a key element in cognitive linguistic studies since the appearance of Lakoff and Johnson's groundbreaking 'Metaphors we live by' in 1980 (Lakoff and Johnson 1980/2003). The authors argue, persuasively, for metaphor as a basic factor in our mental make-up that mediates and controls the way we interpret and respond to the world. They suggest that basic emotional states such as happiness or depression are both experienced, and communicated, metaphorically (*high as a kite, over the moon, on cloud nine, in seventh heaven, things are looking up; lower* than a snake's belly, beneath the underdog, down in the dumps, at rock bottom, flat as a pancake, etc.).

Metaphors structure our mental models of reality and influence our behaviour, including with respect to the natural environment; as (Keulartz 2007) says, if we see nature as a 'divine text' we may be less controlling towards it than those who regard it as a 'machine'.

From a critical point of view, Arran Stibbe identifies metaphors that conflict with deep ecological wisdom, for example the countless ways in which 'pig' features in metaphors with negative meanings (*greedy pig, drunken swine, unscrupulous swine, fascist pig, fat pig, male chauvinist pig*, etc.). This is not just the case for the unlucky pig, however. As Goatly (2006: 28) showed, the following categories of animals are all associated with negative metaphors: *mammals, cows, sheep, monkeys, dogs, cats, horses, rodents, reptiles, insects, fish, birds, chickens* and *waterbirds*.[4] Like other researchers, Stibbe lists harmful metaphors for nature such as that nature is a *competition, battle, struggle, war* (Stibbe 2015: 68). These conceptions of nature reflect Darwin's influential view of evolution, which popularized concepts such as 'natural selection' and 'survival of the fittest'. At the level of everyday social interactions, as Larson (2011: 75, in Stibbe ibid.: 68) says, this way of thinking slips easily into neoliberal consumerist ideology:

> not only is competition found in societies, but we should actively promote it because it is the way the world works – it is natural.

Another commonly encountered harmful metaphor sees nature as a *machine* (Stibbe 2015: 69). One such metaphor was used by the eighteenth-century philosopher, clergyman William Paley, who argued that the sheer complexity of ecosystems ruled out the role of chance in their creation, and thus God, the 'blind watchmaker', was invoked as a necessary first cause. The negative implications of the machine metaphor, from a deep ecological perspective, are pointed out by Verhagen (2008: 11, in Stibbe, ibid.: 69):

> Nature as a machine and its variant Nature as a storehouse justifies the exploitative and managerial character of Western civilisation, making it seem natural, obvious and normal.

As has been pointed out already, metaphors are no longer thought of in an Aristotelian sense, as decorative resources to adorn a speech and provide aesthetic pleasure. Their role in persuasive discourse, whether it is found in courtrooms, parliaments, advertisements or mass media, is increasingly recognized. These last two metaphors illustrate connections between human cognition – the ideas people have about the world – and behaviour, how these are applied in action. As Goatly points out, it is also possible to 'die' by metaphors (Goatly 1996).

Stibbe also emphasizes alternative metaphors that can be used in positive representation patterns, and thus encourage more holistic relations with the natural world:

> Ecolinguistics can play a role in [. . .] searching for novel metaphors which encourage behaviour that protects the ecosystems that support life, and promoting those metaphors so that they can become new metaphors we live by. (Stibbe 2015: 81)

Some of these metaphors see nature as an organism, a patient, a person, a woman, a work of art, a library and a web. To see nature as a 'patient', for example, encourages us to look after it, to take care of it, to heal it and so on although, as Stibbe points out, it also tends to exclude non-specialists from involvement in these actions. The 'web' of life originated with Native American chief Seattle, who is supposed to have said:

> Humankind has not woven the web of life. We are but one thread within it. Whatever we do to the web, we do to ourselves. All things are bound together. All things connect. (Stibbe, ibid.: 72)

These words express meanings familiar in native America, where they shaped the relations of a whole society with the natural world. The question is how they can be made relevant to worlds such as our own, where the logic of consumerism is so deeply engrained – whether it would be possible for modern Westerners to live by a metaphor like this.

2.5 Ecolinguistics and the natural imaginary

The concept of 'imaginary' occurs across the social sciences, as a way of theorizing social perceptions of phenomena. It concerns the way individuals and societies understand aspects of the real world, from shopping choices to attitudes to immigrants or the existence of God. Imaginaries depend on exposure to ideas that circulate within social groups, are handed down from influential others, appear in mass media and are repeated across social media and so on. The concept has several dimensions and may relate to:

- a culture's ethos or a society's shared, unifying core conceptions;
- a fantasy or illusion created in response to a psychological need;
- a cultural model or widely shared implicit cognitive schema. (Salazar 2012: 864)

Summarizing, Salazar thinks of imaginaries as 'socially transmitted representational assemblages that interact with people's personal imaginings and are used as meaning-making and world-shaping devices' (Salazar ibid.: 864).

As an example of an imaginary, we can consider the case of smoking, which in Western society today is considered a type of antisocial, cancer-inducing drug addiction. Smokers are made to huddle in tiny glass cubicles at airports and cannot even vape publicly because of the apparent dangers of 'passive smoking'. These attitudes towards smokers reflect all three of Salazar's categories, and the imaginary is a useful concept because it unites the private ideas of the individuals that make up a society with more general social attitudes that determine laws and policies, with the *zeitgeist*, the spirit of the times:

> Non-smokers describe smoking as 'a disgusting habit' and smokers as 'outcasts' and 'lepers' marked by their smell ('reek', 'stink', 'stale') and appearance ('dirty', 'brown teeth', 'grey, dry, wrinkly skin'). (Graham 2012)

Yet smoking has venerable traditions as a palliative to the cares of life, as a social ritual, as an ecological and religious act in many indigenous cultures. These conceptions have passed down through centuries from the first moments of contact between the Spanish and Elizabethan explorers and Native American smokers:

> It was smoking, the burning of the herb to produce smoke, that quickly became part of a priestly healing ritual both to diagnose and cure illness, as well as to drive out the evil spirits that had supposedly caused it. (Gilman and Zhou 2004)

In the twentieth century era of mass production, marketing and advertising, cigarettes became a gigantic industry. The imaginary of smoking was linked to a string of assertive, rebellious heroes like James Dean and Humphrey Bogart, by relentless advertising, which also permeated Hollywood films. The ecological connotations of smoking, and an alpha male image, were personified by the 'Marlboro man', a cowboy whose outdoor lifestyle included a pack of cigarettes that seemed, 'naturally',[5] to accompany the horse and the cowboy hat. In the 1950s, the tobacco companies even launched a campaign in America to promote the health benefits of smoking, *More doctors smoke camels* (White et al. 2012).

There are links between the imaginary and the real, in the sense that these ideas and their connotations condition the enactment of legislation on specific issues. For many years, tobacco companies were obliged to print a 'government health warning' on cigarette packets in the UK, to the effect that 'smoking can seriously damage your health'. As attitudes have hardened, recent years have seen significant changes in anti-smoking messages printed on packets, including graphic colour images of damaged lungs and more worrying messages, required by EU law in 2014, such as:

'Smoking kills – quit now' or 'Smoking kills'[6]

The imaginary associated with pipe smoking is more reflective, associated with wizards like Tolkien's Gandalf, or detective Sherlock Holmes by the Baker Street fireside, pondering a 'three pipe problem'.

In the area of ecology, we can therefore think of attitudes to nature as helping to create imaginaries that reflect deep or shallow ecologies, or a complete absence of ecological thinking. These constructs help us to understand the state of public thinking about environmental issues as it has developed through time.

Before looking at ecological imaginaries, a word about their opposites, that is 'un-ecological' or 'anti-ecological' imaginaries. Anthropocentrism may be regarded as a legacy of Judeo-Christianity, the dominant religion in Europe for the past two millennia. Man – the Bible stresses the male gender – was supposedly made 'in the image' of God, and by him given 'dominion' over the natural world:

> And God said, Let us make man in our image, after our likeness: and let them have dominion over the fish of the sea, and over the fowl of the air, and over the cattle, and over all the earth, and over every creeping thing that creepeth upon the earth. (Gen. 1.26–27)

This supposition was a factor in the Elizabethan world picture (Goatly 2006; Tillyard 1960), which conceived of a hierarchy of being as follows: God/Angels/Man/Animals/Plants/Minerals.

It is not easy to identify such explicitly anti-ecological imaginaries in the contemporary mediascape, in the adverts of multinational corporations, in government pronouncements, where the need to appear 'environmentally friendly' currently seems to dominate. For example, under the right-wing Brazilian president Jair Bolsonaro, an area of the Amazon forest the size of Belgium was destroyed by fire.[7] Bolsonaro was well-known as a climate change denier, but his words here explicitly recognize the global importance of the Amazon:

'We understand the importance of the Amazon for the world – but the Amazon is ours. There will not be any more of that sort of policy that we saw in the past that was terrible for everyone', he said. 'We preserve more [rainforest] than anyone. No country in the world has the moral right to talk about the Amazon. You destroyed your own ecosystems.'[8]

Far from justifying the burning of trees, or downplaying its significance to the climate, both of which might have been expected of a denier, his words could be construed as expressing a shallow ecological sensibility. Considering that most Western nations were also once entirely covered with forests, the accusation of hypocrisy is not altogether unfounded.

Or consider the website of Shell, an oil company in the frontline of human destructive exploitation of Earth's non-renewable resources, one which has been responsible for numerous environmental tragedies over the years. They do not advocate, for example, an ideology that justifies an element of environmental damage for the sake of the benefits of the oil they extract. On the contrary. On one page we find words like *sustainability, cleaner energy solutions, social considerations, climate change, the environment, diversity and inclusion, human rights, net-zero emissions, respecting nature, protecting the environment, making a positive contribution to biodiversity*.[9] By these means, Shell present themselves as a company that is fully socially and environmentally aware and responsible:

> We aim to provide more and cleaner energy solutions in a responsible manner – in a way that balances short- and long-term interests, and that integrates economic, environmental and social considerations.

They position themselves as on board with current environmental legislation:

> We fully support the Paris Agreement's goal to keep the rise in global average temperature this century to well below two degrees Celsius above pre-industrial levels and to pursue efforts to limit the temperature increase even further to 1.5 degrees Celsius. We have set a target to become a net-zero emissions energy business by 2050 or sooner.

This well-known business strategy has been called 'greenwashing' (Greer and Bruno 1996); companies frame themselves as environmentally friendly because of the tremendous social cachet of the ideology. The point to note however is that, if even environmental desecrators like multinational oil companies are posing as environmentalists, then some version of an ecological imaginary must have achieved a kind of discursive hegemony.

For a truly harmful imaginary, in the sense of Naess and Stibbe, it is necessary to go back to the beginnings of mass production in the late nineteenth century and the global spread of Fordism (Jessop 1992). The coming world of mass consumption of industrial products was hailed in Italy by the Futurists:

> Marinetti envisaged Futurism as a preparation of 'the imminent, inevitable identification of man with his motorcar, so as to facilitate and perfect an unending exchange of intuitions, rhythms, instincts, and metallic discipline, absolutely unknown to the majority and only guessed at by the brightest spirits'. (Lazareva 2018)

Marinetti envisaged these transformations as the birth of a new consciousness to be attained only by the few, but the masses were brought on board soon enough.

It is easier to delineate the origins and outlines of environmentally friendly imaginaries, which increased significantly in the period of the industrial and agricultural revolutions, as artists and writers across Europe turned to the natural world (Cloudsley 1990). This occurred in response to the first appearances of industrial pollution, to rural unemployment driving the labour force from the land, to over-crowding in city slums, to the manifold social issues that arose in consequence, the natural world was hymned in Romantic poetry. From 1804, for example, came Wordsworth's 'the Daffodils', still one of Britain's best-loved and most quoted poems:

> I wandered lonely as a cloud
> That floats on high o'er vales and hills,
> When all at once I saw a crowd,
> A host, of golden daffodils;
> Beside the lake, beneath the trees,
> Fluttering and dancing in the breeze.

Wordsworth and other Romantic poets describe nature and its objects – trees, lakes, flowers, hills, mountains, caves, canyons, valleys, sunlight, clouds, sea, waves, wind – in broad brush strokes, as in this example. In some of Romanticism's most celebrated poems, nature becomes a sort of comfort blanket for a childhood that experiences the divinity through contact with it:

> Piping down the valleys wild,
> Piping songs of peasant glee,
> On a cloud I saw a child,
> And he, laughing, said to me:
> 'Pipe a song about a lamb!' (William Blake)

Of all the Romantics, the pantheistic sentiment is most clearly and frequently expressed by Wordsworth:

> I have felt; A presence that disturbs me with the joy; Of elevated thoughts; a sense sublime; Of something far more deeply interfused – A motion and a spirit, that impels; All thinking things, all objects of all thought; And rolls through all things. (Tintern Abbey)

> The earth, and every common sight; To me did seem; Apparell'd in celestial light. (Ode: Intimations of immortality)

> To every natural form, rock, fruit or flower; Even the loose stones that cover the highway; I gave a moral life: I saw them feel. (The Prelude)

These lines project the essential features of a Romantic natural imaginary. Indeed, in the last fragment, with its recognition of the 'moral life' even of inanimate natural objects like rocks and stones, the writer expresses an animistic sentiment that is, in some sense, akin to traditional worldviews of the Hawaiian type discussed above. Romantic poetry offered humanity 'a vision of nearly sacred wholeness to replace the apparently fractured vision of contemporary being' (Oerlemans 2002). This vision left traces that have lasted until the present time, and still resurface briefly, for example when Jerusalem is sung, with its evocation of England's 'green and pleasant land'.

The modern period, especially since the 1960s, has seen fully fledged ecological protest movements take off, such as Friends of the Earth, Greenpeace, Extinction Rebellion and Just Stop Oil. Thus, it becomes possible to speak of 'ecological imaginaries', images that refer to various discourses and engage with social attitudes on environmental issues, with the aim of disseminating green ideologies at a popular level (Ponton 2022b). These may regard animals suffering from various problematic manifestations of industrial pollution, for example seabirds covered with spilled crude oil, turtles struggling to be free from plastic refuse or polar bears on shrinking ice flows (Ponton 2023).[10]

In their book on visual design, Kress and Van Leeuwen (2020) say that 'the gaze of represented participants directly addresses the viewers and so establishes an imaginary relation with them'. Though their work is intended to illuminate artistic genres like portraiture and human photography, the words apply equally in a case like this, where the creature engages with the viewer on a footing of equality. This is the first implicit 'meaning' we can find in the image of the polar bear on ice, which is carefully constructed. By copying the generic traditions of posed human photographs or fine art portraits, the photographer confers the same kind of dignity on this non-human figure that a human subject possesses. As occurs with the interpretation of human photos, the image activates certain questions and trains of thought in the viewer. We cannot help noticing that the bear is balancing on an ice floe that is presumably shrinking all the time, and this realization triggers memories of discourses that are circulating in society at large through the news, in social media and so on. Whatever the degree of their environmental awareness, viewers activate background notions such as: *the arctic ice and glaciers are steadily melting; this is due to global warming, which is down to CO_2 emissions; the polar bears are under increasing pressure; they now turn up in unusual places like the edges of cities.* Such social knowledge is necessary for viewers to understand the image at all, and in order not to have these cognitive cues at their fingertips, viewers in a Western society would need to live lifestyles of almost total media deprivation. What the image also does, which elevates it to the status of an ecological 'imaginary', is to engage viewers with deontic propositions. In other words, it not only uses the camera's visual potentialities to show us what 'is', it also suggests what 'ought' to be done about it (Searle 1964). The polar bear's mute gaze contains a tacit accusation and implores specific solutions: you *are* all responsible for my suffering, you *should* all pull together to stop global warming, you *can* make a difference, you *must* act quickly or not just my habitat but all natural habitats will disappear and so on.

This imaginary may be thought of as a 'deep ecological' imaginary, since it rests on assumptions of the following kind: humans are not at the top of a hierarchy of creation but occupy a place alongside the natural world in a living web, a community of beings. If we have the intelligence to create technological devices, it seems appropriate that we should use that intelligence to ensure that the web of life is not harmed by them. The unfolding ecological drama is usually viewed primarily as a human tragedy, that is it is feared because it could mean the end of everything our civilizations rest on. Photos like this suggest that the consequences to the natural world are equally tragic. In this deep ecological perspective, members of the natural world reappear as significant actors whose well-being is a matter for concern.

2.6 Positive discourse analysis

Ecolinguistics has connections with another recently emergent paradigm, positive discourse analysis (Stibbe 2017; Ponton 2022a). Positive discourse analysis, like Ecolinguistics itself, has origins in the work of Michael Halliday and, as its name suggests, it exists in a relation of contrast to the movement which has already been mentioned in several places above, *critical* discourse analysis (Fowler et al. 1979; Kress and Hodge 1979; Fairclough 2015). A few more words about CDA will help us better understand its positive cousin (from now on, *PDA*).

Van Dijk (2001: 352) explains that CDA is concerned with how 'social power abuse, dominance, and inequality are enacted, reproduced, and resisted by text and talk'. Something of the excitement of the early days of CDA is captured in the following quote from Kress (1996: 15), who claims that the intention was to

> bring a system of excessive inequalities of power into crisis by uncovering its workings and its effects through the analysis of potent cultural objects – texts – and thereby to help in achieving a more equitable social order.[11]

These researchers clearly believed in the power of discourse to shape the social world. They shared George Orwell's faith that to shine light on obfuscatory, corrupt or misleading discourse – in terms of the ecology of language discussed above (Section 1.3), in order to revitalize and cleanse language itself – would help improve society.

Critics observed, at quite an early stage, that this approach is flawed because it is the analyst who themselves define what counts as a social injustice, and this may not be the optimum mindset to perform objective, 'scientific' analysis (Widdowson 2004; Bartlett 2012). CDA thus presupposes that there is general agreement on what constitutes a social injustice or an abuse of power, which of course may not be the case. The temptation is thus for the analyst to select data that confirms their own ideological positions on the issue and ignore other data that may not.

It was also criticized by Noam Chomsky, who felt that academic studies were an ineffective tool to achieve social change. The works of academics, he argued, have little effect on public opinion outside the ivory towers of academia and that, if they want to change the world, to go on demonstrations would be a much better use of their time (Beaugrande 1991).

In response to a feeling that, for these and other reasons the project was not delivering on its promises, some research began to shift the emphasis away from a simple focus on the problem towards its possible solution(s). For example, Chouliaraki and Fairclough (1999: 60, in Bartlett 2012) outlined the following steps for CDA which, in essence proposed to study:

1. A problem.
2. Obstacles to it being tackled.
3. Function of the problem in the practice.

4. Possible ways past the obstacle.
5. Reflection on the analysis.

The aim is to accompany critique of a social problem with practical suggestions for its solution, in an attempt to make linguistic research relevant outside the confines of academia.

In the early 2000s, perhaps in response to a sense that there were some serious issues with the project of CDA, the positive approach was fleshed out in some prominent publications, mainly by James Martin (Martin 1999, 2004; Martin and Rose 2003).

On the one hand, Martin clearly sees benefit to the analyst in this kind of work and recommends that the focus should be on 'discourse that inspires, encourages, heartens, discourse we like, that cheers us along' (Martin 1999: 51–2). On the other, he reaffirms the social constructivism of the emerging paradigm, and argues that, after all, a more effective means of bringing about social change could be to stress the positive note rather than continually harp on about negatives:

> The lack of positive discourse analysis [. . .] cripples our understanding of how change happens, for the better, across a range of sites – how feminists re-make gender relations in our world, how indigenous people overcome their colonial heritage, how migrants renovate their new environs and so on. And this hampers design and perhaps even discourages it since analysts would rather tell us how the struggle was undone than how freedom was won. (Martin 2004: 182)

For ecolinguists the way is thus open for in-depth approaches to environmentally sound discourse such as the examples provided above (Sections 2.2.ii, 2.3.iii, 2.4.iv, 2.52.v.), to discourse that embodies aspects of a deep ecological perspective.

Martin's work also appears to question the ethical and political positions of CDA, which as well as subjective could appear judgemental and, at times, Manicheistic. Some of them portray the social world as one full of multiple abuses – racism, sexism, exploitation of resources, corruption, group violence, militarism, abuse of power and so on – but neither offer a picture of what an alternative picture might look like, nor consider nuances or extenuating circumstances that might excuse the abuser(s) of a degree of blame.

Rather than the kind of neo-Marxist positions that can be traced in the enthusiastic words by Kress cited above, Martin sees the possibilities for a more gradual approach to social change. We need, he says:

> a complementary focus on community, taking into account how people get together and make room for themselves in the world – in ways that redistribute power *without necessarily struggling against it*. (Martin 2004: 183, my emphasis)

As Stibbe (2017) points out, and as we also see in this extract, Martin's intention was that PDA should *complement* CDA rather than replace it.

Stibbe himself has begun to explore the ecological potentials of stories, and cites Ben Okri (1996: 21, in Stibbe 2017: 170):

> Stories are the secret reservoir of values: change the stories that individuals or nations live by and you change the individuals and nations themselves.

He critiques some of the current stories or 'myths' that our societies currently live by, including *growthism* (see Section 1.2) as well as 'progress, individuality, omnipotent science, commercial freedom, life as a competition and nature as a machine' (Midgley 2011, in Stibbe 2017: 170). He then confirms the socially committed aspect of PDA, describing it as

> a search for new ways of using language that tell very different stories from those of the current industrial civilization – stories that can encourage us to protect the ecosystems that life depends on and build more socially just societies. (Stibbe 2017: 170)

Hopefully it will be seen in the latter part of this book that the two case studies – case *stories*, we may call them – do precisely this.

2.7 Greta and the modern ecological context

Greta Thunberg's arrival on the public scene came thanks largely to a speech she made at the UN in 2019, during which the teenager presented a dramatic 'j'accuse' to the world leaders in attendance:

> You have stolen my dreams and my childhood with your empty words. And yet I'm one of the lucky ones. People are suffering. People are dying. Entire ecosystems are collapsing. We are in the beginning of a mass extinction, and all you can talk about is money and fairy tales of eternal economic growth. How dare you! (Greta Thunberg, speech to the UN 2019)[12]

Greta's words here would be incomprehensible without knowledge of the ongoing climate crisis. It is necessary to have a basic understanding of media representations of scientific data, as well as a degree of political awareness, for her speech to make much sense. In order to understand who is meant by 'you', quite delicate pragmatic/linguistic analysis is also needed. We need details of the context in which it was delivered, an important event at the United Nations, a Climate Action Summit; to an audience, in other words, consisting of world leaders, politicians, bureaucrats, journalists, scientists, representatives of NGOs and so on – in short, to a group of adults with highly responsible social positions. But we also know that the speaker is not just speaking to those present – after all, it would be unfair to blame the climate crisis on the few adults who happen to be attending in person. She knows that the speech will be broadcast to a global audience, and therefore 'you' must also apply to some of them. So, who are 'they'? From her reference to her 'stolen childhood', and from the staged contrast between her visible youth and the adulthood of the listening audience, we might interpret her words as pragmatically constructing an us/them opposition consisting of an in-group of young people and an out-group of adults. The latter are all responsible for the negative phenomena described – stolen childhoods, people suffering and dying, collapsed ecosystems, mass extinction. This is not the whole story, however, as she narrows down the out-group considerably by adding 'all *you* can talk about is money and fairy tales of eternal economic growth'. 'You', then, means bankers, financiers, economists, capitalists, businesspeople, which is still a substantial number of people, and presumably world leaders who oil the wheels of industry, and massive institutions like the World Bank or the UN itself are also involved. From the point of view of a critical analysis of this speech these questions are relevant, arising from the application of a familiar critical tool, that of *pronoun reference* (Oktar 2001; Oddo 2011; Fairclough 2015; Gardelle and Sorlin 2015). However, the accusation in the speech is not limited to these just-mentioned groups. The cry 'how dare you?' is a generic response to abuse, and the plural pronoun 'you' directly addresses every listener, whether or not they have any involvement in financial matters. Indeed, the text does imply a broad, generational blame that applies to adults everywhere – nurses, teachers, shopkeepers and so on – all are engaged in a system that depends for its continuance on their compliance, their patterns of consumption, their aspirational striving after more and better material things.

The above is a kind of critical reading of Greta's speech, but in both CDA and PDA, what anthropologists refer to as a 'thick description' (Geertz 2008) of the social context in which the language to be analysed occurs is understood as necessary. The context of this speech concerns ecological issues such as species loss, collapsing ecosystems, which also form the backdrop for this book as a whole. Thus, it will be useful to consider the current state of environmentalism, before moving on to the case studies and linguistic analysis presented in a later part of the book.

2.8 Environmentalism

Greta's speech signalled an important moment in the establishment of environmentalism as a key player in today's counterculture (Eder 1990; Peterson Del Mar 2014; Forte 2020). Environmentalism is indeed a powerful ideological motivator, the inspiration of Green movements and political parties in many Western countries. Greta Thunberg's emergence as a young person's leader on environmental themes did not happen in a vacuum, but rather sprang out of a social context that had nourished these aspirations for generations. In America, the ferment of the 1960s saw hippies and others turn full-scale to nature in the back-to-the-land movement (Jacob 1997), an affirmation of a naturalistic vein found in American culture as long ago as the nineteenth century. In *Walden*, for instance, Thoreau describes a pond thus, attributing not just life to an inanimate natural phenomenon, but also the human sense of sight:

> 'It is Earth's eye', he decides, 'looking into which the beholder measures the depth of his own nature'. (Howarth 2017: 48)

The 1960s also gave impetus to the affirmation of a slew of holistic practices that in their different ways express deep ecological perspectives – veganism and vegetarianism, Zen and other kinds of Buddhism, Taoism, meditation, yoga, Tai Chi, Feng Shui, health food, natural therapies, homeopathic medicine, rebirthing, natural healing, permaculture, tree hugging, bio dance and many more. In 1974, Lovelock and Margulis proposed the 'Gaia hypothesis', or the hypothesis 'that the total ensemble of living organisms which constitute the biosphere can act as a single entity to regulate chemical composition, surface pH and possibly also climate' (Lovelock and Margulis 1974). Their landmark paper is a work of geochemistry and a hard read for the non-specialist, but at a popular level it launched the idea that the Earth itself is a kind of living organism. There are clear parallels with a notion such as the Gaia hypothesis and the traditional understandings of life described in Section 2.2.

Many of these practices spread across the Western world, including to Britain, where traditional outdoor practices and sports received an added stimulus from these fashions and their underlying ecosophy. Cycling or walking to work rather than using cars (Caimotto 2020; Loland 2021) became more popular, as did growing your own fruit and vegetables in rural gardens and town allotments (Diamant and Waterhouse 2010; Joyce and Warren 2016). The beneficial effects of physical contact with nature also feature in therapeutic contexts such as the 'care farm' movement (Hassink et al., 2014), where social services combine with farmers to treat a range of conditions.

The picture Greta draws of Earth's biospheres recalls a notion, current in media for some years now, that the very survival of life on Earth is at stake. Not just Greta, but an overwhelming majority of the scientific community believe that human-driven climate change is real, and that unless CO_2 emissions are brought under control very soon, planetary catastrophe will occur (see Khan 2012; Peters and Darling 1985). There is also scientific consensus that global warming is mainly due to unprecedented, human-driven increases in CO_2 emissions (Hamilton 2014; Oreskes 2004, Cook 2020, etc.). Therefore, though conspiracy theorists and industrial apologists deny it (Uscinski et al. 2017; Wong-Parodi and Feygina 2021), human-driven climate change has today attained the status of an objective fact.

Alongside terms for the geological ages of the Earth such as Pliocene, Pleistocene, Holocene has appeared a new one – the 'Anthropocene' (Steffen et al. 2007, 2011; Ponton and Sokół 2022), which suggests that human impact on natural systems is now comparable to that of the great forces of nature. Among negative effects of Anthropocenic processes on the biosphere is species loss, which is reaching dramatic levels. In 2017, a group of world scientists published a 'Warning to Humanity', claiming: 'we have unleashed a mass extinction event, the sixth in roughly 540 million years, wherein many current life forms could be annihilated or at least committed to extinction by the end of this century' (Ripple et al. 2017: 1).

By contrast with this toxic picture of the contemporary situation, Steffen et al. point out that humans have had a negligible effect on their environment for the greater part of their existence:

> For well over 90% of its 160,000 year history, *homo sapiens* have existed as hunter-gatherers only. During that time our ancestors had demonstrable impacts on their environment, even at scales approaching continental, through, for example, fire-stick farming and hunting of mega-fauna during the latest Pleistocene. However, these human impacts registered only slightly at the global scale, and the functioning of the Earth-System continued more or less unchanged. (Steffen et al. 2011: 741)

Reports on the state of the environment produced by Earth System scientists like Will Steffen trace a gloomy picture: a range of key indicators such as population, real GDP, foreign investment, urban population, primary energy use, fertilizer consumption, large dams, water use, paper production, transportation, telecommunications, international tourism all evince significant increases since the 1950s, with most shooting up at faster rates since the year 2000 (Steffen et al. 2015: 84). Steffen et al. comment:

> One feature stands out as remarkable. The second half of the twentieth century is unique in the entire history of human existence on Earth. Many human activities reached take-off points sometime in the twentieth century and have accelerated sharply towards the end of the century. The last 50 years have without doubt seen the most rapid transformation of the human relationship with the natural world in the history of humankind. (Steffen et al. 2004: 131; cited in Steffen et al. 2015: 82)

Thus, we now live in a period that began after the Second World War, termed by Earth System scientists the 'Great Acceleration', a period when industrialization and city-living have spread across much of the world.

The ambivalence of the political classes towards this accumulating mass of data is shown by the fact that, though periodical global climate summits are held, and ambitious agreements signed, these are not matched by events on the ground, key nations refuse to participate and anti-environmental practices like fracking continue to be consolidated (Soeder 2021). The protocols and recommendations produced by these climate initiatives, though they stimulate popular awareness of the problem, thus largely prove ineffectual (Dryzek 2013: 47).

Moreover, in their report for the German Federal Ministry of Economic Cooperation and Development, Eckstein et al. (2021) say that these processes are having their most severe effects in developing countries. They call climate change a 'reality' that is manifesting around the world in 'an increased volatility of extreme weather events' (ibid.: 6). Natural disasters like wildfires, droughts, typhoons, tornadoes, floods, hailstorms and landslides are all on the increase, while other climate-related disasters concern heavier monsoon rains, damage to coastal areas from rising sea levels, increase in skin cancer and deaths from extreme heat because of global warming.

Regrettably these phenomena, though largely originally provoked by the industrial processes of so-called developed countries, will have the heaviest impact on the countries with the fewest resources to deal with them (Timmons Roberts 2001).

2.9 Modern farming methods and the environment

Key themes in this book concern agricultural practices in modern economies and the husbandry of rural land. A relevant work on this, already cited, is Rachel Carson's *Silent Spring*, a milestone in environmentalism in the 1960s. Carson, a marine biologist, was convinced that caution should be exercised in using the new 'miracle' pesticide, DDT, because of its collateral effects.[13] Her work does not focus on DDT alone, but problematizes some of the basic assumptions behind modern agriculture, especially in its use of chemicals:

> Chemicals sprayed on croplands or forests or gardens lie long in soil, entering into living organisms, passing from one to another in a chain of poisoning and death. Or they pass mysteriously by underground streams until they emerge and, through the alchemy of air and sunlight, combine into new forms that kill vegetation, sicken cattle, and work unknown harm on those who drink from once pure wells. (Carson 1962)

Silent Spring drew public attention to the often conflictual relationship between modern scientific methods of pest control and the health of ecosystems, and the concerns she raised over that controversy play into environmentalism generally in the second half of the last century. Among other crucial insights, her work identifies the reason why modern agriculture needs pesticides in the first place, which concerns the intensification of agriculture and the focus on production of single crops. This system, she says, 'sets the stage for explosive increases in specific insect populations'. Her work stresses that to apply scientific-technological rationalism to agriculture runs counter to traditional understandings of our place in nature:

> Nature has introduced great variety into the landscape, but man has displayed a passion for simplifying it. Thus he undoes the built-in checks and balances by which nature holds the species within bounds. One important natural check is a limit on the amount of suitable habitat for each species.

In passing, we should note the correspondences with Gaia-thinking (see Section 2.7) in this depiction of 'Nature' as a self-regulating system that, in a quasi-conscious manner, applies its own 'checks and balances'. The environment, then, is not just threatened by pesticides, but also by far-reaching reforms in farm size, mechanization, techniques of sowing, harvesting and food production, genetic modification of crops and other changes. These have seen significant increases in output (Trautmann et al. 2015), but at a cost of dramatic alterations in rural landscapes in most nations of the first world (Sheail 1995; Hansen et al. 2001). Sheail's paper outlines the history of the relationship between town and country in twentieth-century Britain, the birth of the notion that wildlife could represent 'a heritage of the people as a whole' (Edlin 1952, in Sheail 1995: 83). He describes the thankless predicament farmers were to find themselves in as they attempted to balance the need to constantly increase food production with the demands of the emerging environmental lobbies. He presents a summary of one of the first government-backed reports on the state of the countryside, which appeared in 1984, and painted a striking picture of at times 'catastrophic losses of existing habitat':

> Agricultural intensification had damaged or destroyed the wildlife interest of 97% of Lowland neutral grasslands since the war. Some 80% of the sheepwalks of chalk and Jurassic limestone country had been significantly damaged, largely by conversion to arable or improved grassland. Half the lowland fens, valley and basin mires had been lost or damaged through drainage operations, reclamation for agriculture and chemical enrichment of drainage water. (Nature Conservancy Council 1984)

There were significant changes to the appearance of Britain's countryside, with the removal of centuries-old features like hedgerows, random woods, wild flower field borders and farm ponds:

> The most damaging practices have been the removal of hedgerows and the ploughing up of un-cultivated field margins, together with the reclamation of scrub and woodlands; the reduction in rotations and fallows; the replacement of permanent pasture by leys and arable cropping; land drainage and the elimination of standing water and farm ponds; and the treatment of grassland and arable land with selective herbicides and insecticides. (Ogaji 2005)

The notion that modern farming relies too heavily upon commercial fertilizers, insecticides and herbicides to be sustainable is increasingly found in traditional farms as well as organic (Morton et al. 2013).

For the above reasons, the modern period has witnessed a growing interest in organic farming, which has also been motivated by a reaction against the increasing homogenization of the fruit and vegetables found on supermarket shelves. Organic farms were originally 'driven by an emerging environmentalism and health concerns about exposure to pesticides, antibiotics and hormones' (Seufert et al. 2017: 11), but now represent one of the fastest growing sectors of food production in first world countries. As the FAO (1999) explain, such agriculture is a 'holistic production management system which promotes and enhances agro-ecosystem health, including biodiversity, biological cycles, and soil biological activity'. It emphasizes the regional qualities of specific farming areas and avoids the use of synthetic materials.

However, over the years since organic farming began, the tendency has been for the promotion of biodiversity to be forgotten about. As Seufert et al. (2017) mention, the reasons why consumers choose organic products are overwhelmingly because pesticides are not used in these systems. It is the perceived improvement in food quality that gives organic farms their market edge, especially in the niche sectors where people are prepared to pay more for such products. For these authors, organic farming is defined by a 'chemical-free management system', one that relies on 'natural substances'. They point out that this is not enough for such farms to be considered sustainable or even necessarily 'environmentally friendly', since many relevant indexes, such as the maintenance of water resources and the protection of biodiversity, come low on the list of priorities.[14]

Though the organic trend in farming in its ideal form may be positive in terms of achieving environmental goals, it is too early for a reliable assessment, especially given its scarcity when compared with large-scale traditional farming. In 2010, only 2.1 per cent of farmland in Europe is devoted to organic farming, the figure rising to 5.1 per cent within the EU (Tudorache and Sàrbu 2013). More research would also be needed to explore the question of the promotion of biodiversity within contemporary organic farming.

2.10 The war on wildlife

Traditional farming appears to carry on a war against wildlife, which includes animals (Carson, ibid.) that we think of as occupying an intrinsic place in the British countryside. For example, researcher David Macdonald tells the story of his group's efforts to tag foxes in Westmoreland, and how he became aware of the real state of our relations with foxes:

> My own introduction to the love-hate relationship of farming and wildlife was made through foxes. My prying into their private lives led me deep, and wide-eyed, into the underworld of agriculture. There, I learnt from men deeply knowledgeable about nature, who became my closest friends more often despite, rather than because of, their actions towards it. For example, Westmoreland shepherd, Edwin Dargue who, taking pity on my derided efforts to radio-tag foxes in sheep country, persuaded a hostile community to offer me a deal: they'd

enter their terriers into the fox-earth, and I'd start digging – if I got to the fox before the dogs killed it, they'd spare it. After one such life-and-death excavation, choked on dirt and hands bleeding, men who'd measured themselves by the foxes they'd killed introduced me to their companions in a tiny fell-side pub – 'This is David, he chews nails and spits rust' – then they spoke for hours, almost reverentially, of foxes against which they'd waged war – always concluding with the consolation 'But I'd never kill the last one'. So, I was introduced to the War and Peace that is farming and wildlife, and learned, to quote Leo Tolstoy, that 'One of the first conditions of happiness is that the link between man and Nature shall not be broken'. How is that link holding up? (Macdonald and Feber 2015)

For Tolstoy, the 'link between man and Nature' is fundamental to human happiness, but from a farmers' perspective foxes simply constitute a menace to livestock.

The story does not provide the author's demographic details. From certain cues (e.g. 'wide-eyed', 'taking pity on my derided efforts', etc.), we can see him as a rather naïve young man, possibly a townie, an academic – in short, as someone without a real understanding of country life. By contrast, the farmers are depicted as 'men deeply knowledgeable about nature', who 'measure themselves by the foxes they'd killed' and so on. It pits two kinds of understanding of nature against one another: the first kind is unrealistic, possibly 'idealistic'. The author's ideas about Nature (which is capitalized in the original text) derive from books like those of Tolstoy, an idealizer of country life and the Russian peasantry. The other perspective is realistic, that of men whose daily jobs engage their energies in destroying these animals. There is no room for poetry in their mindset, though they do display something of 'reverence' for the foxes. For the purposes of agriculture, it appears that there is no place in the countryside for the fox (Feber et al. 2006).

From the perspective of (ecological) CDA, it may be useful to consider patterns of representation in this text, and in some other scientific discussions of the fox, remembering the notion of animal 'erasure' in Section 2.3 (Stibbe 2012). In one text, on the introduction of the fox into Australia, they are called 'pests', 'noxious animals', 'baneful disturbing influences' or 'key threatening processes' (Saunders et al. 2010). In another, the fox is referred to as an 'indiscriminate predator' and a 'vicious pest' (Baker and Macdonald 2000). This use of *negative evaluative language* (Martin and White 2005) discursively positions the fox as a 'problem'. Another way of describing this would be to say that the fox is 'framed' (Alexander 2009; Croney 2010; Goffman 1986;

Lakoff 2010; Lakoff and Johnson 2003) as a *problem*, which creates an expectation in the reader that a *solution* will be proposed somewhere else in the text (Winter 1977). This problem-solution pattern reflects the human psychological need for closure: if we read of 'baneful disturbing influences', for example, it is natural for the reader to wish them to be removed. From the deep ecological perspective (Section 2.2) however, these representation patterns strip the fox of any right it may have to exist as a conscious, thinking being, with its own place in the biospherical web. Descriptions of the 'solution' do the same thing, employing Orwellian euphemisms (see Section 1.3) for what happens to them: instead of represented as being 'killed', they are 'managed', 'controlled', 'excluded', 'baited', 'reduced', 'suppressed', 'abated', 'shot', 'trapped', 'fumigated', 'targeted' and so on (Saunders et al., ibid., Baker and MacDonald, ibid.). One effect of representation is to distribute emotional responses and consequent ethical/axiological judgements: to hear of the 'management' or 'control' of a 'vicious pest', for example, is likely to elicit positive responses among readers. By contrast, to hear of foxes 'being killed' may disturb environmentally aware readers. David's story, with its graphic details of the foxes' life-and-death struggles, its 'wide-eyed' interest in the lives of foxes, the 'reverence' they inspire even among those who kill them, is likely to influence readers in quite a different way.

Proverbially cunning, the fox has a strong cultural footprint in the UK thanks to its numerous appearances in children's entertainment (Brer Rabbit, Disney's Robin Hood), TV entertainment (Basil Brush) and significant literature (Aesop's Fables, La Fontaine). They even crop up in a witticism by Oscar Wilde, who spoke of fox-hunting as 'the unspeakable in full pursuit of the uneatable'. Another large mammal, the badger, has a similar or even greater claim to affection, since it features prominently in one of the best-loved of all British children's books, Kenneth Grahame's *The Wind in the Willows*. As Cassidy (2012) describes, its situation in contemporary Britain is analogous to that of the fox:

> Badgers occupy a significant position in British society, whereby they benefit from extensive legal protection and a highly visible and enthusiastic network of local support groups (the Badger Trust), yet at times continue to be subject to (illegal) human practices of badger 'baiting' (fighting for sport), 'digging' (digging out a sett and/or sending terrier-type dogs in to hunt the animals), and 'control' activities from farmers and gamekeepers.

Not only that, but they are systematically killed – the Orwellian euphemism for this is 'culled' – because of the perception in the UK that they spread Bovine TB to cattle herds. Though not a linguist, Cassidy (ibid.) recognizes the importance of representation, and quotes research that confirms the evaluative patterns just indicated in the case of foxes. She speaks of 'pestilence discourses', which 'often present exaggerated claims of the damage animals do, and represent them as dirty, violent, criminal, cunning, highly numerous and out of control'.

Against such depressing pictures of the way animals are treated and represented, as well as the undeniable facts of environmental devastation in the modern era, it is hard to look for positive perspectives. However, it should also be recognized that the last century saw the birth of political groups that increasingly spread positive environmental ideals, such as private organizations already mentioned like Friends of the Earth, Greenpeace, or supranational quasi-political bodies such as the Global Alliance on Health and Pollution or the Global Green Growth Institute.[15] Green parties, which began appearing in the 1980s, are no longer marginal groups but have a significant presence in many European countries (Haute 2019). As we have just seen, badgers have activists that campaign for their rights, while fox-hunting stimulated unheard of levels of environmental concern before the Hunting Act made it illegal in 2004 (Ponton 2007).

3

Aspects of Ecolinguistic Methodology

3.1 Narrative

3.1.1 Narrative functions

The social importance of language and its repercussions for our lives and for the worlds we live in have been covered at some length in the first part of this book. A book which proposed a new view of metaphor was mentioned: 'Metaphors we live by' (Lakoff and Johnson 2003), which argues that metaphor is not just an essential component of political rhetoric, as Aristotle believed, but a vital part of the human cognitive apparatus (see Section 2.4). The authors suggest that metaphor plays 'a central role in defining our everyday realities', and make the strong claim that 'the way we think, what we experience, and what we do every day is very much a matter of metaphor' (Lakoff and Johnson 2003: 4). In a broader sense, what may be true of metaphor also applies to *narrative*, which features in literature and poetry, but may also be found in stories, fables, folklore, parables, sayings, proverbs, prayers, nursery rhymes, anecdotes, newspaper texts, advertisements, jokes, songs and many other discourse genres. In the contemporary world, these established forms are added to by social media posts on sites like Facebook and Instagram, by emails, tweets and so on. In words that recall the work of Lakoff and Johnson, Polkinghorne (1988: 11) calls narrative 'the primary scheme by means of which human existence is rendered meaningful'.

All of the above text-based narrative forms reflect patterns of thought and feeling that are shared, to a degree, across the speech community. We come across all kinds of stories, on a daily basis, that fulfil a variety of social functions. Aesop's fable of the ant and the grasshopper, for instance, cropped up recently in a university exam, where I assisted in the defence of the final theses of some Economics graduates. One student's topic was Covid and EU assistance funds. In the technical discussion a professor mentioned Aesop's fable: some of the states (the 'ants') had contributed to these funds in times of relative plenty. Others, such as Italy, had not, and these were the so-called grasshoppers. His point was that certain countries which had contributed nothing to the funds were among those that had benefited most from them. By explaining the issue in this way, he was able to communicate the rights and wrongs of an abstruse economic subject to an audience that consisted mostly of the students' relatives, for whom the specialist lexis of Economics would have been problematic.

Such narrative genres as the fable, proverbs, parables, cautionary tales and so on have an essentially didactic function. They transmit moral codes, ethical principles and practical guidelines across the speech community in which they occur, like Greek or Roman didactic poetry in the ancient world (Toohey 1996). One of their functions, then, is precisely that of spreading social values around a speech community – to convey notions of right and wrong, for example – but without invoking a religious or other kind of normative framework. In our societies there is a bedrock assumption that we are socialized into from birth, which can be explicitly expressed verbally in different ways. For example, in the case just described: *it's impossible to get something for nothing, you can't expect others to work for you while you sit by doing nothing, you only get out what you put in* and so on.

In fables like those of Aesop, the point of the story is signalled by the presence of a 'moral' which follows it and gives explicit guidance in how the tale should be interpreted. Here is another well-known example:

> A Nightingale, sitting aloft upon an oak, was seen by a Hawk, who made a swoop down and seized him. The Nightingale earnestly besought the Hawk to let him go, saying that he was not big enough to satisfy the hunger of a Hawk who ought to pursue the larger birds. The Hawk said: I should indeed have lost my senses if I should let go food ready to my hand, for the sake of pursuing birds which are not yet even within sight.
>
> Moral: A bird in the hand is worth two in the bush.[1]

In this fable, the moral has no special ethical connotation, but refers to the practical dimension of everyday life: it would not be immoral for the hawk to release the nightingale, just very foolish. Since the time of the ancient Greek storyteller, humans have found that it is better to be content with what one has than give it up for the mere prospect of obtaining something better. The fable serves to teach this message to children inexperienced in the realities of life, as well as remind them of its wisdom later, when they may be in danger of forgetting it.[2]

This picture of the role of narrative in constituting a sort of psychic bedrock, common to all members of a speech community, is complicated by the fact that it is easy to find contradictory examples, both in terms of textual discourse and also human behaviour. For example, it may be the case that we learn from Aesop the value of prudence and pragmatism, but clearly those who gamble are either deaf to the meaning of the 'bird in the hand' fable, or are guided by other sources of folk wisdom. Kipling's 'If', for example, which has headed recent lists of the UK's favourite poems, includes the verse:

> If you can make one heap of all your winnings
> And risk it on one turn of pitch-and-toss,
> And lose, and start again at your beginnings
> And never breathe a word about your loss.

The poem portrays gambling as admirable: these words appear as part of Kipling's attempt to pass on to his son the quintessence of manly virtue. It preaches other virtues too, mainly those of Stoicism, but from a narrative-pragmatic perspective there is a connection between this well-loved poem and the social trends that have seen the UK's online betting industry become the current world leader in this sector (Orford 2003).[3]

3.1.2 Analysing narrative

Narrative has been extensively studied in many fields, especially linguistics and literary criticism, but also in sociology, anthropology, education, philosophy and psychology. For the purposes of this book, there are two relevant questions that emerge from the field of narrative research: first, what exactly constitutes a story (Prince 1973, 1982; Ricoeur 1984; Cortazzi 1994); and second, whether the same perspectives apply equally to fictional and real-life contexts, that is, whether the everyday anecdotes people tell can be seen as stories and assessed with similar tools to those used in literary analysis (Georgakopoulou 2007). Finally, as the above discussion (in Section 3.1.1) has indicated, we need to ponder the pragmatic function, or dialogical significance of both kinds of stories, to consider their effect in real-world terms (Oliver et al. 2019).

For the first question, literary theory has proposed that in order to constitute a story, a text needs three conditions to be present: *temporality* (a sequence of events that unfold through time with beginning, middle and end), *causation* (the middle action causes the end) and *human interest* (Prince 1973; Ricoeur 1984, in Cortazzi 1994: 158). These elements occur in classical poetry, such as in Coleridge's *Rhyme of the Ancient Mariner*, whose narrative unfolds through time and abounds with human interest. Causation can be observed in the logical structure to the tragic events that strike the ship, its crew and the narrator, which flow from the key event, the shooting of the albatross. However, to address the second question, they also feature in everyday interaction of all kinds, for example in the following snippet from BBC Norfolk's Countryside Hour. A listener phones in to tell a mini-story:

> Jean says: 'I was lucky enough to see a treecreeper in the woods at Bowthorpe in Norwich where I walk my dogs. Sadly it went round the other side of the tree when I got my camera. And I missed getting a photograph. It's only the second one I've spotted in these woods, but I was thrilled to see a treecreeper.'[4]

This could be analysed as follows:

Temporality:

1. Jean is walking with her dogs
2. She sees a treecreeper
3. She gets her camera/the bird goes round the tree

Causation:
   Her getting the camera (or arriving with her dogs) cause the bird to hide
Human interest:
   Jean's emotional state at seeing a rare bird

A more detailed typology of narrative analysis is the influential model proposed by Labov (1972: 227), which identifies the following (tables 3.1, 3.2):

Table 3.1 Stages of a Narrative (Labov 1972)

Abstract	What was this about? optional element – (summarizes the point or states a general proposition which the narrative will exemplify) Who? When? What? Where?
Orientation	(gives details of time, persons, place, situation)
Complication	Then what happened? (gives the main event sequence and shows a crisis, problem, turning point)
Evaluation	So what? (highlights the point, shows listeners how they are to understand the meaning and reveals the teller's attitude by emphasizing parts of the narrative)
Result	What finally happened? (shows resolution to crisis)
Coda	(Optional way of finishing by returning listeners to present)

Table 3.2 Jean's Treecreeper Story

Text	Labov Stage	
Jean says: 'I was lucky enough to see	Abstract	
a treecreeper in the woods at Bowthorpe in Norwich where I walk my dogs. Sadly it went round the other	Orientation	**Who**: Jean, her dogs, a treecreeper. **Where**: In the woods at Bowthorpe, Norwich
side of the tree when I got my camera. And I missed getting a	Complication	Treecreeper went round the other side of the tree
photograph. It's only the second one I've spotted	Evaluation	Lucky / Sadly / She was thrilled
in these woods, but I was thrilled to see a treecreeper'	Result Coda	She missed getting a photo –

The story of Jean and the treecreeper can be analysed, using this model, as follows:

This is, of course, not much of a story, as stories go, but it will bear examination as an example of the way Labov's model will be applied, in conjunction with other tools of pragmatic enquiry, about which more will be said in due course. It is noticeable that the stages do not necessarily follow a linear progression: here, for example, both the adjective 'lucky' and the evaluative adverb 'sadly', which convey the speaker's emotional response to the story, precede rather than follow the complication stage. As Labov says, the evaluation stage guides listeners' response to the story, it 'shows (them) how they are to understand the meaning'. Overall, the failure to photograph the treecreeper appears the dominant emotional cue in the tale, outweighing the narrator's 'thrill' at seeing the bird and her sense that she has been 'lucky'.

Pragmatic analysis involves looking below the surface, beyond what is explicitly said in search of meanings that can be inferred, supplying invisible connectors between disparate sentences, attempting to connect the words with underlying patterns of thought and trace the speaker's assumptions concerning her listeners. It seems clear, for example, that for Jean being able to take a photograph of a rare bird, when you see one, is a key part of the experience without which something is lost. For her, the thrill of seeing a treecreeper appears, in the end, insufficient compensation for the disappointment of not being able to get a photograph of the bird. This interpretation of the story draws on the social importance in Western culture attributed to photography (Sontag 1973; Diehl et al. 2016), which has only been heightened by the affordances of cell-phone technology (Faimau 2020). The adverb 'sadly', in this reading, would show that Jean expects her listeners to share her sense of disappointment, to respond with empathy to her emotional signals, along the lines of *'you saw a treecreeper? How exciting! But you didn't manage to get a photo of it? Oh, what a pity!'* It should be stressed that pragmatic analysis is not an exact science, and other readings of the story's intended meaning are possible, for example that Jean's excitement is the dominant emotion and her failure to get a photo just a trifling disappointment.

3.1.3 Discourse pragmatics

As Wilson and Sperber (2015) say, pragmatics refers to 'the study of the general cognitive principles and abilities involved in utterance interpretation'. They describe it as a dynamic perspective on meaning that looks beyond lexis and grammatical connectors to include a range of other factors, most obviously the context in which words are spoken. A pragmatic theory of meaning, they explain, is able to account for ambiguities, irony, metaphor and implied or non-literal meanings, all of which are problematic if meaning- transfer is considered purely in terms of the encoding and decoding of messages.

One of the earliest proponents of such perspectives was philosopher John Austin, who identified a category of expressions he called 'declaratory speech acts'; groups of words whose meanings relate to the real-world effects they produce: 'I now pronounce you husband and wife', 'I declare this supermarket open', 'Not out!' and so on. These phrases all have lexico-grammatical meaning, but their actual, or social meaning depends on their being pronounced in certain situations, with specific groups of participants. In the first, for instance, the person making the pronouncement needs to fulfil certain conditions, depending on where in the world the wedding ceremony takes place; hearers must include at least a couple who want to get married and so on. If these conditions are fulfilled, then a specific real-world event will take place; the couple will be married, with all the legal and affective implications that follow. If they are not observed correctly, for example because of the absence of one of the participants (who must respond appropriately to a ritual question along the lines of 'do you take this woman to be your lawful wedded wife?', etc.), then no real-world effect will follow. The statement, in effect, despite having a correct lexico-grammatical appearance, will be null and void, or *meaningless*.

Austin's dynamic perspective on language is described in terms of *locution* (the textual meaning of the words, *illocution* (the context-dependent aspect of meaning) and *perlocution* (the real-world effect brought about by the utterance) (Austin 1975). In the above example, the locution is the denotational meanings of the words used ('I now pronounce you man and wife', etc.), the illocution is 'you are being married' and the perlocution is the fact that the couple, after this phrase is pronounced, are legally wed.

In the same vein, Austin went on to describe other types of speech act in which words are used to 'do' things, such as promise, invite, order, apologise, bet, warn (Cohen 1973). These acts could be explicit; for example in the case of invitations 'You are warmly invited to celebrate Bob and Jane's 25th wedding anniversary at . . . , on . . ., etc. RSVP', or implicit: 'Are you doing anything on Friday evening, because I'm having some friends over?'

Wilson and Sperber extended the range of this research, developing a theoretical framework for a systematic description of the extra lexico-grammatical processes involved in meaning-transfer, known as *relevance theory* (Sperber and Wilson, ibid., Wilson and Sperber 1986). They claim that 'relevance, and the maximisation of relevance, is the key to human cognition' (ibid.: 41). Relevance theory holds that, in conversation, we assume that communicative processes involve a presumption of 'optimal relevance' (ibid.: 45). Here is one of their examples:

a. Peter: Is George a good sailor?
b. Mary: ALL the English are good sailors
   (ibid.: 47)

The intended meaning (in the technical language of pragmatics, the *implicature*) is easy to understand – Mary's answer is 'yes, he is', but how exactly do we understand this?

Cognitive processes of interpretation depend on the application of what the authors term 'the hearer's encyclopaedic and environmental knowledge' (Sperber and Wilson ibid.: 55). In other words, partners in conversation make assumptions about what their interlocutor will know – about the world in general and the topic in particular – and select their language accordingly. The presumption of optimal relevance leads the receiver to view Mary's utterance as a satisfactory response to the question; however, a question remains, namely, why Mary did not reply with a simple 'yes'. This would have been to respect the principle of *brevity* which, in another key foundational notion of pragmatics, philosopher H. P. Grice (1975, 1978) identified as one of four conversational 'maxims'.[5] Sperber and Wilson answer this by suggesting that Mary aimed to achieve 'some additional contextual effects not derivable from the direct answer "Yes", and these will also be implicatures of her utterance'. In their words:

> As this example shows, implicatures may differ in their saliency. For the hearer of (2b), the implicature that George is a good sailor is strongly salient, but there is an indefinite array of further implicatures such as 'The English have much to be proud of', 'England deserves a good navy', which are only weakly salient.

In some contexts, questions require a straight yes or no in reply; others, questions like that about George leave space for more elaborate answers. We can imagine the dialogue taking place at a dinner party, for example, in which case the indirect reply is explicable with reference to the speaker's wish to amuse the company, flatter her English listeners or show off her cultural knowledge.

Relevance theory has been widely used in discourse analysis to explore latent meanings in texts, to probe assumptions and speculate about speaker ideologies, prejudices, beliefs and so on. The next section explores the usefulness of relevance theory as a general approach to meaning in environmental discourse.

3.1.4 Pragmatics, narrative and environmental discourse

Stories abound in the BBC Radio Norfolk programme, *The Countryside Hour*, which mainly focuses on the presentation of narratives that concern Chris Skinner's farm. In the following example, a listener writes in from Canada with an incomplete narrative:

> Gudgin:
> It was cleared a hundred years ago and was originally a dairy, but she's talking about some of the wildlife and I think that there are quite a few experiences in common here. She talks about the flocks of starlings that come and visit her on that piece of property, and she says we have lots of birds around the place in the fall. That's the autumn to you and I. We get pretty big flocks of starling who don't eat the fruit, but they work out in the pastures. All except one lone starling who doesn't associate with the flock as they come and go, but rather sits on the power cable. And there is a picture of the silhouette of a starling. Just one. By himself, yes, and she's saying what's going on here?

The first part of presenter Matthew Gudgin's discourse relates to Labov's 'orientation' stage, introducing as protagonists the listener and the starlings. He also provides the 'complication' in the description of the 'lone starling' whose mysterious behaviour provides the interest of the story as a whole. In this case, and in many others that occur in the rest of the book, the category of 'human interest' will be extended to include the natural world, as indeed will the notion of pragmatic meaning. It is noticeable that Gudgin's language is not limited to a factual presentation of events but includes elements that draw on the realm of human interpretations, responses and behaviour. The birds are improbably represented as 'coming to visit her', and he emphasizes the 'loneliness' of the single bird. From the connotations of 'to not associate with' we can infer that a possible explanation of the bird's behaviour is that it feels superior to the rest of the flock or is avoiding contact with them, holding itself aloof, for some private reason. Gudgin's framing of the story, in other words, is somewhat anthropomorphic.

In Labov's terms, what is missing from the story are the 'evaluation' and 'result' stages, and this is the motive behind the listener's email. Without these stages, there is a sense of incompleteness.

> Skinner:
> Yes. Well, that's a nice easy question for me to answer. I had a closer look at the picture, and it's the same species as we have here in the United Kingdom (. . .) what Claire's describing is exactly what I've seen countless times on the farm where we have quite a large flock of starlings feeding on the ground. I think I got you quite close to one of the flocks this summer. They were out on the pastures eating the leatherjackets in the top of the soil just before after it had been wet. The leatherjackets pupated and came up near the top. Starlings knew about that and were feasting on them. And up in the hedge nearby, one solitary starling was sitting exactly the same as Claire's described. This rather lonesome figure sitting up on the line and what you're looking at here is a scout, and he's watching out as the others are feeding or obviously very busy keeping an eye out in the United Kingdom for things like sparrowhawks, kestrels, will spook them, buzzards flying over the top. Anything that might create a danger (. . .) it's often the senior bird as well.

Skinner replies with another, more complete story in which neither the Evaluation nor the Result stages are explicitly included, but both can be inferred. The Result of the bird's behaviour is that the rest of the flock is enabled to feed in tranquillity, while the Evaluation of the bird's behaviour is positive, to the extent that its behaviour will be judged as laudable. Again, Skinner does not use explicit language (*'what selfless, altruistic behaviour'*, etc.), but represents the bird as being 'very busy keeping an eye out . . . for anything that might create a danger', and it is likely that listeners will share a sense that such behaviour is positive. As Labov says, part of evaluation relates to showing listeners 'how they are to understand the meaning'. The only explicit signal Skinner gives in this sense is his mention that the bird is often 'senior', implying that it possesses the wisdom of experience, is a kind of tribal elder and is mindful of the common good rather than dominated by concern for its own hunger.

This kind of analysis is a first step to a broader, pragmatic understanding of both stories, a prelude to situating them in an overall social and ecosophical context. To walk, or drive, past a lone bird on a wire is a daily event for most people, yet it is not often that we ponder the question 'what is going on here?' Even if they noticed that near the lone bird was a meadow where other birds of the same species were busy feeding, most people would be unlikely to think twice about the situation. To wonder about it at all shows a level of concern with the doings of wildlife that is rather rare in our societies, and this enables us to infer, even from such a brief account, much about Claire's underlying ideological/ecosophical mindset. She believes, for example, that it is important to understand why animals behave the way they do (otherwise she would not even notice that the birds' behaviour is unusual in any way, much less take the trouble to contact a radio station about it). Her tale demonstrates a willingness to engage in observation and analysis, which have produced reliable insights in this field (Lorenz, ibid.).

We can also infer other details concerning her life and attitudes, which are not explicitly mentioned but may be derived from a pragmatic reading. Claire is a person with a hands-on relationship with nature, since her property includes 'fruit' and 'pastures'. Possibly her activity involves fruit production, where large flocks of birds may constitute a problem, since she mentions that the starlings 'don't eat the fruit'. Unlike many farmers, her attitude to these birds is not one of hostility but of scientific interest. Casting the net further, we can see how her tale counters the usual anthropocentric mindset of Western societies that regards the natural world with disdain, seeing its inhabitants as motivated by largely random, instinctive mechanisms, incapable of the noble actions found in the human world. Indeed, her expression 'working out in the fields' associates the birds with the quintessentially human activity of working, thereby conferring dignity on the flock as a whole.

Finally, the episode tells us something about expected listeners to the programme. Since we know that radio programmes, to be successful, need to provide entertaining or instructive content that will please listeners, we can infer that listeners will share, to a degree, the kind of environmental perspectives that feature in a story like this. At some level, an editor will have earmarked Claire's email, among scores or even hundreds of analogous emails received during the week prior to the programme's recording, as suitable for broadcasting. To some degree, the story's selection is evidence that it conforms to the implicit ideological framework of the programme designers, the BBC.[6]

3.2 Speaker evaluation

One of the central assumptions of this book is that, in looking at texts through the lens of linguistic analysis, it is possible to have a fuller picture of what is 'going on', to delve beneath the surface of the text in search of ideologies, prejudices, beliefs or attitudes that shape the speaker's framing choices (see Fairclough 2003: 9). Alongside metaphor and narrative, relevance theory and pragmatics, another fruitful area of enquiry to focus on is the speaker's use of evaluation, which Hunston and Thompson (2003: 5) explain as follows:

> Evaluation is the broad cover term for the expression of the speaker or writer's attitude or stance towards, viewpoint on, or feelings about the entities or propositions that he or she is talking about.

A focus on such language not only reveals the speaker's own standpoints but also tells us something about how society at large tends to assess the phenomenon in question. In Hunston and Thompson's words, evaluative language serves both 'to express the speaker's or writer's opinion, and in doing so to reflect the value system of that person and their community' (ibid.: 6). Thus, it is possible to show how speakers use evaluation to flag up their agreement or disagreement with views that are current in media, to construct in- or out-groups of opinion, to signal virtue and so on, and to appreciate nuances in the mindset they verbally manifest (Martin and White 2005; Ponton 2022).

Consider the following:

> Mexico stands as a nation for the principle that a healthy environment is essential for the common future of humanity, with particular stress on the quality of life our children will inherit.[7]

Evaluation can be explicit, for example via an adjective (*healthy* environment, *essential*), or implicit. Here, in fact, the overall drift of the text is that, since Mexico 'stands for' this admirable principle, it must be a praiseworthy country. Not only is it represented as united – it stands 'as a nation' – but it does so not just for Mexican citizens but for the whole world, not for this generation alone but for all futurity. Thus, the positive evaluation of Mexico is conveyed by these converging implied meanings, rather than stated explicitly. It should be noted that this account of the dynamic role of evaluation depends on the kind of pragmatic mechanism outlined in Section 3.1.3. The speaker/writer takes for granted that abstractions like 'the common future of humanity' and 'the quality of life our children will inherit' will be seen as important by readers and by global public opinion alike. The ends of evaluation will only be served if readers share the writer's notion of the importance of a healthy environment. Readers who work for oil companies, climate change deniers and the like will most probably have a negative response to the text.

Evaluation helps speakers signal their belonging to communities of all kinds, as in the following example of a virtual community, created on YouTube around a video of turtles on a Hawaiian beach.[8] In comments below the video, two of the first respondents signal their positive assessment through explicit evaluative adjectives (*beautiful, gorgeous*):

- *Beautiful* video of the turtles I'm glad u shared this!
- Such *gorgeous* animals, thanks for sharing :)

At this point the poster enters the conversation. Her comment expresses positive evaluation through an indication of subjective stance:

- This video is a little different . . . but *I really liked* the footage of the turtles and wanted to share it with you. Do you like it?

Notice that her evaluation is strengthened by the presence of 'really' before the verb. We can also see that she engages directly with an imagined community; though the video is available for a global audience, it seems that she has a specific viewership in mind (I . . . wanted to share it *with you*). The next viewer buys into this virtual community by using the poster's first name:

- Kasia!!! This is so *cool*! Love the message you shared in this, and that's amazing that you had the opportunity to see so many of them basking!

Her positive evaluation is strengthened by the use of multiple exclamation marks, as well as repetition of the word 'so' before the positive adjectives 'cool' and 'amazing'. Other viewers string along with the trend:

- I am also a nature lover I love to experience it without disturbing it, at it's best *glory*

- I'm so glad you were able to see them. What an *amazing* experience. Hawaii is on my bucket list.
- Wow that's a lot of turtles! What a *cool* experience :)
- How *cool!!* I'm so glad you shared this, even though it's not your normal type of video. I would die of awe if I saw them in the wild like that. :)

Partly through their use of bland, catch-all positive adjectives (*amazing, cool*), which are taken up by others, these respondents signal convergence around a proposition, that it is good to spend time close to turtles; this becomes the touchstone for membership in this transient community. We find other common positive adjectives like *awesome, great, really nice* and *cute,* as well as references to positive emotions (*glad, love, dear to my heart, relaxing*) or other positive lexis (*a privilege, the best thing*). Evaluation is also conveyed through exclamation, most commonly *Wow,* and the negative emotion of jealousy, which also conveys positive evaluation of the post, since the viewers say they are '*so jealous*' of the experience. Thus, this typical YouTube page may be seen as a microcosm of human social behaviour; though it is a virtual, not a real community, it operates in analogous ways as 'members' clearly conform their responses to a rather restricted range of possibilities. There is an in-group of would-be members who signal their willingness to participate by using various textual devices that show their suitability. There are no negative comments, no member who does not like turtles, thus the out-group is constituted by those viewers who simply do not post or by those who do not find turtles *great, amazing* or otherwise deserving of enthusiasm.

The most comprehensive account of evaluative language within linguistics is found in systemic functional linguistics, Martin and White's Appraisal Framework (see Martin and White 2005). They boldly divide the entire lexis of the English language into three macro semantic categories which, as Hunston and Thompson (2003: 142) explain, constitute a systematic typology of responses to experience:

> The enormously varied lexical choices [. . .] are seen as construing [. . .] a small range of general categories of reaction. The main category or sub-system is AFFECT, which deals with the expression of emotion (happiness, fear, etc.) Related to this are two more specialised sub-systems: JUDGEMENT, dealing with moral assessments of behaviour (honesty, kindness, etc.), and APPRECIATION, dealing with aesthetic assessments (subtlety, beauty, etc.).

Each instance of evaluative language in a text is coded using shorthand semantic categories, and the system also allows for implicit meanings to be registered; results can be positive or negative, of normal, raised or lowered intensity. Briefly to see how it works, consider these examples, from the YouTube turtle video comments:

For instances of explicit evaluation, the key text is underlined; the coding follows in brackets with a + or − sign indicating positive or negative evaluation. The main semantic category is then indicated, with the specific subcategory in which the instance belongs.

Martin and White suggest that the emotional category is fundamental, since evaluation itself is a type of emotional response: in iii., for example, the writer expresses her evaluation of an abstract thing (a topic) in emotive language, while in v. a response to the turtles is construed through the description of a (hypothetical) emotional reaction.

AF deals with implicit evaluation by italicizing the relevant stretch of text:

> *I am also a nature lover* (t + Judgement: propriety)

The subcategory of propriety relates to judgements of ethical questions. Here, the writer suggests that to love nature is a good thing, alluding to a relevant value frame that applies to all would-be members of this community. The pragmatics of 'also' suggest implicit meanings along the lines of: *I am a good person, like you yourself, the poster of this ecological video, and all the other posters interested in the topic*. But nothing is stated explicitly – she does not add '*and to love nature is a good thing*'.

At times, as in examples iv. or vii., the framework is quite straightforward to apply, but there are some complex effects which it struggles to deal with, such as v., with its reference to 'awe'. Should to 'die of awe' be coded negatively because of the fearsome connotations of dying, or positively because it expresses wonder?[9] The area of implicit evaluation also has problematic features, for example in the following:

> It's extremely sad (− Affect: Unhappiness, intens.) to see the impact and damage that pollution has caused these magical creatures (+ Appreciation: Value).

The appraisal patterns in the text are collected in table 3.3:

Table 3.3 Turtle Video, Appraisal

i. I'm glad u shared this! (+ Affect: happiness)
ii. This is so so so cool! (+ Appreciation: Value, intensified)
iii. This topic is very near and dear to my heart. (+Appreciation: Value)
iv. What an amazing experience (+ Appreciation: Value)
v. I would die of awe if I saw them in the wild (−/+ Affect: Fear)
vi. Your editing and camera skills are awesome (+ Judgement: Capacity)
vii. These beautiful and majestic animals (+ Appreciation: Quality)

Here the writer expresses two distinct explicit evaluations, one of the turtles ('magical' creatures) and the other of her overall emotional reaction to the damages of pollution. But it is hard not to feel that her real concern in this text is with more complex, large-scale processes like industrial activity, pollution and environmental damage; and in sum, with the humans who are responsible for these things. All that is registered is her sadness at their effect on the turtles; any implied condemnation of multinationals, corrupt politicians and the like is simply impossible to include in the coding process.

Despite these difficulties, the appraisal framework offers a handy method of bringing out these features of a text and, if viewed within a pragmatic framework, will help open windows into intriguing domains of meaning.

To a degree, Martin and White's system can be seen as expanding Labov's own views on evaluation:

> Evaluative devices say to us: this was terrifying, dangerous, weird, wild, crazy; or amusing, hilarious, wonderful; more generally, that it was strange, uncommon, or unusual – that is, worth reporting. It was not ordinary, plain, humdrum, everyday, or run-of-the mill. (Labov 1972: 371)

The difference would be that Labov's main concern with evaluation appears to have been its role in storytelling as an attention-getter since, for him, these adjectives can be used to justify a speaker's monopolizing talk, answering the listeners' impatient question: 'so what?' (ibid.: 366). Martin and White, by contrast, are concerned first with the semantic distinctions represented by separate lexical items, and second, with their possible pragmatic effects when used in context. The analytical model used in the second part of the book blends these two approaches by incorporating a more semantic/pragmatic understanding of evaluation into a Labovian framework.

Stibbe (2015: 83–4) concisely explains the importance of evaluation and its potential influence on the way we think and act:

> Appraisal patterns are of key interest in Ecolinguistics because of their power to influence whether people think of an area of life positively or negatively. If inundated with statements that economic growth is good then the message may penetrate deep into people's minds and become a story that they live by. This story, once in their minds, then has an influence on their behaviour and how they treat the systems which support life.

Here Stibbe too takes 'appraisal patterns' in a semantic/pragmatic, or a broadly Hallidayan sense.

3.3 The movies

For the title of his well-known 2015 book *Ecolinguistics: Language, Ecology and the Stories We Live By* Stibbe borrowed from Lakoff and Johnson, adapting their title to narratives in an ecological context. In this book, he insists on the social constructivist potentialities of language, as outlined in Section 2.6 (Fairclough 2015; Kukla 2013). As mentioned above, CDA views language as fundamental in shaping social realities. It is essential, in this time of ecological crisis, to understand its role in mediating our relationship with the natural world. Stibbe encourages us to contemplate the stories our societies currently run on; how we are herded by mass media into patterns of consumerist behaviour (Ball-Rokeach et al. 1984), and how these processes end up in an inevitable conflict with ecological principles.

The cinema is one of the most significant distributors of stories in our culture, and its approach to narrative often illustrates the way a covert, persuasive ideology of consumerism nestles inside the ostensible narrative function of the medium. As an example, consider the plot of the acclaimed 1988 film *Rain Man*, starring Dustin Hoffman as an autistic idiot-savant and Tom Cruise as his ambitious, materialistic, driven brother. From one point of view, the story is a tale of human development as Charlie (Cruise) discovers that his father has left his fortune to a brother of whose existence he was unaware. Painfully, he learns to care for Raymond (Hoffman), finding a tender, human dimension and a sense of responsibility in his own identity which he had previously lacked. However, his need for money leads him to the gambling tables of Las Vegas, where he uses Ray's uncanny autistic fixations to rack up huge winnings. The film thus degenerates into an advertisement for Las Vegas, whose money-obsessed values are imported uncritically into the film: 'You've got to love this town!' cries Cruise gleefully as Ray wins again. It could be suggested that, by contrasting brotherly values with those of materialism, the film actually aims to develop a critique of consumer society, whose apotheosis is represented by Las Vegas. But the sexiest, most memorable scenes occur in the context of Cruise's pursuit of a quick buck. The good life is one of fast, flashy cars, glamorous women, liquor, lurid night spots, rock music and adrenalin pumping; it is not spent in painstaking conversations with a disabled person, developing a meaningful relationship. A similar critique could be made of many successful films, from Hollywood and elsewhere.

Product placement (Newell et al. 2006) is a further indication of the penetration of consumerist ideology into the practice of film-making. Film companies take money to use the products of specific manufacturers in their films, with which they thus perform a covert advertising function while telling their stories. Balasubramanian (1994: 30) considers such films as 'hybrid messages', which include 'all paid attempts to influence audiences for commercial benefit using communications that project a non-commercial character', and he goes on to highlight that audiences

> are likely to be unaware of the commercial influence attempt and/or to process the content of such communications differently than they process commercial messages.

The phenomenon has been widely studied, for example, in the cases of cigarettes (Charlesworth and Glantz 2005), Coca Cola (Redondo and Bernal 2016), Starbucks (Zhang 2011). In some cases, the products are simply an unobtrusive part of the background, while in others they play a prominent role. Russell (2009) describes how the 2000 Tom Hanks movie *Castaway* featured a Wilson volleyball, which was 'on screen for over 10 minutes and mentioned in the film 37 times'. In the 1992 remake of the Italian classic *Scent of a Woman*, Al Pacino's character has a scene where he drives a Ferrari, and the following dialogue occurs:

Charlie: I guess you really like women.

Slade: Oh, above all things! A very, very distant second . . . is a Ferrari.

Again, it may be possible to interpret the blind, egocentric colonel's obsession with this luxury car as a veiled critique of materialism, as his stunt driving the Ferrari undoubtedly endangers the lives of Charlie, pedestrians and other road users. However, it is more likely that most viewers, 'unaware of the commercial influence', will simply see the scenes as comic relief, while on some level they register the name of the car.

The post-Cold War opening of previously closed societies like Russia and China, as well as their supposed embrace of capitalist values, offers another opportunity to witness the way that media help spread the values of consumerism. In Russia it has been suggested that film-makers 'extol the virtue of solid Russian cars and the evils of foreign luxury brands' (Grosso et al. 2015: 39), and a certain 'cultural sluggishness' (Grosso et al., ibid.) has so far prevented the wholesale adoption of Western values, despite Russia's post-Communist exposure to Western media. By contrast, Paek and Pan (2004) say that advertising has functioned as the vanguard of the emerging consumerist society in China (Chaffee et al. 1997; Wei and Pan 1999). While traditional Confucian and Communist values emphasize respect for elders and social equality, adverts instead appeal to youth, modernity and status (Lin 2001). Paek and Pan conclude that 'mass media, along with advertising as their "intimate partners", act as a conduit for the global consumer culture' (ibid.: 508).

3.4 Naturalization and framing

Stibbe understands stories in a twofold sense, depending on whether the focus is on the individual or the collective s/he lives in:

> Stories are cognitive structures in the minds of individuals which influence how they perceive the world. Stories-we-live-by are stories in the minds of multiple individuals across a culture. (Stibbe 2015: 6)

Stibbe's idea is to critique the latter sort of story if they produce harmful ecological effects, and to suggest different possible stories that would be beneficial to the environment, the natural world and to humanity in a holistic, deep-ecological sense (see Section 2.ii.ii). This approach leads him to synthesize in a few words what is felt to be the takeaway or the message of a narrative, for example:

> THE PURCHASE OF PRODUCTS LEADS TO WELLBEING (ibid.: 26)
> CONSUMERS MAXIMISE THEIR OWN SATISFACTION THROUGH PURCHASE (ibid.: 27)
> IF SOMEONE BUYS SOMETHING THAT THEY WANT THEN THEIR LIFE IS IMPROVED (ibid.: 38)

Such stories are frequently found in advertising. For example, in 2016, IKEA launched a campaign devoted to what they call 'retail therapy', thus blending consumerist practices with discourses from the domains of psychotherapy and personal wellness:

> A product that might help you improve your relationship at home. Or just remind you of the fact that our products are inspired by your life, for real. So whether it's a snoring husband, a never ending gaming son or any other relationship problem you have, IKEA can come to the rescue.[10]

Naturally, the claim that shopping at IKEA will resolve any 'relationship problem' you have is an absurd one, but there is no legal obligation on advertisers to justify their assertions. The point is rather that such a story, by leaving traces in shoppers' minds of the notion that THE PURCHASE OF PRODUCTS LEADS TO WELLBEING, acts to strengthen the dominant ideologies of consumer capitalism. In fact, the notion of 'retail therapy' is not limited to the context of IKEA products alone but has rapidly spread across consumer cultures everywhere.

In this context, Stibbe quotes Macy and Johnstone (2012), who focus on the story of 'business-as-usual' that 'sees economic growth and technological development as the way forward for society' (Stibbe, ibid.: 5). Though not primarily linguists, they echo a key notion of CDA, that of 'naturalization', when they remark: 'When you're living in the middle of this story, it's easy to think of it as just the way things are' (Macy and Johnstone 2012: 15).

Naturalization is a key notion of CDA, one that owes a debt to Roland Barthes (2006), and has already been touched on briefly (see, e.g., Section 2.ii.iv). For Barthes, an image of a black soldier saluting the French flag is a kind of 'alibi of coloniality' (Barthes ibid.: 129): that is to say, the fact that one of the supposed victims of French colonialism is saluting the flag absolves the phenomenon of moral blame, rather making it seem worthy of honour and respect. 'Everything happens', he writes (ibid.), 'as if the picture *naturally* conjured up the concept'. For CDA scholar Norman Fairclough (1989: 92), naturalization, which is connected to the notion of common sense, is an 'effect of power'. In Barthes's example, it is not necessary for anyone to argue the case that French colonialism was a good thing; of course it was, since we can all see the love and respect which this black soldier evidently feels for it. The positive value of French colonialism has thus become part of 'the way things are'.

This linguistic phenomenon is of importance in the ecological context, since it crucially influences cognition, and hence, behaviour. For example, consider the term 'alternative energy', used for comparatively clean sources such as hydro-, wind or solar. The term 'alternative' helps to naturalize the idea that the typical or default means of getting energy is from fossil fuels (Ponton 2014).

Connected to the notion of naturalization is that of *framing*, and it is possible to see Stibbe's potted story-meanings in this light. Framing studies (Goffman 1974; Entman 1993), which are common across the humanities, are concerned with the organization of information in such a way that a particular reading of a message is encouraged (Edwards 2005: 15). As an example, consider the phrase 'self-made man', which is used in the following mini-story, told about John Major, a Conservative prime minister in the 1990s, during a radio phone-in:

> I think that is actually something that I like about him, the fact that he left school early, that he did actually have to struggle. He's a <u>self-made man</u> and that sort of

thing [. . .] Well he's inherited an army of people sleeping rough. But he could have done something quite dramatic and significant there. What has he done? How has he shown that this man, who's come up from poverty, understands poverty and is prepared to do something about it. I don't think he's shown much, do you?¹¹

Here the phrase 'self-made man' acts as an organizing principle – as a *frame*, in short – that guides listeners in understanding the story, in appreciating the speaker's meanings. Indeed, in this example, the implicit connotations of 'self-made man' are spelled out by the caller. He tells us that Major 'had to struggle', he 'came up from poverty', both of which imply that a 'self-made man' is determined by materialistic criteria. The frame works to underline Major's shortcomings since he, a man who has overcome poverty himself, and therefore 'understands poverty', is doing little to help the homeless in this current crisis.

Advertisers exploit the persuasive power of frames:

To help Cinderella catch midnight, give her the Swiss International Watch Company's 150,000 Grande Complication timepiece.¹²

This ad depends on the fact that all readers have an intimate knowledge of the Cinderella story, from Disney and other media sources. This circumstance guarantees that its nuances and connotations are deposited in obscure corners of their minds, ready to help interpret the inferences of such a text. Readers have no difficulty in decoding the message, and they perfectly understand why Cinderella would benefit from possessing an accurate wristwatch.

From an ecological point of view, both this ad and the Cinderella story are problematic. The latter is essentially a materialistic fable, whose meaning could be summed up by the label RAGS TO RICHES. The girl's grinding poverty is overcome by a triumphant marriage to a prince, and the doors to the good life, of luxurious consumerism, are flung wide. These meanings also help explain why the story offers a suitable frame for selling a high-end timepiece.

From a social perspective, naturalization and framing affect the reception and transmission of narratives and play a crucial role in shaping our cognitive responses and behaviour. As Halliday (1992) and Stibbe (2015) emphasize, the meanings MORE IS BETTER or GROWTH IS GOOD feature in countless narratives we encounter daily and form a sort of psychic bedrock underpinning Western capitalist societies today. So strong is this tendency that statements like the following will almost always be seen as positive:

In Africa, we forecast economic growth to outpace the global growth rate.¹³

Yet, as we have seen, the question of how 'positive' economic activity is, per se, is highly debatable, since indicators typically only assess monetary indexes such as gross national product, average income, levels of inflation. Other factors that might reflect more subjective dimensions to the well-being of a nation such as health, physical fitness, suicide rates, churchgoing, availability of social services, ethnic and racial integration, as well as environmental matters like pollution, protection of biodiversity, availability of green spaces, nature reserves and parks, are seldom part of the debate. Naturally, such accounts also completely ignore statistics relating to the natural world.

The following case studies apply these linguistic perspectives, and the inherent ecosophy outlined in the first section of the book, to narratives of nature found in two contexts, one in the UK, the other in Italy. The aim is to explore the role both of macro-narratives, or what Stibbe refers to as 'stories-we-live-by' and micro-narratives or the kind of 'small stories' produced by individuals using the sites, in order to bring out nuances in patterns of natural representation, and shed light on the infinitely varied relationships of Western industrial humanity with the environment and the natural world.

4

Situated Narratives (1) High Ash Farm and the Countryside Hour

4.1 High Ash Farm

In this part of the book the focus moves from general ecolinguistic approaches and background to the two specific contexts that provide the linguistic data for our study, beginning in the UK with High Ash Farm; Priolo Saltpans, the reserve in Sicily, will be introduced in a later section.

High Ash Farm is located at Caistor St Edmunds, a village 2 miles south of Norwich in East Anglia, one of my favourite parts of the UK. I came across this remarkable farm via its appearance in a BBC local radio programme, the Countryside Hour, whose podcasts I have followed for some ten years. The protagonist is farmer/naturalist Chris Skinner, who discusses topical ecological issues, answers listener questions and takes a BBC journalist, usually Matthew Gudgin around the farm, telling him what has been going on during the past week. It is a simple recipe, enriched by interactive segments like the 'rural riddle', where Skinner plays a sound recorded on the farm and challenges listeners around Norfolk to guess the animal or, more frequently, the bird, which makes it. Possibly these riddles, which show how little I know about birds, sparked my interest and kept me coming back; gradually, after repeated listening I found it possible to identify the songs of Great Tit, Green Woodpecker, Greenfinch, Blackcap, Chaffinch, Song Thrush, Blackbird, Starling, Nightingale and so on. More infectious still was Skinner's enthusiasm for nature in all its diversity. Lengthy sections of the programme are often devoted to creatures that most humans largely ignore or treat as pests to be eliminated – spiders, ants, wasps, snails, slugs, hornets, bats, hover flies. He drools over nuances in hoverfly colouring and calls them 'stunningly beautiful', a favourite catchphrase. He not only tolerates ants, but actively encourages them to occupy his front porch and, on young relatives' birthdays smears their name in honey on the table so that the ants will spell it out. His account of the ants' great marriage day, when they all leave the porch in droves to mate on the wing, is spellbinding. His tolerance extends to moles, who are given free rein to disfigure the lawn with their digging.[1]

In the square mile of High Ash Farm, among many other species, are:

> red deer, fallow deer, muntjac deer, Chinese water deer, hares, badgers, foxes, buzzards, goshawks, little owls; Green, Greater and Lesser-spotted woodpeckers, all kinds of birds, butterflies and moths, trees, flowers and fungi, insects, spiders and snakes. (Ponton 2022a: 39)

At times Skinner's deep ecosophical feelings emerge, in homely phrases like 'they've all got just as much right to be here as I have', or in more serious critiques of our wildlife blindness and harmful ecological practices, our 'war on nature'. Over time, I became aware that the programmes touched deep ecological chords, and I came to see the back catalogue of podcasts as a significant educational resource.

When Skinner inherited the farm, a family business, it was mainly used as a shooting estate, and his narratives occasionally dive into social history that reveals the dramatic changes that have taken place in agricultural methods and rural contexts since the Second World War. In one moving episode, he describes the sparrows that beset wartime fields, how he would pass a shotgun loaded with scatter-shot to his father, to make great holes in the hordes. Today sparrows have become so scarce that Skinner provides them with a long row of nest boxes in the farmyard. Gradually the farm's identity changed, and now it is set up for growing grain and niche bio products, and also provides stabling and other facilities for horse-riding. In fact, High Ash Farm today is open to visitors who can walk or ride their horses in ample designated areas.

Through his appearances on the long-running radio programme, currently in its third decade, Skinner has acquired a small but significant platform for disseminating a particular ecological vision. His mottos are the promotion of biodiversity and sustainable farming, and the fact that, unlike other organic farmers he does have access to public discourse makes him a controversial figure. It is not just that his preference for protecting foxes, badgers and other so-called pests leads him into inevitable conflict with neighbouring farmers. 'I've been smiling a lot lately. . . . I heard you were dead', said one of these, bumping into him in a local pub. It is rather that what he is doing at High Ash Farm raises wider questions about farming methods, about our relationship with the natural world; ultimately about free-market capitalism tout court, and the social and psychological transformations it has ushered in. More will be said in later sections on each of these three counts: for the first, in brief, it is worth asking if it is sustainable to destroy centuries-old habitats like hedgerows and copses to create vast areas for arable production, which depend on the use of toxic chemicals and intensive mechanization. For the second, Skinner's guiding principle is that animals, birds, trees, flowers have lives, destinies, vital interests of their own, which we deny when we view the natural world solely in an instrumental light. The third topic pits principles against profits: if we are willing to grant the dignity of consciousness to fleas, flies, gnats, bats, harvest mice, spiders, badgers – to the whole panoply of extra-human actors – then we cannot simply exterminate them en masse whenever their most vital activities provoke negative movements on someone's balance sheet, or otherwise disturb human tranquillity. Foxes in the outskirts of Norwich are making so much noise at night that residents complain to the authorities. The foxes are shot, since a human's right to a good night's sleep is more important than the foxes' right to live (Ponton 2022a). Badgers are culled – an Orwellian euphemism for 'killed' (see Section 1.3)[2] – because of their links to bovine tuberculosis in cattle (Downs et al. 2019); moles are destroyed everywhere, not just to protect bourgeois lawns, but because:

> The soil they push to the surface gets into grassland silage fed to cows and sheep in winter months, potentially contaminating meat and milk with listeriosis bacteria.[3]

Skinner's activity is thus carried out on a border which it helps to delineate, where sustainable agriculture and unfettered biodiversity clash with the logic of the marketplace, with product standardization, increasing productivity, protection of the bottom line.

By contrast with better-known British naturalists like Sir David Attenborough and Chris Packham, Skinner's status as a professional farmer enables him to present society with an even more basic challenge. Nature documentaries may raise public awareness about the fragility of ecosystems (Zemanek 2022) and popularize the sense that creatures possess beauty and value (McKay et al. 2022). However, their actual effect on levels of environmental awareness may be slight (Arendt and Matthes 2016) and, through glossy productions for prime-time entertainment, such programmes also seem to commodify the natural world (Fürsich 2003). It has been argued that they represent animals in ways that deny their individuality (Mills 2015), and promote a reductive view of wildlife through an endless focus on courtship rituals and hunting scenes. Since they show animals in extant natural habitats, they may also disguise the rate at which these are being lost.

Implicitly, Skinner invites us to wonder how far High Ash Farm could be a model for other British farms, to consider the effects which a number of such farms could have on our declining wildlife, to ask ourselves what sacrifices we might be prepared to make to live in a rich, diversified biosphere. Research suggests that the ends of agriculture are in conflict with the needs of the biosphere, or as Green et al. (2005: 552) says, 'the biodiversity value of farmland declines with increasing yield'. Though many UK farmers claim to have positive attitudes towards their captive animals, or that conditions in intensive farms are better than life in the wild (Serpell 1999), still a lack of tolerance towards wildlife appears to be an intrinsic feature of modern agriculture (Conover and Decker 1991).

It is hard to answer the question whether High Ash Farm is, after all, a sort of 'rural theme park', its biodiverse environment propelled by one man's green whimsy; or whether it and similar farms may instead represent a credible alternative to large-scale, modern commercial farming. This is a crucial point since it asks if economic and ecological goals may combine in the field of agriculture, or if they are indeed fundamentally opposed, as has been suggested (Shmelev 2012). Many people would regard an optimum set-up for the British countryside as consisting of a rich biosphere that exists alongside an efficient, economically viable farming sector. In this regard, an interesting practice that Skinner undertakes is to annually seed enormous fields with what he calls 'over winter wild birdseed mix'. This produces a wild flower rich habitat which has powerful impacts on biodiversity of all kinds, especially for insect and bird life, as well as for small mammals and their predators. It enables many species of bird to overcome the so-called hunger gap in the winter months when their usual food sources, seeds and insects become scarce. However, this is a practice whose feasibility for farmers would need to be assessed in studies of agricultural sustainability. Currently the scheme is funded by the government, a positive signal that, for the time being at least, it is willing to support farmers in ecological initiatives.[4] But the question is what would happen to these birds if the government withdraw funding, or if farmers like Skinner who are willing to make the effort and support the scheme no longer apply.

4.2 Country Diary

Some of the themes that will be explored in more detail below can be seen in the following analysis of a text found on the *Guardian*'s Country Diary pages, written by Kate Blincoe, who appears from the text to be Chris Skinner's daughter (table 4.1, line 13):

Table 4.1 Countryside Diary

1	The massive oak trunk lies close to where it fell, now
2	carved into a bench. I sit there, feeling the balm of long-
3	awaited spring sunshine on my face. Across the valley,
4	the hay meadows are greening up, promising bales and
5	bales of goodness for the horses. The hum of the bypass
6	is, for a few minutes, overpowered by the piercing trill of
7	a skylark, rising up just a few metres from me. I smile at
8	the walkers passing by. As Spring revives the landscape,
9	so too does it beckon people.
10	Much of the local countryside here is inaccessible, often
11	behind barbed wire and 'keep out' signs. Here at High
12	Ash Farm, miles of wide grass tracks are freely accessible
13	to the public; my dad has even created a small parking
14	area for walkers. Being close to a city brings some
15	difficulties, but also opportunities to share nature. It
16	means hundreds of people care about the farm and
17	become unofficial custodians, picking up litter and
18	reporting broken fences. Maybe, as tenant farmers, my
19	brother and dad have an in-built knowledge that this land is not theirs to possess.[1]

[1] Country Diary. Online at: https://www.theguardian.com/environment/2023/apr/19/country-diary-a-question-of-land-use-that-has-no-easy-answers, retrieved 19.04.2023.

Typical of 'diary' entries, this seems at first to be a piece of impressionistic writing rather than a coherent narrative with a specific point. If it is viewed through an ecosophical lens, we notice how frequently agency is grammatically conferred on natural and non-human subjects (Goatly 1996, 2017), and how this technique gives life to parts of the piece. It should be remembered that grammar typically represents agency and even consciousness as exclusively human features, reserving subordinate or passive roles for natural phenomena; through these means, humanity tends to position itself at the centre of creation (Heuberger 2007; Fill 2015). For example, the writer says she feels 'the balm of long-awaited spring sunshine on my face' (2–3), where the spring sunshine has no agency and we are mainly interested in its therapeutic effect for a human subject. The metaphorical connotations of the word 'balm' underline the instrumental, human-centric values ascribed to the sunshine, and her representation of it as 'long-awaited' further confirms a subjective impression. We are drawn into her subjectivity as she foregrounds her presence in the scene ('I sit there', 2) and invites readers to share her 'feelings' (2).

This pattern is confirmed in the second paragraph, where the agents are humans who are represented, implicitly and explicitly, as 'doing' things, which we can observe by focusing on the verbs used. Humans (implicitly) make the countryside inaccessible (10) by putting up barbed wire and keep out signs (11), make miles of grass tracks accessible (12) to the public who – again implicitly – 'use' them (12–13). Her dad has 'created' (13) a parking area for walkers. Once more, this is an implicit representation of human activity by unnamed human actors who park their cars and go walking. Hundreds of people (16) 'care' about the farm, they 'become' unofficial custodians (17), they 'pick up' litter and 'report' broken fences (18). Finally, her brother and dad are represented as 'knowing' that they do not 'possess' the land. The pattern in this paragraph is quite a typical, anthropocentric representation of human interaction with a natural landscape.

In the first paragraph, however, agency is grammatically attributed to natural phenomena. The oak trunk 'lies' and 'falls' (1), the hay meadows 'green up' and 'promise' (4), the bypass 'hums' (5), a skylark 'rises up' (7), Spring 'revives' (8) and 'beckons people' (9). Moreover, the 'promise' of the greening meadows circumvents human activity altogether – it is made directly to horses, with no reference to the intervening human labour of harvesting, baling, distribution and so on that must mediate these processes. In (5), the bypass is metaphorically represented in the happy human activity of humming. That this noise is cast as a pleasant, rather than an oppressive backdrop to events is clear from the rapidity and lack of protest with which it disappears at the skylark's song (6–7). Moreover, the key fact described in the passage as a whole, the seasonal revival of the landscape, is carried out entirely by a non-human process, or 'Spring' (8).

The salient features of the 'story' can be appreciated if we view it via Labov's interpretative schema:

Table 4.2 underlines the rather haphazard nature of this text, considered as a story. Typical of the 'diary' genre, the first-person perspective is relevant, and the tale flits in a random manner from one sense perception to another, as the multiple possibilities in the *orientation* section for the 'what (is this story about)'? category make plain. In the first paragraph alone possible topics are: oak trunk, spring sunshine, valley, bypass, skylark, walkers, Spring. Yet the story does have a point, which a consideration of *evaluation* will elicit. Though there is little explicit evaluation, there are many elements in the first paragraph where the writer signals positive evaluations, beginning with the opening:

The massive oak trunk lies close to where it fell, now carved into a bench (1–2)

Nothing is wasted; benches for passers-by to sit and enjoy meditative or restful moments immersed in nature are public utilities. From the writer's perspective,

Table 4.2 Countryside Diary, Narrative Structure

Abstract	-
Orientation	Who? I (2,7) When? Springtime (8) What? Oak trunk, valley, skylark (etc.) Where? High Ash Farm (11–12)
Complication	Much of the local countryside [. . .] keep out signs (11–12)
Evaluation	(explicit) +ive: balm (2) (implicit) +ive: Spring revives the landscape (8) (explicit) –ive: difficulties (14), litter (17) (implicit) –ive: barbed wire and 'keep out' signs (11)
Result	hundreds of people care about the farm (15–16)
Coda	Maybe, as tenant farmers [. . .] this land is not theirs to possess (15–16)

both walkers who use the bench for these purposes and those whose thoughtful husbandry put it there are admirable. Everything in the first paragraph is positive: the 'balmy' Spring sunshine, the promise of 'goodness', the skylark's 'piercing trill', the landscape's 'revival'.

The second paragraph immediately changes tone, with the introduction of the *complicating action*:

> Much of the local countryside here is inaccessible, often behind barbed wire and 'keep out' signs

Thus, people who are 'beckoned' by Spring find it impossible to enjoy its benefits. It is possible to trace what Martin and White (2005,) call an 'implicit negative judgement' here, on the farmers responsible for the exclusion. At this point she introduces what turns out to be the real protagonist of the story – High Ash Farm – and things begin to fall into place. High Ash Farm is cast as a solution to the problem (Winter 1977)[5] that has been described, and a tone of implicit positive evaluation returns in the following details (for explanations of abbreviation, see Section 3.2):

- *miles of wide grass tracks are freely accessible to the public* (t+ *Judgement*);
- *my dad has even created a small parking area for walkers* (t+ *Judgement*);
- *opportunities to share nature* (t+ *Judgement*).

- *hundreds of people care about the farm (t+ Judgement)*
- *become unofficial custodians (t+ Judgement),*
- *picking up litter and reporting broken fences (t+ Judgement)*

For the writer, it is a good thing to make the countryside available to the public, to provide parking areas, to share nature, and these evaluations implicitly praise members of her family. It is also good to care about the farm, to become a custodian, to pick up litter and report broken fences, and here she praises members of the public for their ecological sensitivities (Labov's *result* phase).

The *coda* (15–16) returns the focus to her family members and underlines the story's basic idea, that of *sharing* nature as epitomized by High Ash Farm, in contrast to the exclusive practices of other farms in the area.

This kind of linguistic, narrative-based analysis is helpful for several reasons. First, it enables us to appreciate how texts are not neutral but inevitably carry traces of the writer's ideological positions, which in this case relate largely to environmental or ecosophical questions. In the first paragraph the ecosophy is manifest, in the writer's appreciation of natural and non-human elements of the scenery – oak trunk, Spring sunshine, hay meadows, bales of goodness and so on. These things all give her pleasure, a feeling which colours the evaluative picture. Applying pragmatic logic (Section 3.1.4) we can draw the further inference that they also give pleasure to the walkers (walkers would not be there unless they were among those 'beckoned' (9) by such things, etc.). This positive emotional shading also transpires from the fact that the writer 'smiles' at the walkers (7–8), a not infrequent cultural practice in East Anglia between strangers in country places like this one. The smile can be seen as a token of recognition, that they share a common awareness of the reviving potentialities of Spring. We can also learn much about the writer's ecological sensibility in a cognitive sense by these means: for example, she has specialist knowledge of a detail such as the importance of greenness in horse hay (4–5), a topic that the research group Equinews sums up as follows:

> Greenness indicates the hay was not subjected to any adverse conditions during curing or storage, thereby suggesting the forage is nutritious and free of molds. Green hay is often rife with carotene, a precursor to vitamin A, and vitamin E.[6]

She can recognize a skylark by sight and/or song (6–7). From the fact that she mentions that it is 'just a few metres from me' we can realize that for her such unusual closeness has value, and that she expects her readers to also feel delight in getting up close to the natural world (see Ponton 2022c).

Moreover, once the text's implicit meanings are probed in this way, its dialogical potentialities emerge more clearly. That is to say, it engages in a subtle way with ongoing normative debates about the correct way to organize rural spaces and run an agricultural property. In the first paragraph the appeal is more axiological or value oriented. In other words, she is engaging with readers, pointing out the holistic benefits they may receive if they too learn to love nature as she does: *look around you, the natural world is wonderful, Spring is a reviving force, get out there and enjoy it!* is her implicit message. The second paragraph is more aggressive, splitting the farming world into two groups, an out-group that consists of most farmers in the area who put up barbed wire and keep out signs, and an in-group consisting of High Ash Farm and its users, where public access is part of an overall environmental project. Thus, the text has a bearing on national debate, since the same patterns of behaviour that are found in Norfolk also apply at a national level, and there will also be other eco- or bio-farms in other places around the country who, like High Ash Farm, are trying to go against the current.

4.3 UK farms and the environment

At this point we consider the context in which High Ash Farm operates, the UK farming industry, to see how far Skinner's practices might reflect an atypical balance between the interests of biodiversity and those of food production. To appreciate nuances in the narratives that centre on the farm at the analysis stage, we need to understand the degree to which its environmental practices conflict with the overall ecological habitus of conventional farming.

In the UK, appreciation for wildlife and the importance of a healthy biosphere date back at least as far as the foundation, in 1895, of the 'National Trust for Places of Historic Interest or Natural Beauty', which later became 'the National Trust'. Sheail (1995) documents some key moments in the evolution of twentieth- century notions of ecology and wildlife protection, as well as the emerging sense that the mechanization of agriculture, deforestation, the use of pesticides and other features of modern farming all represented serious threats to the maintenance of Britain's traditional rural heritage (Benton et al. 2003). Towards the close of the last century, during national debate on these issues, farmers were coming under fierce criticism from the ecologically minded:

> Brainwashed into thinking it was their duty to cater for the different interests of nature conservation, landscape beauty, historical and archaeological sites, and recreational amenities, it often happened that the most disadvantaged farmers, such as those of the marginal farming-areas of Exmoor, were the most called-upon to meet the cost of an urban society's desire to maintain agriculturally-outdated landscapes. (Sheail 1995: 84–5)

In great numbers, people had migrated away from their country-based, traditional lifestyles to urban centres, where rural pursuits had little or no meaning; still, they wanted to know that the idyllic 'English countryside' survived (Williams 1975).

Many studies have gathered significant evidence of the extent of the damage to the environment from modern farming methods (Conway and Pretty 1991, Krebs et al. 1999, Usubiaga-Liaño et al. 2019, Pretty 2000, Williams et al. 2021), and this may be grouped under a number of headings:

a) Habitat loss: As a number of these studies highlight, converting natural habitats to farmland can lead to the loss of biodiversity and the fragmentation of habitats, which in turn can reduce genetic diversity and resilience of ecosystems. The draining of wetlands for agriculture can lead to the loss of habitats for wetland species like birds, fish, amphibians (Morris et al. 2002).

b) Pesticides: Their use in agriculture can have negative impacts on biodiversity by reducing the number of pollinators, insects and other wildlife that depend on healthy ecosystems. Neonicotinoid pesticides, for example, have been linked to declines in bee populations in the UK, with negative implications for pollination of crops and wildflowers (Woodcock et al. 2016).

c) Fertilizers: The use of fertilizers in agriculture can lead to eutrophication of water bodies like ponds and lakes, which can harm aquatic biodiversity by promoting the growth of algae and reducing oxygen levels (Withers et al. 2014). Fertilizers can also lead to soil acidification and nutrient imbalances, which can reduce the productivity of the soil and limit the diversity of plant species (Goulding 2016).

d) Monoculture: As Varah et al. (2013) point out, increasing productivity at all costs is key in modern farming, and one strategy used to this end is that of 'reducing environmental complexity in order to grow large areas of monocultures with better economies of scale'. It is obvious that to grow a

single crop entails a reduction in biodiversity, since it reduces the diversity of plant species and limits habitats for wildlife.
e) Soil erosion: Soil erosion caused by intensive agriculture can lead to the loss of soil organic matter and nutrients, which can reduce soil fertility and, again, limit the diversity of plant species (Boardman et al. 2009).

These examples highlight the potential negative impacts of intensive agriculture in rural UK, and the consequent need to promote sustainability in agriculture and support the conservation of biodiversity.

There are several types of farm which, for a variety of reasons, carry out environmentally friendly methods of food production:

Organic Farms. These use natural methods to improve soil health, reduce the use of synthetic pesticides and fertilizers and promote biodiversity (Heckman 2006). They typically use crop rotation, composting and cover crops to maintain soil fertility and reduce the use of synthetic inputs. Organic farms often provide habitats for wildlife in hedgerows and wider field margins than are found on conventional farms. As DeGregori (2004) shows, the historical origins of organic farming lie in religious and cultural movements outside the mainstream, in currents that are considered to be counterculture or even occult.[7] Trewavas (2004) follows DeGregori in his dismissal of farming methods based on so-called cosmic forces, and accounts for the organic trend as follows:

> Human beings recognise the natural world and often feel a strong kinship with it because we are living organisms too. Simplistically this turns into 'natural' equated with 'good' and human activity as 'synthetic' equated with 'bad'. This view is self evidently, a version of original sin. (Trewavas 2004: 764)

His paper opposes the view that organic food could be better for you, or that organic farms are more ecologically sustainable than conventional farms. Rather, he attributes environmental damage from conventional farming simply to bad management, and claims that environmental goals should be pursued by 'incorporating the good points of organic agriculture [. . .] combined with a flexibility in approach with the goal of environmental improvement but most efficient use of land' (ibid.: 777).

Agroforestry Farms: Agroforestry is a farming system that combines trees with crops or livestock to create a more diverse and sustainable ecosystem; it has measurable positive impacts on bird and pollinator populations (Varah et al. 2013). These farms can provide a range of environmental benefits, such as reducing soil erosion, improving water quality and promoting biodiversity.

Permaculture Farms: Permaculture is a holistic approach to farming that aims to create sustainable and self-sufficient ecosystems. It is currently a niche activity, with roughly half of its UK practitioners engaged in other employment (Genus et al. 2021). Permaculture farms use a range of techniques to promote biodiversity, such as intercropping, companion planting and natural pest control methods.

In response to voices of concern over the environment and political pressure from increasingly influential green social currents, ecological ideas began to feature in the thinking of conventional farmers about their businesses. Today, many appear to encourage a degree of biodiversity in their farms through practices like protecting hedgerows, planting wildflowers, creating wildlife habitats and using natural pest control methods. Some already see biodiversity as essential for maintaining healthy ecosystems and improving long-term crop productivity (Feltham et al. 2015). As Omer et al. (2008) argue, although increasing the number of species on a farm may reduce productivity levels of the main crop in the short run, this increased biodiversity, 'by providing ecological services (e.g. through pollination, soil nutrient enhancement and integrated pest control) may increase agricultural output in the longer run'.

The UK government also supports biodiversity conservation through various funding initiatives such as the Countryside Stewardship Scheme, which has the ambitious goal of making Britain 'the healthiest, most beautiful place in the world to live, work and bring up a family'.[8] Its aims involve: 'increasing biodiversity, improving habitat, expanding woodland areas, improving water and air quality, and improving natural flood management' (ibid.). The support of biodiversity is to be realized through practices such as the protection and planting of hedgerows, creating ponds and managing grasslands for wildlife.

There are also a number of well-known conservation organizations in the UK that work with farmers to promote biodiversity, such as the Royal Society for the Protection of Birds (RSPB) and various wildlife trusts. They offer advice and support to farmers on how to manage their land to support a wide range of wildlife and biodiversity. There is, therefore, a growing recognition in the UK farming industry of the importance of biodiversity, and many farmers have realized that it is necessary to promote and protect it. Thus, these positive trends in farming work against the harmful ecological practices that have already been described. The picture is a complex one in which positive initiatives struggle to become established against a general current of environmental indifference or even hostility.

4.4 The Countryside Hour

4.4.1 A farmer's identity

In this section we consider some data from the Countryside Hour that may shed light on some of the questions raised in the last section. In an episode from the programme, recorded on 19 September 2016, Skinner was joined by an executive from the Norfolk Wildlife Trust and a conservation advisor from the RSPB, to discuss the release of the RSPB's State of Nature report. This online document naturally focuses mainly on birds but, since their well-being is closely bound up with the maintenance of varied rural farmland habitats, it also pays attention to more general environmental issues. Apart from birds, it provides data for most species of animals as well as plants and lichens.[9] As Sir David Attenborough makes clear in his introduction, the overall picture is a mixed one, including facts that, from an environmental perspective, are both negative and positive. The text, in fact, conforms to the 'problem-solution' pattern described in an earlier section (2.10), as Attenborough highlights first of all the problem: 'the severe loss of nature that has occurred in the UK since the 1960s', and underlines this with references to 'escalating pressures', 'serious trouble', the 'need for help' and 'struggling species'. Overall, though, the text is positive, pointing out recent successes and it concludes on a bright note:

> But the State of Nature 2016 report gives us cause for hope too. The rallying call issued in 2013 has been met with a myriad of exciting and innovative conservation projects. Landscapes are being restored, special places defended, and struggling species are being saved and brought back. Such successes demonstrate that if conservationists, governments, businesses and individuals all pull together, we can provide a brighter future for nature and for people.

The following extract is of interest because it allows us to focus on the role of one modern farmer in the person of Chris Skinner, and appreciate his place in a complex social context where the UK's food production needs are balanced against those of its wildlife:

Table 4.3 Countryside Hour Story One: 'Success/Failure'

1	Well, ten years ago less one month . . . so almost the ten-year scheme that High Ash
2	Farm embarked on is just coming to an end and at the beginning of it I was full of
3	trepidation and I've received a lot of criticism from farmers that I'm a kind of deserter
4	because I've gone to farming wildlife and if you like receiving these environmental
5	payments as opposed to production agriculture and I was always really keen with my
6	farming . . . good yields of sugar beet on variable land, wheat, barley all the traditional
7	farming crops, but the opportunity came to enter a quite a large-scale environmental
8	stewardship scheme called 'higher-level scheme' and it embraced most of the farm and
9	because I was a professional farmer, I want to do the Norfolk motto and 'do different'
10	and become a professional wildlife producer, and that's what I've done with absolutely
11	incredible success. Flocks of linnets 15, 16, 17,000 in a single flock, open to the public
12	365 days a year and hedge, pond creation, hedge planting, 27,000 hedge plants gone in,
13	three new areas of woodland, an area of successional woodland also open to the public
14	and the environmental benefits are absolutely stunning, but we couldn't have done that
15	without the regular annual payments and the capital payments to put all fencing in.
16	Public access gates, a small car park, and about three weeks ago the rug was pulled
17	from under us. We'd applied three months ago to enter another five-year high-level
18	scheme. We failed hugely, even despite that massive success with all the public access
19	and all the wildlife benefits.

Table 4.4 shows the narrative structure of this section of text:

Table 4.4 'Success/Failure' Narrative Structure

Abstract	-
Orientation	Who? I (3, 5, 8, 9, 10) We/Us (14, 16, 17) High Ash Farm (1) When? Last ten years (1–2) What? Food crops (5–6), Stewardship Schemes (7–8, 17), Where? High Ash Farm (1), Norfolk (9)
Complication	Rug pulled from under us (16)
Evaluation	I was full of trepidation (2) (− Affect: Fear); I've received a lot of criticism from farmers (3) (−J: propriety); A deserter (3) (−J: propriety); I was a professional farmer (9) (+J: capacity); absolutely incredible success (10–11) (+J: capacity, intens.); environmental benefits are absolutely stunning (14) (+ App: Quality, intens.);
Result	Incredible success (10–11), A 'huge' failure (17–18)
Coda	-

As the frequent use of the first-person pronoun 'I' indicates (table 4.3, above), Skinner's own experiences are central to the story's purpose. However, since he is a professional farmer (9), like other farmers engaged in the full-time business of food production (5–6), his account is not simply provided as autobiography, but rather as the testimony of an informed representative. He documents his own transformation from engagement in one professional occupation, that of food producer, to that of 'professional wildlife producer' (10). Such a transformation is viewed by other farmers as a kind of betrayal. Skinner is criticized (3), called a 'deserter' (3), and admits to feelings of 'trepidation' (2) which, we can imagine, would depend at least in part on the fear of being ostracized by his peer group. His bold claim to a broader identity, based on the Norfolk motto 'do different' (9), sounds like bravado, since it is plain that his choice was a minority one, supported by few of his fellow farmers.

In the end, the story invites a complex response because of its approach to framing. On the one hand, Skinner appears to present a classic problem/solution frame, where environmental 'problems' – here, implied rather than stated – are solved via grants and funding schemes, and farmers switching over from full-scale food production to focus instead on wildlife. The solution is described in terms of intense positive evaluation, and also via specific details of the vast flocks of linnets, improved public access, new hedges, ponds, woods and so on (11–16) that have resulted from Skinner's activities. However, the final evaluation is not one of success but rather failure, as the grant on which all these wildlife benefits depend is not renewed (17–19).

Perhaps because of this final evaluative ambiguity, the story leaves an unsatisfactory aftertaste. Unlike Attenborough's positive environmental message, which suggests that all could be well if the social actors involved collaborate, it rather highlights tensions that work against happy environmental outcomes. Before entering the Stewardship Scheme, Skinner had been a successful professional farmer, producing sugar beet, wheat, barley and 'all the traditional farming crops' (8–10). His text gives no clue as to where the lost agricultural output would be made up, if the High Ash pattern were to be followed on a large scale by other UK farmers. In other words, he does not address the question of sustainability. Moreover, the dependence of his farming practices on outside funding is plain: 'failure' is not determined by the logic of the marketplace, but rather by the external factor of not qualifying for a certain scheme.

Thus, the story underlines the presence, in the farming vs. wildlife debate, of wider political and socio-economic currents, and returns us to the substantial and weighty considerations that have already been amply delineated. Members of the public who want to live in a green and pleasant land with a rich and diverse biosphere would celebrate as 'success' a farm that manages to 'produce' a single flock of seventeen thousand linnets. Whether there would be a widespread willingness to put up with the eventual shortages in food supplies that may accompany such results is another question. It is also unclear to what extent such environmental grants could be politically expedient in the long term, given the dominance of the post-Thatcher, neoliberal economic philosophy that ascribes primacy, first and foremost, to the material value of things.

4.4.2 The Countryside Hour: Thanks, ants!

In this section the focus shifts towards the ecological dimension of High Ash Farm and the Countryside Hour. The episode discussed in the last section was rather atypical of the programme's normal format, consisting in a formal debate on topical environmental issues. Normally episodes are recorded at the farm itself, and feature Chris Skinner discussing its flora and fauna, their seasonal variations and other local happenings that might interest listeners.

Here we deal with a lengthier monologue by Chris Skinner on the subject of the ants with which, as mentioned, he is happy to share his porch. The text is divided into a series of mini stories on different topics, though all concern aspects of ant behaviour. The extracts will all be analysed using the same methodology, which focuses on the speaker's evaluation, the narrative structure, some considerations of the framing involved and the overall pragmatic effect.

The first text includes a curious anecdote that perhaps tells us more about Skinner than about the ants themselves:

Table 4.5 Countryside Hour: Ant Story (1)

1	If I stand up and walk over into the corner I have a little dish here. And the sun, just as
2	it's setting, still shining on it. And it's a tiny little dish. It's not much bigger than a
3	teaspoon, and in that dish each evening I top it up with honey, some just <u>fine, runny</u>
4	honey and just a few drops into the bottom of the dish and it's away from all the pots
5	and the shelves and things. It's just sitting out by itself, and the ants form a <u>lovely</u>
6	circle all the way round this tiny little dish that I have, little ceramic dish. And they
7	form a <u>very neat</u> circle, and sometimes the birthday of some of my grandchildren I
8	write their name in honey on one of the shelves, something like Fern, and then the ants
9	will come and write there, the child's name in ants all the way round, they'll make little
10	lines all the way around the honey at that time of the year, June and July, there's
11	absolutely masses in the colonies. So ants are <u>fascinating</u> to me

Table 4.6 shows the Labovian narrative structure analysis, which shows that, as in other stories already dealt with, the Abstract and Coda stages are missing, nor is there any Complication to speak of. In Labov's terms, this latter stage deals with what is called 'the main event sequence' (Section 3.1.2), but in this story there is clearly no 'crisis, problem' or 'turning point'. Since there is no complicating action, there is also no discernible 'Result', which in a typical tale would refer to the resolution of some crisis. Despite these missing stages, there is

Table 4.6 Countryside Hour: Ant Story (1), Narrative

Abstract	–
Orientation	Who? I/me (1, 3, 6, 7, 11) Ants (5, 6, 8, 9, 11), Skinner's grandchildren (7, 8, 9) When? June–July (10) Where? Skinner's porch (mentioned before the extract)
Complication	–
Evaluation	Ants are fascinating (11)
Result	–
Coda	–

Table 4.7 Countryside Hour: Ant Story (1), Evaluation

Line	Relevant Text	AF Code
3–4	fine, runny honey	+ App: Quality
5	a lovely circle	+ App: Quality
7	a very neat circle	+ App: Composition (intens.)
11	fascinating to me	+ App: Impact

no doubt in our minds that we are listening to a kind of story, the theme of which could be 'curious ant behaviour' or 'what happens in the Skinner household on grandchildrens' birthdays'. This ambiguity of focus can be seen as resulting from the numerous references to a variety of social actors in the Orientation stage. In particular, the presence of a consistent number of references to the first person (I, me) could suggest an autobiographical intent:

There is an Evaluation stage (table 4.7, above) and this, to quote Labov (1972), 'highlights the point, shows listeners how they are to understand the meaning and reveals the teller's attitude'. Probably Skinner's emphatic Evaluation shifts the balance towards the ants and away from the children, in terms of identifying the focus of the story. The speaker's overall intention may thus be interpreted as to explain to his audience why he finds ants fascinating – rather than, for example, to tell listeners how he spends the weekend, or suggest novel ways of entertaining kids at birthday parties.

A focus on his use of evaluative language shows an exclusive focus on the evaluation of phenomena, via terms from the semantic domain that Martin and White term 'Appreciation':

The 'circle' formed by the ants on the honey ring is singled out among the other components of the story for the most prominent use of explicit evaluation;

the first reference is a generally positive term ('lovely') which is then refined to the more precise 'very neat'.

These evaluations of the ants' circle are fundamental in the story's use of framing (see Section 3.4). Their behaviour has the kind of ritual, geometrical precision associated with human spectacles – opening ceremonies for important sporting events, dances, processions or musicals, and – at least from this anecdote – this would appear to be the source of the ants' 'fascination' for Skinner. His use of the conjunction 'so' (11), in fact, is expressive of the meaning '*to sum up then, this is why*'. It is almost as if the ants, in forming these circles, and writing the childrens' names, did so not because they were randomly crowding onto the shapes traced in honey, but rather in response to some mysterious spontaneous impulse, and this is why Skinner finds them fascinating.

This rather fanciful interpretation is supported by a consideration of the aspect of agency, and the specifics of Skinner's representational style. The ants are portrayed as performing the identical actions as Skinner, in the same grammatical form, with the same construal of agency:

> I write their name in honey on one of the shelves (7–8)
> The ants will come and write there, the child's name (9–10)

There is a difference between Skinner's choice here and the following hypothetical formulation of the same event where the unconscious nature of the action in question, the spelling, is made explicit:

> *The ants all crowd onto the honey and their bodies spell out the letters of the girl's name*

Of course, for sophisticated adult listeners, there is no mystery here, but it should be noted that young children are crucially involved in the tale. Very young children will perhaps not make these connections – for them, it may appear that the ants themselves have joined in with the birthday party. Thus, the pragmatic significance of this story is concerned not just with Skinner the naturalist and his objective 'scientific' fascination with ants; rather, it relates to the creation, in the impressionable minds of children, of patterns of relations with the natural world. As we shall see, below, one typical human frame for ants, especially when they turn up indoors, is that of 'pest to be eliminated', or at the very least, 'driven from the house'. To see the ants, instead, as participants in a birthday celebration is to view them in a more holistic fashion altogether. To push pragmatic analysis one degree further, we could see a levelling parallel between the ants' enjoyment of the honey's sweetness and the children's excitement about the sweetness of birthday party fare: a fondness for sweet things is something common to both.

The whole mini-episode could thus be viewed in a didactic perspective. Skinner is using this honey trick to pass on a holistic, eco-friendly message to this group of children, which in plain terms runs as follows: *ants are not simply pests, they may be entertaining beings who love sweet things and are capable of putting on an aesthetically pleasing show*. The message, via this micro-story, is also shared with the mainly adult audience that listens to the Countryside Hour.

In the next two extracts, Skinner provides reasons based on strictly biological considerations for finding ants fascinating:

Table 4.8 Countryside Hour: Ant Story (2)

1	Or as I said come back to the same colony, but why I'm talking about black garden
2	ants which fascinate me, many aspects of their life, they're very social. They will learn
3	to milk aphids so they'll stroke the back end of an aphid to exude what we call
4	honeydew, you know, if you park under something like a Maple tree in June and July
5	your car bonnet will all be sticky and that's the honeydew which aphids exude
6	normally. Well, ants learn to farm the aphids and stroke their rear ends, and you get
7	little tiny drops of honeydew which the ants gather and bring back to feed the queen or
8	the larvae in the nest

In this short fragment there is no explicit evaluation, and the implicit evaluations invite us to further explore the difference between two of Martin and White's subcategories of Judgement, what they call 'capacity' and 'propriety' (see Section 3.2). The former refers to how well something is done (*playing tennis, speaking French*, etc.) and the latter to how ethically correct an action might be. In the case of ants, the ability to milk aphids (2–3), for example, would clearly concern a type of capacity judgement (the ants are able – that is, they have the *capacity* – to perform this action); however, the attribution of 'propriety' judgements (2,7–8) to non-human social actors could have problematic features:

Though this is only a short 'story' it touches on two central and wide-ranging themes in this book and in ecological studies generally – the potential of the natural world to fascinate, and possible differences between human and non-human consciousness, and should therefore be worth looking at in some depth. This potential of the natural world to fascinate throws up an issue for the Appraisal Framework's coding system, as the question mark in the AF code column in Table 4.9 suggests. A *thing* such as a book or a puzzle that is 'fascinating' can be assessed readily as +App: Reaction, a semantic category that consists of reactions to phenomena, in which 'fascinating' is included by Martin and White as a guide word alongside others such as 'exciting, sensational, engaging, dramatic' and so on (Martin and White 2005: 56). The problem is that ants are not 'things' but conscious entities,[10] and although people can also

Table 4.9 Countryside Hour: Ant Story (2), Evaluation

Line	Relevant Text	AF Code
1–2	black garden ants which fascinate me	t+J: ?
2	very social	t+J: propriety
2–3	they will learn to milk aphids	t+J: capacity
3	they''l stroke the back end of an aphid	t+J: capacity
6	ants learn to farm the aphids . . . stroke their rear ends	t+J: capacity
7–8	ants gather . . . in the nest	t+J: capacity/propriety

be 'fascinating' there is no indication in Martin and White's classic book on Appraisal theory to suggest how this attribute of a person should be assessed. As we have seen, they record appraisals of people via the 'Judgement' system, which is subdivided into five categories: normality, capacity, tenacity, veracity and propriety (ibid.: 53). Of these five, perhaps the first, 'normality' would be the appropriate category for 'fascinating', but this is quite problematic and the point would require detailed investigation. Just to raise one aspect of the matter: presumably a person is 'fascinating' to the extent that they differ in some way from 'normality' (otherwise all ordinary people would be fascinating too). It seems counter-intuitive if a fascinating person – someone with a gift or some other attribute that marks them out as more interesting than the common run of the mill person – should be seen as meriting a + Normality judgement. Yet, since the intent is usually to praise the person, the judgement can clearly not be negative either. To come back to the ants, it is obvious that Skinner means to say something nice about them by saying that they 'fascinate' him, but it seems most unlikely that this has anything to do with their 'normality'.

On the second point, whether the quality of being 'social' as it appears in ants and other animals may be seen as an instance of positive evaluation at all, or if instead it is merely a descriptive adjective, is open to debate. Even in the human context, it is possible to see behavioural traits such as sociability either as innate character features, or as 'social skills' to be acquired, as learned behaviour, a perspective which would locate this aspect in the 'capacity' category.

My suggestion, in analysing this and the next text, is that when he calls ants' behaviour 'social', Skinner is making a positive ethical judgement. Here some readers might feel that we are in the realm of Sperber and Wilson's 'weakly salient implicatures' (see Section 3.1.3), though I think that both the context and what we know about Skinner's general ecological outlook support this hypothesis. The point is not insignificant because it is precisely the social orientation of many animals that may be adduced as one of the most significant differences between non-human and human ways of being in the world, their consciousness and patterns of behaviour (Caracciolo 2020). Perhaps we do not usually consider animal behaviour as bound by analogous ethical considerations to those that affect the human sphere (Ayala 2010), but Darwin's observations led him to propose a different view:

> Looking at Man, as a Naturalist would at any other Mammiferous animal, it may be concluded that he has parental, conjugal and social instincts, and perhaps others. These instincts consist of a feeling of love and sympathy or benevolence to the object in question. Without regarding their origin, we see in other animals they consist in such active sympathy that the individual forgets itself, and aids and defends and acts for others at its own expense. (Charles Darwin, in Richardson 2013)[11]

Darwin's account of social orientation in this passage, in particular his concept of 'active sympathy' and 'self-forgetting', seems to attribute behavioural qualities to animals that we would conventionally consider highly ethical if they were found in the human world.

Or consider the following definition of morality, outlined by Musschenga in his study of animal ethics:

> Morality cultivates and regulates social life within a group or community by providing rules (norms) that fortify natural tendencies that bind the members together – such as sympathy, (indirect) reciprocity, loyalty to the group and family, and so on – and which counter natural tendencies that frustrate and undermine cooperation – such as selfishness, within-group violence, and cheating. (Musschenga 2016)

It is plain, then, that in considering the essential nature of ethical behaviour, an emphasis on relations with the social group is crucial, whether the discussion regards the human or non-human world.

It is on the basis of these background considerations that it is possible to view Chris Skinner's use of the term 'social' as a positive evaluation of animal behaviour. It is clear from the co-text, from the other extracts on the topic of ants, that part of his enthusiasm for them, his oft-repeated claim to find them 'fascinating', derives precisely from this tendency to evince collective rather than individual behaviour. In fine, it will not be necessary for us to debate the substantial issue of animals' potentials for ethical behaviour any further: what is relevant is that discussion and analysis are able to shed light on the *speaker's attitudes* in this regard, since, as ecolinguists, all we are concerned with is to arrive at a clear understanding of his meaning.

The narrative structure (Table 4.10) below is rather patchy, with missing stages, numerous social actors and a Complication – the sticky car bonnets – that is not resolved:

Table 4.10 Countryside Hour: Ant Story (2), Narrative

Abstract	-
Orientation	Who? I (1,2), You (4), black garden ants (1, 2, 3, 6, 7), aphids (3, 5, 6), the queen (7), larvae (8) When? June and July (4) Where? Garden (1), Under a Maple tree (4), the nest (8) What? Ants' social behaviour
Complication	Bonnet will be all sticky (5)
Evaluation	1–2 *black garden ants which fascinate me* 2 very social t+J: propriety 2–3 they will learn to milk aphids t+J: capacity 3 they'll stroke the back end of an aphid t+J: capacity 6 ants learn to farm the aphids . . . stroke their rear ends t+J: capacity 7–8 ants gather . . . in the nest t+J: capacity/propriety
Result	The ants have food to feed the queen or larvae (7)
Coda	-

In point of fact, mention of the car bonnet is incidental to the story, an intrusion of the human world into a story that regards non-human social actors – ants and aphids – and their interaction.

The fact that ants 'farm' aphids is quite well-known, though it is perhaps less appreciated that, as Nielsen et al. (2010) report, there is also a gain for the aphids, who the ants guard and shelter from natural insect enemies.

As in the first extract, Skinner's use of framing assimilates the ants' world to that of humans. Their behaviour is termed 'farming' (6). The strictly human activity of 'milking' cows serves as a metaphor to illustrate non-human behaviour. They also 'learn' (2,6) to farm the aphids, to stroke their rear ends, another verb that refers to an institutionalized form of human behaviour. The pragmatic significance of this frame is thus to reduce the gulf that separates humanity from the natural world. If this tiny being can perform this delicate task, and has the cognitive capacity to organize relations with another species that can readily be described as a kind of 'farming', then we must look elsewhere for the species exceptionalism that has traditionally lifted *homo sapiens* above the rest of creation. There is also something about the picture of younger ants being taught how to perform the stroking, of knowledge being passed on across the generations, that gives the lie to the crude idea that animal behaviour is directed by an impersonal, mechanistic 'instinct' (Tinbergen 1989).

In the final extract of this sequence, Skinner reiterates the social nature of ants:

Table 4.11 Countryside Hour: Ant Story (3)

1	But I've noticed something which I've never ever seen before. I sit and have my
2	usually <u>burnt</u> supper which I've cooked for myself in the porch, here in the sunshine
3	and in this little dish with the honey in it, I started to notice lots of grains of sand in
4	the dish and I couldn't understand where it's coming from. So I've been watching over
5	several evenings. We've had some <u>lovely sunny</u> evenings and occasionally, an ant will
6	get stuck in the honey. It will try to run across the top of the honey and get stuck.
7	And so what happens? Would you believe this, *other* ants will go off and get grains of
8	sand and drop into the edge of the honey so that the ant that's stuck in the honey can
9	manage to get itself back out. It's an <u>amazing</u> sight. I've just been watching it over and
10	over again because I couldn't quite believe my eyes as to why there's grains of sand
11	and little bits of silt were ending up in the honey dish. So there we are. The life of the
12	black garden ant and there's lots, lots more to learn about them. And about the
13	environment we spend and share the Norfolk countryside with. So before you go off to
14	the shops when they're open and buy some more ant spray just have that second
15	thought before you do it. They're <u>really social</u> little insects and of course they're <u>great</u>
16	food. If you love things like green woodpeckers, the largest of our three species of native
17	woodpecker, and they absolutely love the ants and gobble them up with their long sticky
18	tongues which they probe down into the ant colonies. They can't do that in my porch
19	because they're in amongst the cacti. Fascinating to watch them. Always lots more to learn.

As we can see in Table 4.12, the narrative structure is more complete:

Table 4.12 Countryside Hour: Ant Story (3), Narrative

Abstract	*I've noticed something . . . coming from* (1–4)
Orientation	Who? I (1, 2, 3, 4, 5, 9, 10) ants (5, 6, 7, 8, 9, 11, 12, 15, 17, 19), we (5, 11, 12, 16), you (7, 13, 14, 15), green woodpecker (16–19) When? June–July (given information) Where? Skinner's porch (given information) What? Ants rescuing a comrade stuck in honey
Complication	*an ant will get stuck in the honey* (5–6)
Evaluation	*So before you go off to the shops when they're open and buy some more ant spray just have that second thought before you do it* (13–14)
Result	*the ant that's stuck in the honey can manage to get itself back out* (8–9)
Coda	Fascinating to watch them. Always lots more to learn (19)

The story opens with what Labov calls the 'abstract', in which Skinner outlines the 'problem' which the rest of the story will resolve, that is where the grains of sand in the honey are coming from. Again we notice the narrator's self-inclusion via personal pronouns, but there are also many references that suggest an other-orientation. There is dialogical engagement with listeners, for example via a rhetorical question like '*Would <u>you</u> believe this?*' (7), hypothesis about possible listeners' attitudes: '*If <u>you</u> love things like green woodpeckers*' (15–16), as well as use of the first-person plural pronoun to construe commonality with them, as in

'We've had some lovely sunny evenings' (5), 'there we are' (11), 'the environment we spend and share the Norfolk countryside with' (13). Above all, there is an explicit attempt to point out the moral of the story via the rhetorical device of apostrophe: *before you go off to the shops when they're open and buy some more ant spray just have that second thought before you do it (13–14)*. This message represents the Labovian Evaluation stage, which 'highlights the point, shows listeners how they are to understand the meaning'.

In terms of evaluation, it is noticeable that Skinner highlights once more the 'fascinating' quality of the ants, and once again stresses their 'social' qualities:

Table 4.13 Countryside Hour: Ant Story (3), Evaluation

Line	Relevant Text	AF Code
2	burnt supper	+ App: Quality
5	a lovely sunny	+ App: Quality
7–9	Other ants will go off . . . back out	t + J: propriety
9	An amazing sight	+ App: Quality
12	*There's lots, lots more to learn about them*	t + App: Impact
13–14	*Before you go off to the shops . . . ant spray*	t-ive J: propriety
15	Really social little insects	+ J: propriety
19	*Fascinating to watch them*	t + App: Impact

In terms of framing, the human world is once more evoked via an emergency/rescue frame: an ant struggles in the honey and will perish, so the nearby colony members produce an escape route constructed from the materials nearest to hand. On the basis of the discussion of animal morality above, it is possible to view Skinner's description of the ants' rescue activities (7–9) as encapsulating the essence of the story. They stop what they are doing, engage in extra work, collaborate in order to save the life of a fellow, and for Skinner this is 'social' behaviour and carries a positive ethical connotation.

From a pragmatic perspective, it is fruitful to ponder Skinner's response to his own observations, which he characterizes as amazement (9) and even disbelief (10). From his rhetorical question ('would you believe it'?), we can see that he also expects his listeners to react in the same way. From this we can infer that the ants' behaviour demonstrates a level of intelligence or, at the very least, practical know-how that surpasses general human expectations for this species.

Thus, we can also understand his appeal to listeners to avoid an automatic use of ant-spray. It depends on listeners joining up a series of cognitive dots, to revise their thinking about ants – if, that is, they formerly considered them to be nothing more than semi-automated bugs, rampant pests to be swept unthinkingly from the house. He presents them as motivated by a form of altruism, guided by a strategic intelligence, by a value system that places the group's survival above that of the individual. Therefore, he argues, they merit more from our hands than chemical destruction.

Finally on this text, it is worth remembering that pragmatic analysis tends to concern possible, rather than absolute, meanings, on the basis of hypotheses selected according to the principle of salience, which was discussed above (Section 3.1.3). In the case of Skinner's use of the term 'fascinating', more evidence can be found in the co-text to support the hypothesis advanced above, that is that it is the ants' capacity for social behaviour that Skinner is claiming as their outstanding, most 'fascinating' feature. He concludes the anecdote – significantly, from a narrative perspective – in the 'coda', Labov's optional stage which has a summing up function, underlining the relevance of the story:

> Fascinating to watch them. Always lots more to learn (19)

Thus, he underlines the possibility that there is a connection between fascination, observation and the potential to 'learn' about ants (thus excluding, e.g., the idea that the fascination is in some way related simply to the spectacle they provide, as in the case of the honey ring anecdote). It is plain that what has been learnt in the story of the sand in the honey concerns the ants' capacity both for strategic thinking and social action: significantly, a reference to the ants' profoundly social orientation immediately follows the rescue episode:

> They're really <u>social</u> little insects (15)

In this case, then, Sperber and Wilson would use the term 'strongly salient' for the implicature that what Skinner finds 'fascinating' about the ants relates in some way to their social orientation, as well as to the fact that they demonstrate surprising qualities of intelligence and strategic thinking.

4.4.3 Carrion Crows and Pheasants

The Carrion Crow does not enjoy a good image. Something to do with the name, perhaps, though a lot of other birds are equally happy to feed on carrion. Like all corvids, their presence in the countryside is problematic for farmers for several reasons. First, they tend to eat seeds, as an old sowing rhyme puts it:

> One for the rook, one for the crow, one to die and one to grow

Another reason for the enmity of part of the rural community towards crows is their habit of eating the eggs of birds earmarked for shooting such as partridges, quails and pheasants (Montevecchi 1976). Hence, the crow is widely considered as one of the chief enemies in our 'war on wildlife' (see Section 2.10). As Gregory and Marchant (1996) explain, all corvids are regarded as 'pests' to be 'controlled' in the agricultural context, and the UK had to negotiate an exemption from EU regulations in this regard. This is the theme of Skinner's story in this section, one of the most complete and coherent narratives so far studied:

Table 4.14 Carrion Crows and Pheasants Story

1	Now, I said I was going to introduce you to two of my top conservation birds at High
2	Ash farm and that will explain why I have all these Pheasants around me. It would
3	gladden the heart of any gamekeeper, any conservationist, because in front of me is a
4	row of Ash trees in the hedge right in front of me, I'm looking almost into the sun, so
5	I'm facing due east and interspersed in those trees about 20 meters apart are a few
6	Oaks as well, they're all now coming into leaf and in the very first tree, about 25 feet
7	up just over halfway up in an Ash tree, right above one of the permissive walks at
8	High Ash farm is a Carrion Crows' nest. Right, (laughter) all the gamekeepers start
9	frothing at the mouth. What are you doing letting Carrion Crows nest on your farm,
10	and why have they got anything at all to do with conservation? Well, the answer is
11	something I've found over the last 20, 25 years of leaving nature to do its own work,
12	and I have one pair only of Carrion Crows and in a few minutes we'll drive round to
13	the other end of the field and see my single Magpies' nest as well. Both species and
14	members of the Crow family. Notorious egg thieves . . . yep, so how many of us woke up
15	this morning and had eggs for breakfast? And that's probably quite alright. And these
16	are natural birds, and this is a natural habitat for them, and they're just doing what they
17	do. So I stand back and allow nature to kind of rule the roost, if you like, and make the
18	decisions here at High Ash farm. The farm's not big enough for a full scale rewilding
19	project and on many rewilding efforts, some form of control is still carried out, which
20	is really sad. So this Carrion Crows' nest in front of me, the female is still sitting on
21	the nest. I'm probably 80 to 100 yards away. She's incubating, the eggs will be
22	hatching quite soon. And they're extremely territorial. And I mean, extremely
23	territorial. Talk about bad neighbours! (laughter) They will not tolerate other Carrion
24	Crows to nest in this area. I'm actually over the boundary in this particular field,
25	Caister's down in the valley there and I'm actually sitting in Stoke Holy Cross. And
26	the Carrion Crows' territory extends over most of High Ash farm, which is getting on
27	for a square mile and well into Stoke Holy Cross. So fingers crossed these . . . this pair of
28	Carrion Crows are not going to be controlled or shot because the extreme territorial
29	behaviour they exhibit prevents any other birds – Carrion Crows, in other words
30	nesting in their territory, they've become dominant. They've formed this relationship,
31	which has lasted several years now, and this is the third year in succession the same
32	pair of birds have used this nest. And so what they're doing is, yep, they'll take a few
33	Pheasants' eggs. There's lots of Pheasants here in front of me. Pigeons' eggs, other
34	eggs and small mammals. Small birds, fledglings if they can catch them. But they're
35	not doing enough harm to affect in any meaningful way the number of species nesting
36	at the farm or reductions in species. They're doing the gamekeeping for me, if you
37	like. They're doing all the hard work. I don't have to be out early in the morning, I
38	don't have to be setting traps or whatever or shooting them, they're doing the work for
39	me, and the Pheasants are all pondering off in front of me now into one of the hedges.
40	There's lots of thick, grassy bottoms and so lots of nests for them and yep they may
41	steal a nest or two and take all the eggs, and at this time of the year, the Pheasants
42	certainly can rear another clutch. But there's – we're absolutely stuffed with Pheasants.

This stretch of narrative begins with a clear abstract in which Skinner announces that he will tell his interlocutor how it is that the Pheasants on the farm are so numerous (2):

Table 4.15 Carrion Crow. Narrative Structure

Abstract	Now, I said [...] why I have all these pheasants around me (1–2)
Orientation	**Who?** I (1, 4, 5, 10, 11, 16, 20, 22, 23, 24) top conservation birds (1), Pheasants (2, 32, 38, 41, 42) gamekeeper (3, 8) conservationist (3), Carrion Crows (9, 12, 16, 19, 20, 21, 23, 25, 27–38, 40), Magpie (13), Us (14) **When?** Spring (5–6), over the last 20, 25 years (11) **What?** Role of Carrion Crows in conservation **Where?** High Ash farm (1–2), Stoke Holy Cross (25)
Complication	Notorious egg thieves (14)
Evaluation	+J: capacity: <u>top</u> conservation birds (1) +Aff: happiness: It would <u>gladden the heart</u> of any gamekeeper (2–3) -Aff: (dis-)satisfaction, *intens.*: all the gamekeepers <u>start frothing at the mouth</u> (8) –ive J: propriety: <u>Notorious</u> egg thieves (14) t-ive J: propriety: *so how many of us woke up this morning and had eggs for breakfast?* (14–15) +J: propriety: that's probably <u>quite alright</u> (15) t+J: propriety: *these are natural birds [. . .] doing what they do* (15–17) –ive Aff: unhappiness: which is <u>really sad</u> (19–20) –J: propriety: Talk about <u>bad neighbours</u> (23) +J:propriety (*irrealis*): they're <u>not doing enough harm</u> (34–35) +J: capacity: They're <u>doing all the hard work</u>. (37) –ive J: propriety: they may <u>steal a nest or two and take</u> all the eggs (40–41)
Result	We're absolutely stuffed with pheasants (42)
Coda	–

Digressions, as we have seen, are a familiar feature of Skinner's narrative style, and here he goes off the subject with some details about the trees (4–7), a reference to Magpies (13), some remarks on rewilding (18–19) and details of where he finds himself (24–25); however, the rest of the text has a bearing on the story, which winds about in various directions but returns to conclude perfectly on topic (41–42).

In common with the ant story which also made a specific point, that is that we should not simply reach for pesticide when we find ants in the house, this text attempts to engage with listeners who may have different views. It may be seen as a sample of another genre, which has been extensively studied in the analysis of political discourse, a more overt category of persuasive, or 'rhetorical' text (Virtanen and Halmari 2005; Ferretti and Adornetti 2021; Chilton 2004; Ponton 2017; Kjeldsen 2017). This kind of text frequently involves arguing from 'is' to 'ought' (Searle 1964), that is it starts from a description of a real-world situation and proposes appropriate courses of action to resolve a problem. Most linguistic approaches to such texts identify one or more propositions that are carried forward in an 'argument', which can usually be expressed in the standard form for syllogisms, an approach that dates back as far as Aristotle (Damer 2012; Aristotle and Bartlett). In the Crow text this would be something like the following:

> Since: The Carrion Crow is extremely territorial (21–22) and, if not controlled by gamekeepers, will prevent other Carrion Crows from nesting in an area of more than a square mile (26–27; 27–30);
>
> (And Since): Gamekeeping is extremely hard work (35–39)
>
> Therefore: We should not waste time, energy and other resources in 'controlling' them but rely on nature to regulate the business (17–18)

There are certain assumptions that are not specified; the speaker takes for granted, for instance, that his listeners will know that crows are regularly shot by gamekeepers, that this happens because they prey on Pheasants' eggs, that there is a lucrative business that centres on Pheasant shooting and so on. There are some more subtle implicit assumptions, too. The conventional solutions practised by gamekeepers, referred to in the text like setting traps and shooting (37–38), must be deficient in some way. If this inference is not recognized, then the argument falls to the ground: If the gamekeepers' way works just as well in terms of limiting crow population, then why do things Skinners' way? One of two meanings must be relevant here: either there is some intrinsic problem with what gamekeepers are currently doing, or Skinner's meaning is likely to be that, if the gamekeepers did things his way then they would have more time and energy for other useful projects.

As can be seen from the Who? section of the Orientation in Table 4.15, the main social actors in the story are Skinner himself (as usual!), Carrion Crows which dominate the narrative, a few other bird types, gamekeepers, conservationists and a solitary reference to 'Us', the inclusive 'we' by which Skinner means British people as a whole. The solitary reference to 'us' occurs in connection with a crucial ethical point, and it is worth exploring this reference in some detail, since it will shed light on the way storytellers interact with their imagined audience. Skinner has just proclaimed that corvids like Magpies and Crows are <u>notorious</u> egg thieves (14), a case of Martin and White's serious ethical category, 'negative judgement: propriety'. For this reference to be applied to a human subject, the person in question would have to break the law or commit some other manifestly unethical action.

Skinner acknowledges that this is the usual social judgement on corvids, especially among the gamekeeping fraternity, but immediately engages with the implications of the inference by asking a rhetorical question to 'us' concerning behaviour in the human world:

> Notorious egg thieves . . . yep, so how many of us woke up this morning and had eggs for breakfast? And that's probably quite alright. And these are natural birds, and this is a natural habitat for them, and they're just doing what they do (15–17)

Once again it is possible to trace the contours of the implicit argument made here:

> Since: Humans also eat eggs, commonly for breakfast on a daily basis (14–15)

> And since: We see nothing wrong with this (15)[12]

> Therefore: It is unreasonable to use strong negative judgements like 'notorious thieves' (14) to describe Crows' behaviour

Just as it is 'natural' for us to go to the supermarket, or open the fridge and fry an egg, Skinner applies the adjective with equal justice – indeed, arguably, with more – to the actions of the crows. Later in the same episode when the focus has switched to Magpies, Skinner continues in the same vein to discuss Magpies' habit of removing all eggs from a nest and storing or cacheting the 'extra' food:

> If you have a food shortage, what do you do? Go to the local shop and stock up – Magpies will do that.

When Skinner suggests that animals and birds, on the one hand, and human beings, on the other, have common issues that they deal with in similar ways, he closes the distance between human and non-human world and encourages a more sympathetic response from the former to the latter. Another instance in this tale is his reference to neighbours:

> Talk about bad neighbours! (23)

Here the negative judgement: propriety on the birds' behaviour, by contrast with the egg thieving reference, is not opposed, since it seems that all corvids will always behave aggressively to other birds who attempt to move into their territory.

On one level, then, in this section of the story, Skinner engages with the general public, attempting to absolve the crows from what Martin and White term the 'social sanction' associated with wrongdoing. However, another important human target is perhaps more relevant, the gamekeepers whose solutions to the problem of corvids are represented as unnecessary. In another episode of the Countryside Hour, Skinner discusses gamekeepers' practices in the context of Magpies, who represent them with identical problems. The more they trap, destroy, shoot at or poison Magpies, it seems the more the birds multiply and resist destruction. Skinner recommended the same solution as that outlined here, since a pair of Magpies will occupy a territory and prevent other pairs from nesting and breeding in it.

Gamekeepers, along with farmers, are key social actors in the farming industry, people at the frontline of the war on wildlife, people whose everyday actions are decisive in determining the shape of the biosphere and our relations with the natural world. Gamekeepers are not just represented in the text with the aim – for example – of discrediting their views with the general public. Rather, they make an appearance in it as dialogical partners when Skinner addresses them as a group directly:

> Right, (laughter) all the gamekeepers start frothing at the mouth. (8–9)

Skinner then temporarily becomes a representative gamekeeper as he enacts, or voices, the likely response of the whole category to his proposition:

> What are you doing letting Carrion Crows nest on your farm, and why have they got anything at all to do with conservation? (9–10)

The gamekeepers' response is a hyperbole, since to 'froth at the mouth' is a sign of extreme rage. Together with the questions that follow it, this signals that what Skinner is proposing is regarded as a radical and absurd course of action, anathema in the profession. Yet this is not simply a disagreement on a technical point of governance – rather it is something deep seated, something that provokes a visceral and angry reaction, which Skinner mocks by laughing as he impersonates the typical gamekeeper. Interestingly, the second of their questions allows the inference that gamekeepers themselves are concerned with conservation. This reading arises if we pause to ask, in a pragmatic sense, what are the likely causes of the gamekeepers' supposed anger. From the first of their questions, the strongly salient implicatures concern the damage which Carrion Crows will do to the Pheasant population as they steal eggs, with consequent harm to the yearly shoot. In the second, we can infer that gamekeepers as a category care about biodiversity, that the objection to Carrion Crows concerns the harmful environmental effects that they would produce if allowed to breed undisturbed.

The connection between gamekeeping and conservation also emerges right at the outset of the story, as Skinner introduces them in the same breath:

> It would gladden the heart of any gamekeeper, any conservationist . . . (3)

As with the anger just discussed, joy is a basic emotion, and here gamekeeper and conservationist share a strong positive emotional response to the scene Skinner is describing, a rural idyll of pheasants in a setting of hedges, the sun shining on Ash and Oak coming into leaf (3–7). The gamekeeper, then, as a category, is aligned to a degree with the conservationist, since both have an identical emotional response to nature. Remembering that Martin and White (2005) consider emotional responses to be fundamental in determining an individual's scale of both aesthetic and ethical evaluations, this emotional convergence is suggestive of other resemblances of a cognitive type.

This positive presentation of gamekeepers is quite surprising, since they represent one of the principal poles of opposition to the kind of conservationist policies which he advocates. It must also be remembered that, though gamekeepers share Skinner's concern with protecting Pheasants' eggs, their reasons for wanting the same thing are very different. Skinner's overall outlook is expressed in his reflections on rewilding (16–19). Nature should 'rule the roost', should 'make the decisions', and his joy at witnessing a flourishing community of Pheasants reflects his sense that, in a small way, the Carrion Crow control mechanism proves that the rewilding option is effective in terms of promoting biodiversity. Gamekeepers' actions are determined by the bottom line, and a genuine concern for the Pheasants' well-being is no part of their efforts to protect the species.

The story's conclusion emphasizes the healthy state of the Pheasant community under the Carrion Crow's protection. Again we notice engagement with the gamekeepers' position in a reiteration of the text's argument:

> yep they may steal a nest or two and take all the eggs, and at this time of the year, the Pheasants certainly can rear another clutch. But there's – we're absolutely stuffed with Pheasants . . . (40–42)

As in lines 14 and 32, the 'yep' here acknowledges another voice, it summarizes the meaning *'yes, I know what you're about to say . . .'* In this case the contrary voices are those of gamekeepers, farmers, the shooting fraternity and their sympathizers. Skinner's homely phrase 'we're absolutely stuffed with Pheasants' (41–42) seems to carry on the dialogical exchange with this group of social actors.

Finally on this story, there is an apparent slip of the tongue from Skinner:

the Pheasants are all <u>pondering</u> off in front of me now into one of the hedges (39)

Whether this is a term from a Suffolk dialect or an accidental neologism is uncertain. However, the mingled semantics of 'to wander' and 'to ponder' seem particularly well suited to capture the bird's slow, purposeful gait.

4.4.4 Chris Skinner the naturalist

Before moving on from High Ash farm, some observations regarding the relevance of the type of enquiry presented in the last sections, which may be useful for the non-specialist reader, unused to this kind of linguistic digging. They might wonder why it is necessary to pin down the precise implications of Skinner's choice of words; they may ask, if it matters so much to know *exactly* what he means, why not send him an email? In an ideal world, the dimension of pragmatic linguistic enquiry could perhaps be explored using a simple questionnaire which people could fill in to explain precisely 'what they meant' by saying this X or that Y. However, it might be objected that, although there is a certain amount of truth in the notion that only the speaker knows what s/he really means, it is also true that most of us use language in a rough and ready way, without necessarily being aware of all the cognitive steps involved, or calculating possible alternatives that may express our ideas more precisely. Does Skinner himself know why he finds ants fascinating? Is it not probable that his interest in ants is multifaceted, has grown up over time, is part of an overall ecosophy or way of life that is part emotional, part intellectual, part spiritual – and therefore cannot easily be put into words?

In this study the central focus is the language that a wide range of people use to represent nature, which can provide us with keys to explore how they think about it. Some of these people are pop singers (Section 1.2), Hawaiian fishermen (Section 2.2), Native American chiefs (Section 2.4), institutional social actors such as politicians and oil companies (Section 2.5), Romantic poets (Section

2.5), environmentalists (Section 2.7), a marine biologist (Section 2.8), BBC radio listeners, modern internet users (Section 3.2) and so on.

Skinner's perceived importance in this study derives from two considerations: first, because he is deeply enmeshed in the practice of farming which, whatever directions the world takes to deal with the current planetary crisis, must continue in some form or another. It is thus appropriate to consider his views on our relations with the natural world, how farming practices can be organized in the future to balance agricultural returns with environmental goals. Second, as a seasoned broadcaster on these topics, it is plain that his views – like those of other prominent environmentalists like Chris Packham and Sir David Attenborough – have an enormous potential to influence public attitudes about the natural world and everything connected with it.

These considerations, ideally, give a certain weight to the analyses conducted in the last section. It appears significant, for instance, to tease out whether Skinner's 'fascination' with animals like ants depends simply on the fact that it can be of scientific interest to study them, entertaining to use them in party tricks or whether instead we are to view them as endowed with consciousness and faced, like us, by ethical dilemmas. Under the influence of the Romantic natural imaginary, this notion reminds us of the thoughts of a poet like William Blake:

> Am not I
> A fly like thee?
> Or art not thou
> A man like me?
> (William Blake, 'The Fly')

If we were to suppose that such thoughts, instead of the poetic 'fancies' they are generally taken for, represent important insights into the human (and non-human) condition, then we might treat the natural world differently. We might find that solutions to the problems of modernity have always been closer to hand than we thought.

As we have seen, Wordsworth believed himself able to perceive a stone as endowed with a 'moral life' (Section 2.5), and something of this deep ecological comprehension appears to infuse Skinner's own 'fascination' with the ants' behaviour. As Naess writes (Section 2.2):

> The ecological field-worker acquires a deep-seated respect, or even veneration, for ways and forms of life. He reaches an understanding from within, a kind of

understanding that others reserve for fellow men and for a narrow section of ways and forms of life.

The suggestion, then, would be that Skinner's discourse might provide models for the spread of this 'kind of understanding' which, if shared by a critical mass of the population, could effect a real transformation in the kinds of 'stories we live by' in modern societies, and hence help the emergence of a range of genuinely sustainable, ecologically directed social practices.

5

Situated Narratives (2) Priolo Saltpans

5.1 Introduction

In this section the focus switches from the UK to Sicily, from an examination of agriculture and environmental sustainability to the broad problem of environmental devastation caused by industrial processes. In the first case study the overall takeaway regards the possibility of including what Skinner calls the 'production of wildlife' among the goals of agricultural activity. Here the terrain is perhaps more familiar, the debate over environmental protection that has accompanied the capitalist-industrial project since its beginnings in the industrial revolutions of the eighteenth century (see Sections 1.2 and 2.7). As in the first case study, this part of the book will present some stories about a site and analyse them using some of the linguistic tools that have been described.

Every time I take the bus to or from Pozzallo, a small town on the south-east coast of Sicily, to Catania, the city on the southern flank of Etna where I work, the journey leads past a long strip of industrial plants that disfigure what would otherwise be a wonderful close-up view of the Mediterranean. Over the years, as I have got to know the realities of my chosen home, I have learnt more about the history of this area, which goes back to the times of Magna Graecia and beyond.

The story begins in the immediate post-war period, in the efforts of Italian governments to rebuild the devastated nation and meanwhile to address other social issues that had arguably been mishandled from the outset of the national unification project that began in 1861. Such problems included analphabetism and poverty and the attachment, especially in the South, to rural patterns of economic activity and ways of life. Italy was beset by a regionalism that manifested in cultural and linguistic diversity, and this fed into a South/North split, whose most visible result was a population drift from the former towards the latter. Industry, flourishing urban centres and technological progress were features of the northern regions, while the abandoned South was marked by backwardness, resource depletion and the remnants of feudalism, all of which tended to support the development of organized criminality (Moe 2002; Dunnage 2022). To site petrochemical plants in Sicily therefore enabled the government to address several problems at once, and projects began in the coastal towns of Gela (1960), Milazzo (1961) and Priolo-Gargallo (1950).[1] The choice to site these heavy industrial sites in the South served a range of purposes. Not only could the government claim to be modernizing living conditions, increasing incomes and thus helping to kick-start local economies in the South, but they also avoided civil opposition that might have resulted from placing them near northern urban centres.

The (hi)story of the Priolo/Augusta petrochemical complex is charted by the World Health Organisation. Their account makes it clear that, from the first, local communities welcomed the plants, mainly because of the employment prospects they afforded:

> Despite a heated debate (Trimboli 2004), these political choices were not opposed by local populations, as plans for industrialization promised new hope for a better and wealthier future. Also, the occupational and economic benefits expected were estimated to more than compensate for environmental and health costs, which the public undervalued in the 1950s and 1960s. Moreover, the moderate environmental legislation in place misleadingly appeared to be a sufficient guarantee for land protection. (Mudu et al. 2014: 108)

With hindsight it is easy to see factors that could not be fully appreciated in that historical moment. As the text makes clear, the risks of damaging the environment and human health were both undervalued, and not just in Italy. Moreover, stimulated by the Marshall Plan, Europe's nations were engaged in reconstruction, in creating employment opportunities, and hence potentially negative aspects of these initiatives were overlooked.

The emergence of mass tourism as a key global industry, one with a much lower environmental impact, exposes the catastrophe of Sicily's post-war industrial choice. A 30-kilometre stretch of coastline containing several sites of outstanding historical importance from classical Greek times, a rich maritime ecosystem with sandy beaches, bays, estuaries – all this prime territory for tourism was wasted, for the sake of the second largest petrochemical complex in Europe. The anticipated economic spin-offs for Sicily failed to materialize. The towns closest to the Priolo-Gargallo plant were Priolo, Melilli and Augusta, and they experienced initial growth but in very short order turned into what

Taylor (2014) terms 'toxic communities'. As the WHO study clearly shows, levels of air, earth and sea pollution have risen beyond safety horizons for human health: toxic chemicals such as mercury have simply been dumped in the sea. When the refineries were in full swing, a palpable smog hung over the road to Catania, and the acrid odours could be smelled by passing traffic. The area is notorious for provoking deaths from cancer and other related diseases among those who worked there – at its height, the plant was like a small town with a 'population' of around twenty thousand souls.

Documentary journalist Elena Chernyshova uses dark (at times, hyper-) realistic images to capture the awful state of this area under industrial control. The accompanying text on the web page accentuates them, creating such an overwhelmingly negative impression of Priolo Gargallo that the rhetorical notions of 'environmental recovery', 'sustainable future', 'pink miracle' and so on with which we shall shortly be concerned seem to fade away like insubstantial shadows:

> The intensive industrialization brought rampant pollution damaging the environment, and the situation was made even worse with wheeling and dealing between criminal networks and public authorities, taking advantage of silent and submissive local communities terrified at the prospect of the economy collapsing if the industrial plants closed down. High levels of pollutants have been released into the air, industrial waste has been illegally dumped and buried on land, and toxic sludge and mercury have been discharged into the sea, with an estimated 500 metric tons of mercury dumped in Augusta Bay since 1958. The death rate from breast cancer in the region increased from 8.9% in 1951 to 29.9% in 1980. The prevalence of congenital malformations went from 1.9% in 1989 to 5.6% in 2000, producing the highest rate for abortion and spontaneous abortion in Italy. In 1998, a coastal area of 5,815 hectares and a maritime area of 10,068 hectares were officially recognized by the Italian government as a site of national interest, requiring compulsory decontamination of land, surface water and groundwater. Today, only one small zone has been cleaned up.[2]

In the less dramatic words of anthropologist Mara Benadusi:

> The zone is exposed to 'frictions' – ecological, energetic, heritage-related – which need to be seen in the light of historical factors that are often obscured by strategic alliances created for the promotion of specific territorial interests. These factors are linked to political economy that make sense of this crisis and allow for its manifestations in urban and rural landscapes, but also to affect the most vulnerable among human subjects. (Benadusi 2018a)

The gravity of the situation is also manifest in the following text, in which nested evaluations both conceal and convey the writer's stance towards the phenomena in question. As befits the objective style of a scientific text, the writer is not concerned with attributing blame or responsibility but with outlining the facts, yet we notice that they can hardly avoid straying into the field of moral outrage:

Table 5.1 The Priolo-Melilli industrial pole

Line	Text	AF Value
1	First of all, the water emergency brought about by the	
2	indiscriminate use of groundwater, which has produced	–J: propriety/capacity?
3	the lowering of the water table by procuring severe	
4	insalination processes . . . the *industrial emission of macro-*	t–J: propriety
5	*and micro-pollutants*; the frequent phenomena of thermal	
6	inversion; the formation of smog by photosynthesis of	
7	ozone and non-methane hydrocarbons; the presence of	
8	organic and inorganic dust; the degradation of marine	
9	waters, linked to illegal industrial discharges, with *the*	–J: propriety
10	*production of oil and mercury pollution phenomena*	t–J: propriety
11	accompanied by processes of eutrophication and genetic	
12	transformation of fish fauna; *the lack of safe distance* of	t–J: propriety
13	plants and storage areas from population centres; *the high*	
14	*production of waste.* . . . In addition to these reasons, it	t–J: propriety
15	should be added that *the area is also considered to be at*	
16	*high seismic risk and that the industrial settlements* have	–J: propriety
17	compromised *both the archaeological site of Megara Iblea*	t–J: propriety
18	*and the surrounding naturalistic areas.*[a]	

[a] Original Italian text: In primo luogo l'emergenza idrica determinata dall'uso indiscriminato delle acque sotterranee che ha prodotto l'abbassamento della falda procurando severi processi d'insalinazione . . . l'emissione industriale di macro e micro inquinanti; i frequenti fenomeni d'inversione termica; la formazione di smog per fotosintesi di ozono e idrocarburi non metanici; la presenza di polveri organiche e inorganiche; il degrado delle acque marine, legato agli scarichi industriali abusivi, con la produzione di fenomeni di inquinamento da petrolio e da mercurio accompagnati da processi di eutrofizzazione e di trasformazione genetica della fauna ittica; la mancanza di distanza di sicurezza degli impianti e delle aree di stoccaggio dai centri abitati; l'elevata produzione di rifiuti. . . . A queste motivazioni va aggiunto che l'area è anche considerata ad alto rischio sismico e che gli insediamenti industriali hanno compromesso sia il sito archeologico di Megara Iblea, sia le aree naturalistiche limitrofe.

From Adorno (2007: 44).

The bites of information that make up the bulk of this text are mainly processed and represented as noun phrases, which is typical of the genre of scientific writing. The noun phrase tends to encode pragmatic meanings suggestive of objective states, abstract processes, natural phenomena and the like, as in:

the formation of smog by photosynthesis of ozone and non-methane hydrocarbons (6–7)

This is the language of the scientific textbook or report, a description of processes at work in the objective 'out there' world of physical realities. It is precise and technical, hence inaccessible to the man in the street, who generally lacks the appropriate knowledge to decode such messages. This perspective on the transformation of processes into things has been identified as 'nominalization' within linguistics and plays an important role in early CDA (Billig 2008). By these lexico-grammatical means, such texts may obfuscate the role of human agency in – and hence also, responsibility for – these processes (Wang and Hu 2023; Biber and Gray 2016; Halliday 2006). To formulate information in this way automatically sidesteps the political realm with its questions of blame and responsibility (whose fault is this? Why is this happening?, etc.). This is the case even with terms that clearly relate to non-technical matters, where human agency is explicitly indicated and evaluation of behaviour expressed, as in the following:

> the <u>indiscriminate</u> use of groundwater (2)

Here, the text proceeds immediately to focus on the results of this 'indiscriminate use', that is:

> which has produced the lowering of the water table by procuring severe insalination processes (2–4)

The cause–effect structure, again typical of scientific discourse (Hao 2018), leads to a focus, for writer and reader, on the outcome of the process in question. If the text at this point were to enquire, instead, into the identities of those responsible for this indiscriminate use, this would represent a significant departure from the generic pattern and would give quite a different flavour to the text as a whole.

For this reason, if we look at the analytical column in Table 5.1, we notice the presence of *tokens* (see Section 3.2), where the critique of human behaviour is said to be implied rather than stated explicitly. Alongside these insinuations are two instances of explicit negative evaluation, which tend to guide interpretations of the implicit content. The first of these, 'indiscriminate' (2), occurs at the beginning of the text, in a description of an 'emergency' provoked by the plants in the context of a vital resource, water. The second, <u>illegal</u> (9), openly states that the processes outlined in the text are against the law; this is thus an explicit reference to the human normative domain, to moral choices, the domain of crime and punishment.

These explicit references enable readers to infer blame in passages where the judgements are implied rather than stated, such as:

a) the *industrial emission of macro- and micro-pollutants (4–5)*
b) *the production of oil and mercury pollution phenomena (9–10)*

c) *the lack of safe distance* of plants and storage areas from population centres (12–13)

d) *the area is also considered to be at high seismic risk (15–16)*

In all of these fragments, pragmatic processes of interpretation lead to the attribution of blame, for example c) *lack of safe distance* – Why were these dangerous plants situated so close to population centres? Whose idea was that? What political figures were involved? Has anyone been punished for this? Just how dangerous are these plants and storage areas? Are they still in place?

Taken in a cumulative sense, these implied references build up into a damning critique of the choices of unnamed social actors and give weight to the final instance of explicit evaluation, the verb 'to compromise':

> *the industrial settlements* have compromised *both the archaeological site of Megara Iblea and the surrounding naturalistic areas (16–17)*

This is both a scientific assessment of a situation in the physical world and, at the same time, an implied critique of the choices that were made by the human beings responsible for these processes. It is noticeable, however, that actual agency is still not attributed; rather, it is the 'industrial settlements' that produce these outcomes, not the human beings involved in decision-making: companies, boards of directors, bankers, local dignitaries, national and local politicians, populations and so on.

The overall failure of the project to achieve its ambitious social and economic goals led to the sites being known among Sicilians as 'cathedrals in the desert', and a still more evocative nickname for the area, the 'triangle of death'. Despite local environmental protests, and growing awareness of the risks of living and working in the neighbourhood, the populations in the immediate vicinity were reluctant to change lifestyles, for example by relocating or changing jobs. No other jobs were available for one thing, and the dominant sentiment in the area could be summed up by a local saying expressing the well-known Sicilian fatalism – 'better to die from cancer than from hunger'.[3] Benadusi (2018b) captures the cruel bind in which the local populations found themselves:

> like the fumes rising from an industrial smokestack, 'oil culture' seeps into the imaginaries and epidermis of the people for whom petroleum represents both a blessing and a curse.

The devastation visited on one of the most beautiful stretches of Italy's coastline appears even more tragic today in the light of Sicily's booming tourist industry.

If correctly managed, its combination of sites of outstanding natural beauty and cultural heritage might have provided a more sustainable pathway towards economic growth in the region.[4]

In such a context, it is normal that local flora and fauna will suffer damage, but in 2000 a nature reserve was opened, on old salt marshes that stand between the northern perimeter of the city of Siracusa and the southern fringes of the industrial area. This was a joint initiative on the part of the Regional Department for the Environment and the Italian League for the Protection of Birds (LIPU). Its main aim was to protect the ecosystems that were used by thousands of migratory birds including the flamingo, which rapidly became the symbol of the reserve itself. The reserve won a national award for environmental protection in 2008, and today it hosts terns, dunlin, sandpipers, avocets, cormorants, herons, marsh harriers, black-winged stilts and little egrets, as well as the purple swamp hen, a species that had become extinct in Sicily. Pride of place, however, is the colony of breeding flamingos, a powerful magnet for visitors. Nowhere else in Sicily are flamingos known to breed, though they do frequent many other sites.

As Benadusi (2019) explains, the reserve developed with the significant cooperation of the industrial plants themselves, which included Italian energy giant Enel, the Industria Acqua Siracusana purification plant and the refineries of ISAB; the latter were taken over by Lukoil and face an uncertain future following Russia's 2022 invasion of Ukraine. She writes:

> The reserve – approximately 55 hectares of land, partly covered by *pantani*, the wet, shady areas typical of various parts of the Sicilian south-eastern coast – is so deeply sheltered among the factories that it would go entirely unnoticed from sea if it were not for several flocks of migratory birds flying over the smokestacks. (Benadusi 2019: 88)

There is an evocative contrast between the fragile beauties of these saltmarsh ecosystems and the backdrop of smokestacks, clearly visible behind the reserve. According to the site's long-term director, Fabio Cilea (2009: 13), the reserve is 'an oasis among the smokestacks', a formula which, as we shall see, has been taken up by the industrial giants to associate themselves with discourses of sustainability and renovation.

Perhaps it is the juxtaposition of a wetland with a flourishing avian population, on the one hand, and this monstrous manifestation of industrial damage on the other, that makes a visit to Priolo Saltpans so memorable. As many visitors with whom I have spoken confirm, it has its own unique fascination.

5.2 'Pink miracle' and pinkwashing

Since its earliest days, the Priolo Saltpans oasis has been represented in ways that emphasize the collaboration between LIPU and the industrial complex that contributed to its origins, downplaying the latter's controversial environmental impact. Benadusi (2019) suggests that the multinational corporations, especially Enel, exploit the 'flamingo factor' and the reserve itself by incorporating them in promotional campaigns for a so-called sustainability agenda, one that suggests an essential harmony between the aims of nature protection and those of industry.

The following text, for example (Table 5.2), appeared on Enel's website in 2018, accompanying a striking image of a group of flamingos with their grey fledglings, below a large headline:

The Pink Miracle of Priolo Gargallo

Table 5.2 Enel Promotion[a]

1	A coloured ring to wish you a pleasant journey. Another 104 pink flamingos
2	were born in the Priolo Gargallo Saline Reserve, the LIPU oasis north of
3	Syracuse from which they will take off in a few weeks. This little environmental
4	miracle was made possible by the Enel Archimede plant which, by maintaining
5	the water levels of the Sicilian salt pan, allows these large migratory birds to
6	nest and reproduce. A very rare phenomenon in Italy and in habitats occupied by
7	man.
8	On July 26, for the fourth consecutive year, the reserve hosted a ritual that is
9	both a baptism and a farewell. About a hundred volunteers and technicians from
10	ISPRA (Higher Institute for Environmental Protection and Research) have
11	ringed the legs of the young flamingos with a colour and an alpha-numeric code,
12	making it possible to record their movements in the wetter areas of the
13	Mediterranean, trace their story and recognize them when they return home next
14	year.
15	The Priolo Gargallo Reserve was established in 2000 and for some years it has
16	been considered one of the most beautiful oases in Italy. The arrival of the pink
17	flamingos is the symbol of environmental restoration and good bio-marine
18	balance of the area. Our Archimedes combined cycle power plant plays an
19	important role by pumping sea water into the basin, guaranteeing a constant
20	water level, which is essential for creating a welcoming environment. The
21	flamingo, in fact, is a demanding animal: it needs a lot of food, optimal levels of
22	water which has to be very clean. In the summer of 2013, the birds nearly died
23	because of the dryness of the marsh. Thanks to Enel's intervention they were
24	saved and, since then, they have not stopped coming back and nesting. A
25	spectacle for ornithologists and birdwatchers. Egg-laying takes place in April:
26	the parents take turns incubating them, for a period of about 28 days. The chicks
27	stay close to their parents for 80 days, then they start flying.

[a]ENEL. Online at: https://corporate.enel.it/it/storie/a/2018/08/ripristino-ambientale-saline-priolo, retrieved 08/07/2023.

It tells the story of the birds' arrival at the reserve, putting a strong accent on the role of Enel. Early in the story they claim sole responsibility for the 'little environmental miracle' (3–4); later on they state that it was 'thanks to Enel's intervention' that the flamingos were saved (23). These references effect a specific strategy of *framing* (Section 3.4), a process which is described by Entman (ibid.: 52) as follows:

> To frame is to select some aspects of a perceived reality and make them more salient in a communicating text, in such a way as to promote a particular problem definition, causal interpretation, moral evaluation, and/or treatment recommendation for the item described.

A key role is played by *selection*. In this case, it is the 'miraculous' element that is highlighted, in the web page title and in the reference to the 'little environmental miracle', which focuses readers' attention on the conventionally joyful event of birth, heightened by the fact that it concerns a beautiful bird, known to be somewhat rare in Italy. But what could justly be said to be miraculous in this event is that it happened in an area made toxic by industrial filth; in conditions which one would imagine flamingos would find intolerable, for whose creation companies like Enel were among those most responsible. In the text, in fact, there is no reference whatever to pollution; rather, its language has the opposite connotations, as what has been termed a positive 'semantic prosody' (Partington 2004) is deployed:

> Coloured ring, pleasant journey, environmental miracle, baptism, home, beautiful oases, pink flamingo, environmental restoration, good bio-marine balance, welcoming environment, optimal levels of water, very clean, saved, a spectacle, etc.

All these lexical items have nice connotations and thus contribute to the 'positive' flavour of the text as a whole.

By claiming such primacy, moreover, the company excludes the efforts of others in the happy outcome – LIPU most of all, but also the numerous other social actors like local politicians, volunteer groups, activists, environmentalists, who devote their time and energy to the reserve. Indeed, the volunteers are mentioned (9–14), but their contribution is not so much to 'save' the flamingos which, as we have seen, is ascribed to Enel alone, but rather to perform more mundane tasks of documentation (11–12).

From a glance at the narrative structure (Table 5.3) it is plain that the story is 'about' flamingos:

Table 5.3 Enel Promotion, Narrative Structure

Abstract	A coloured ring to wish you a pleasant journey (1)
Orientation	**Who?** Flamingos (1, 5, 11, 16–17, 21, 22–25), Enel (4,23), Volunteers and technicians from ISPRA (9–10), ornithologists (25) **When?** – **What?** The birth of flamingos **Where?** Priolo Gargallo reserve
Complication	the birds nearly died because of the dryness of the marsh (22–23)
Evaluation	t+Aff: Happiness: *This little environmental miracle [. . .] to nest and reproduce* (3–5) +App: Valuation, *intens.*: A very <u>rare</u> phenomenon (6) +App: Quality, *intens*: one of the most <u>beautiful</u> oases in Italy (15) +App: Valuation: <u>good</u> bio-marine balance (17–18) +App: Valuation: plays an <u>important</u> role (18–19) t+J: propriety: *Our Archimedes combined cycle power plant [. . .] a welcoming environment* (18–20) +App: Quality: a <u>welcoming</u> environment (20) –J: propriety: a <u>demanding</u> animal (21) t+J: propriety: *Thanks to Enel's intervention they were saved* (23–24)
Result	since then, they have not stopped coming back and nesting (24)
Coda	-

The references to Enel, though few, are key in understanding the overall meaning of the story, as are the patterns of evaluation in the text. As we saw in an earlier section (3.1.2), evaluation in text addresses the listener/reader's implicit question 'So what?'; it 'highlights the point, shows listeners how they are to understand the meaning' (Labov, ibid.: 227). In this story the role of positive evaluation and its relation to framing stand out, for example, in the following sentence:

> The Priolo Gargallo Reserve was established in 2000 and for some years it has been considered <u>one of the most beautiful</u> oases in Italy (15–16).

This is an instance of positive evaluation, intensified by the formula 'one of the most . . .', a claim justified by the national award won by the reserve in 2008. However, the actual truth value of the claim is open to question. Is Priolo Gargallo's nature reserve truly 'beautiful' – would that be the assessment of most visitors, their takeaway from the experience? As I have suggested throughout this chapter, the Priolo reserve has, at best, what Yeats called a 'terrible beauty'[5] – it is a beauty that derives from the contrast of fragile natural elements with a backdrop of an overwhelming, monstrous, industrial threat. What the Enel text does is exclude industry altogether from the picture, and instead trace a conventional, picture postcard kind of 'beautiful oasis' that consists of trees, flowers, water and so on, all conducive to a context in which the pink miracle may nest. Indeed, the pattern of positive evaluation is suggestive of an *ideal* environment for flamingos to nest in: the water is 'clean', its levels are 'optimal' and 'constant', the bio-marine balance (whatever that is) is 'good', the environment has been 'restored' and is thus 'welcoming'.

Thus, the presence of a breeding colony of flamingos reflects well on Enel's environmental credentials; it proves the positive effects of what they do, since this outcome is a 'very rare phenomenon' not just in Italy but in any 'habitat occupied by man' (6–7).

In terms of the emotional aspect of the text, or the 'Affect' dimension, the pattern here is implicit rather than overt. The writer expects their reader(s) to respond with happiness to the text's overall message, that is *thanks to Enel flamingos have nested in Priolo Gargallo every year since 2013, the oasis is beautiful, Enel controls water flows to optimize environmental outcomes, everything is spectacular for bird-watchers* and so on.

Clearly, the main pragmatic effect of this story is to position Enel as a significant player in the flamingos' success, to show that it is not only aware of the importance of environmental values but is willing to invest in projects that carry them forward. This supposed environmental aspect to Enel's mission is not only evident from their hands-on involvement in the flamingo project, but also by the way that the text wields the specialist knowledge of the birdwatcher or naturalist in sentences like:

> Egg-laying takes place in April: the parents take turns incubating them, for a period of about 28 days (25–27)

Ironically, while LIPU and Enel are united in representing the flamingos' presence as a symbol of environmental restoration, the situation is actually much more nuanced. Though its presence constitutes an attraction for a nature reserve like Priolo Saltpans, the flamingo is not always good news for biodiversity, as Benadusi (2019: 91) explains:

> Flamingos tend to expand at the expense of other birds: having chosen a territory, the flocks tend to 'colonize' it [...] thus rendering precarious the reproduction of other nesting birds.

Indeed, she outlines an alarming scenario of the impact of a flamingo colony on other groups of birds:

> In the less exposed everyday life of the nature reserve, I heard stories during my walks about the flamingos that 'steal space' away from black-winged Stilt (Himantopus himantopus) while they are trying to nest, 'ripping the mud from underneath' them and forcing their neighbours to 'take their eggs and emigrate elsewhere'. Raimondo also talks about the 'trauma' experienced by smaller-sized species such as the little tern (Sterna albifrons) that are forced to fight over space with the larger, flashy, and 'abusive' flamingos: the 'hoarse cries' of the flamingos that drown out the 'harmonious songs' of other birds, the 'fussy and foolish features' of these newcomers that clash with the 'elegant movements' of the others. (Benadusi, ibid.)

These facts demonstrate the complexity of environmental interventions, which have to weigh up the relative importance of multiple factors: on the one hand, the flamingo has been called a 'flagship' species (Benadusi 2019). Because of its size, its sheer pinkness, its beauty when the flock flies or feeds, the flashy flamingo has a capacity to attract birdwatchers and members of the ordinary public to sites where it can be seen, and thus it draws public attention to the question of wildlife conservation. Yet on the other hand, its long-term impact on a biosphere could be disastrous for other species of birds, in whose fate the general public is unlikely to be interested.

These perspectives are confirmed by Fabio Cilea, who says:

> The Flamingo is a very cumbersome animal though, it's very important for the enhancement of an area, but if left free to do what it wants, it occupies every space possible or imaginable. To give other animals that can live in that context the opportunity to nest, especially in that context, the area of active management, we're beginning to look at alternatives, to also encourage other species of interest to conservation, like the Little Tern, the Kentish Plover, the Black-winged Stilt, the Avocet.[6]

In other words, in adapting the environment so that flamingos can nest, the LIPU activists and Enel have somehow contrived to render the lives of other birds using the site more difficult, and if flamingos are allowed to spread across the reserve unchecked, their dominance may have tragic consequences for these creatures.

From the holistic, deep ecological perspective, such an outcome simply underlines the destructive effects of human intervention on the biosphere. The flamingo triumphs over these other species of bird not just because they have less pulling power for birdwatchers, but because they are less media-friendly, less spendable in terms of brand building. In short, it would be much harder to commodify a bird like the Little Tern or the Kentish Plover in theme parks or Disney cartoons, or by incorporating them in decorations, lampstands, beach inflatables, cuddly toys or unlikely sex accessories. Because of its intrinsic qualities the flamingo is a star and occupies its own niche in the consumer universe for reasons that, it would seem, have nothing to do with environmentalism.

For the purposes of Enel's self-promotion, it suits them to convey a simple message, one that equates the successful nesting of flamingos at Priolo Saltpans with the achievement of a number of environmental goals. Flamingos are perfect for a project whose aim is to associate the company in the popular mind with current buzz – notions like environmental sustainability, green energy, industrial reconversion. Whether their engagement is more than a branding exercise, a kind of greenwashing – or, in this case, pinkwashing – is not yet clear.

5.3 The flamingos and the drone

Director of the Priolo reserve Fabio Cilea once told me an intriguing story about the flamingos. The flamingos at Priolo Saltpans, he said, are aware that the marshes do not contain sufficient food to sustain the flock, and this explains why they forage in other sites around the area. When there are chicks to look after this is a complicated business, and the flamingos organize a crèche where the young are looked after by a small number of adult birds while the other adults leave in search of food. Next day the birds swap roles, with different birds looking after the young while the others go to feed.[7] This behaviour is not found only in flamingos; the Penguin and the Common Eider, for example, use crèches for protection against predators and/or the cold (Lawless et al. 2001; Munro 1977), while social carnivores like the lion also do something similar (Pusey and Packer 1994). Though the phenomenon has been studied from various points of view, I am not sure that much attention has been paid to the linguistic aspect, for a number of reasons; some to do with the nature of linguistics as a discipline, others with ecological studies and prevailing assumptions about animal communication.

Linguistics, though a remarkably broad church, has so far not seen fit to extend the scope of its concerns to modes of non-human communication that are only controversially viewed as 'languages'. Meanwhile, those whose daily research activities concern explorations of non-human communication have tended to produce mainly functional accounts of these phenomena, and therefore do little to challenge assumptions that birdsong is not really concerned with communicating information in the human sense. Most studies suggest at best a functional account of bird 'language'. As Dave Rothenberg says: 'when asked, "Why do birds sing?" most scientists would answer that birds let out their melodies to establish territories and to make themselves attractive to potential mates' (Rothenberg 2005). In this view bird utterances have meanings that can be paraphrased, as Chris Skinner does here with the meaning of the blackbird's alarm call:

> Other birds learn that alarm call as well so when the blackbird flies off everybody knows there's something wrong and so they may not understand like me what it actually is saying like you know 'there's a bleeding sparrowhawk coming down the track quick get out of the way'.

Meanwhile here is Cilea on the territory building, partner attracting aspect of birdsong:

> A lot of passerines, a lot of Sylviidae, the male builds a territory, builds a nest, then he starts to sing. Because he says: 'Hey, pretty girl, pretty girl, come over here I'll show you my house with my butterfly collection'. And that's why all the girls who go, well, they have to meet him. To the others, to the males, he just puts things very clearly, much less sweetly: 'If you come in here, it's my house, I'll smash your face in'. Just like that.

In these examples both naturalists have used words to express what they take to be the meaning of the birds' utterances, but neither is suggesting that the birds have lexico-grammar whose combinations build these meanings in the way that human language does. Rather, these meaning suggestions are pragmatic interpretations of snippets of birdsound. In the example of the passerine a 'sweet', melodious song is taken to be a pragmatic 'invitation' to a listening female, while a harsh, aggressive sound is a 'warning' to potential rivals. In both of his examples, Cilea presents sentences that people would say in similar circumstances to convey what he takes to be the 'meaning' of the bird's utterance. Birdsound in this perspective is a series of squeaks, squawks, chirps, coos, calls, trills and the like that can be isolated sounds or be combined in melodic patterns, but any transmission from one bird to another of 'meaning' in our sense is absent. The various sounds emitted are not comparable to human words; rather, very basic, 'functional' meanings are exchanged in processes that depend on shared context knowledge and a response to the feeling conveyed by the sound itself.

The crèche phenomenon, in flamingos and other non-human species, could raise the question of whether birds are able to communicate more sophisticated concepts to each other. In other words, whether the sounds they make contribute to meaning-transfer in ways that are comparable to what is going on with human language. Once I put this to Cilea:

Speaker 1: How do they organise this, do you think? How do they communicate among themselves? I mean, you can't call this instinct, or can you? Instinct . . .

Speaker 2: Well probably yes, animals have instinct and they always know what they have to do. How they get organised, who decides what I can't tell you, I don't even know if anyone in the sphere of animal behaviour studies knows, if there are any. . . . To be precise, though, it's a fact that it's clearly a well-organised structure, in the sense that the Germans would recognise.

Speaker 1: That's my interest, knowing about this, that they achieve this organisation without language. They make noises, or what?[8]

Speaker 2: Well, they don't have words, but they have their ways, their ways of communicating as often happens in the animal world, that every animal group has its way of being able to transfer information. If you take the example of ants, well, it's an incredibly fascinating world, made of sociability, made up of organised groups and a chemical communication that always manages to indicate the situation of the moment.

To invoke 'instinct' as an explanation for non-human behaviour is not the most satisfactory response, especially not in a case like this, where the behaviour illustrates what Cilea sees as a 'Germanic' organizational precision. There are at least two mysteries here; first, a question of cognition: How do the flamingos know that the resources of the lake are insufficient to support the flock? Such knowledge, if a comparable situation occurred in the human world, would result from observation, reflection on past experience, problem-solving, study, discussion; it seems scarcely possible that the birds short-cut these processes to arrive instantly at the correct solution by the application of a sort of innate knowledge. The second mystery regards the practical organizational details. How do the birds work out whose turn it is to stay with the chicks, and whose to go elsewhere and feed? Again, in the human world all this would be arranged linguistically (*'It's my turn to feed today. She stayed with the chicks yesterday. It's his turn today! No it isn't!'* etc.). To suggest that all this works by instinct appears to demean the birds in some way,[9] while to imply that the organization is brought about – as it would be in the human world – by some form of discursive interaction would be to acknowledge that there is more to birdsong, and bird *sound*, than is envisaged in the hitherto dominant functional accounts.

The seemingly random nature of flamingo behaviour is in evidence in the following tale of an incident at Priolo Saltpans (Table 5.4):

Table 5.4 The Flamingos and the Drone (i)

1	Fabio Cilea: So some birds nest here, others spend the winter, and the flamingos . . . well,
2	the flamingos don't even have a distinctive migratory habit, the flamingos always wander
3	around looking for the best living conditions; that is, they look for food, tranquillity and
4	the right water level. So those that have nested here in spring in middle or late summer
5	will leave the site, while those arriving from Northern Italy or Northern Europe, you
6	know, from France – actually from Spain in reality or from Comacchio – will stop here.
7	They will stay here for the whole winter and then in spring go back to their nesting sites,
8	while our birds, which could be nearby, say in Vendicari, Pachino or in North Africa in
9	Tunisia, return here to nest. In short then, every season has its birds, but even within the
10	same species there are populations that move in a synchronized way.
11	Interviewer: And do they nest only here, in the salt pans of Priolo, or also in Vendicari?
12	FC: In 2015, for the first time in Sicily, the flamingo nested here in Priolo. It had never
13	nested in Sicily, at least from the historical information we have. That was the situation
14	until 2018, and in ever increasing numbers. Consider that we started with a colony of
15	51 pairs. We moved to around 132 in 2016, 293 in 2017, 403 pairs in 2018. In 2018, in
16	Priolo at the beginning of the breeding season we get a fairly serious disturbance. A guy
17	with a drone descends on the colony practically as soon as it gets established, and the
18	flamingos are very sensitive in the very first phase. These flamingos have not only seen
19	the drone descend just a few meters away from them, but when this gentleman saw that
20	the animals got up and moved away from the nest, he went on chasing them. They flew
21	off and left. Probably because of this disturbance, very probably but it is not an
22	established fact . . . well, the two things happened in an almost synchronized way. These
23	flamingos probably arrive in Vendicari and started to nest there too in 2018. It's just a
24	few couples though. Well anyway, at the beginning there are always a few, there were 15
25	maybe 16 breeding pairs.
26	I: And you say they were the ones who were scared away from here . . . ?
27	FC: Could be, could have been the frightened ones and in the end only two chicks
28	fledged. About the Vendicari ones though, we don't know the motive for the deaths.
29	Well anyway, Priolo Saltpans is still at the moment the most important nesting site,
30	the first nesting site in Sicily. Well, considering the territorial context it's quite a good
31	record . . .

From the 'Orientation' section in Table 5.5, we see that flamingos dominate the story, since apart from a few references to a 'guy with a drone', they are the only social actor mentioned:

Table 5.5 The Flamingos and the Drone (ii)

Abstract	-
Orientation	**Who?** Flamingos (1–10, 14–15, 17–20, 22–28), Guy with drone (16–17, 19) **When?** From 2015–2018 **What?** The response of a group of flamingos to the drone (18–21) **Where?** Priolo Saltpans, Vendicari
Complication	A guy with a drone [. . .] as soon as it gets established (17) - J: propriety: a <u>fairly serious disturbance</u> (16)
Evaluation	t - J: propriety: *A guy with a drone descends on the colony practically as soon as it gets established* (16–17) t - J: propriety: *he went on chasing them* (20) -Aff: insecurity: the ones who were <u>scared</u> (25) -Aff: insecurity: the <u>frightened</u> ones (26) + App: Valuation: the most <u>important</u> nesting site (28) + App: Valuation: the <u>first</u> nesting site in Sicily (28) + App: Valuation: quite a <u>good</u> record (29)
Result	These flamingos [. . .] started to nest there too (23) considering the territorial context it's quite a good record (29–30)
Coda	-

In this example, for the first time in this book, attention is paid to the way stories may develop by integrating what the teller perceives as inferences of their interlocutor(s), a perspective on meaning known as 'dialogical pragmatics' (Ponton 2017). Research in this sphere shows how interlocutors develop scenarios of unfolding meaning by responding to some inferences, warding off others, trying to disambiguate when the other's inference(s) are not clear and so on. In this case, it is noticeable that Cilea responds to one possible inference of the first question, highlighted by the underlined words:

And do they nest <u>only here</u>, in the salt pans of Priolo, or also in Vendicari? (11)

In the light of the foregoing text, this appears a natural enquiry that could be motivated by nothing more than simple curiosity. Up to this point, in fact, the main topic of the story is something like 'where flamingos nest', since this is what Cilea talks about in his first contribution (1–10). Yet if we recall that much has been made in national media and social media of the 'pink miracle', the birth of flamingo chicks at Priolo Saltpans, and even that the reserve's director himself has enjoyed a 5-minute brush with fame as a result of all this – then another inference may appear salient, at least if we look at the interaction from Cilea's perspective. Is the questioner trying to undermine the supposed primacy of Priolo Saltpans by suggesting that the phenomenon is not, after all, unique to this site? If there are other sites in Sicily, like nearby Vendicari, where other groups of flamingos nest and breed, then the prestige of Priolo could be threatened to a degree.

The question is of a simple yes–no type, yet it is noticeable that Cilea does not provide such an answer. The fact that he does not do this lends apparent support to the idea that he responds to what he perceives to be the interlocutor's intended meaning, rather than to the surface meaning of the words. He replies by telling a story that begins with some factual content regarding the presence of breeding flamingos at Priolo from 2015–2018 (12–15), a period during which he asserts that, from the 'historical information we have' (13), it had never nested elsewhere. This information, it will be noticed, does not immediately address the interlocutor's question. Nevertheless, the unwritten rules of behaviour that govern dialogue – Grice's pragmatic maxims, discussed above (Section 3.1.3) – mean that, since these remarks follow a direct question, they will be 'heard' as part of an answer. Such assumptions, by speaker and hearer, depend on the conversational maxim 'be relevant'. Since the surface meaning of the words appears somewhat irrelevant to the question that was asked – once again, notice that a simple 'yes' or 'no' would have served – then this can only mean either that the relevance of all these details to the answer will eventually emerge, or that the speaker is not answering the actual question but responding to what they believe the interlocutor is 'really' asking.

The story goes on to reveal that in point of fact, in 2018, flamingos did nest at Vendicari and breed successfully, but this is not presented as a 'pink miracle'. Rather, the birds involved are framed as a sort of offshoot of the Priolo colony, and the event's significance is undermined in various ways. The numbers involved are minimized: *It's just a few couples* (23–24). The facts are represented with a marker of epistemic modality[10] indicative of the speaker's lack of certainty about the events described: the flamingos that bred in Vendicari were 'very probably' (21) the ones that were frightened away from Priolo in the drone attack. Cilea further undermines the truth value of his story by specifying that this is 'not an established fact' (21–22).

It is noticeable that the questioner picks up on this lack of certainty in his next contribution:

And you say they were the ones who were scared away from here . . .? (25)

Again Cilea's response uses the less-than-certain modal verb 'could':

<u>Could be, could have been</u> the frightened ones . . . (26)

The significance of the event is again played down:

in the end only two chicks fledged (26–27)

The story of Vendicari's breeding flamingos is taken no further, but tails off with a vague reference to 'deaths' (27), presumably of the other chicks which were born but failed to survive. The speaker signals the end of the topic ('Well anyway', 28) and returns the focus to Priolo Saltpans, adding the Coda and thus bringing the story to its close:

> Well, considering the territorial context it's quite a good record (29–30)

This is a curious conclusion to a story that centres on the dramatic event of a man with a drone disturbing a flock of breeding flamingos. More could have been made of negative judgement for such insensitive behaviour, which is actually rather played down, for example through nominalization (see Section 5.1):

> a <u>fairly serious disturbance</u> (16) (- J: propriety)

To thus represent what happened hides the fact that a person was involved in the event at all, lessening the sense that an outrage has been committed. This can be clearly seen by comparing the actual text with sharper interpersonal alternatives: *there was an act of vandalism/of criminal stupidity/lunatic behaviour/a deliberate attack* and so on. Indeed there is negative judgement of the man's behaviour, but at no point does this become explicit; rather, the speaker relies on a shared ethical framework between himself and his interlocutor to imply blame:

> *A guy with a drone descends on the colony practically as soon as it gets established* (16–17) [. . .] *he went on chasing them* (20) (t - J: propriety)

It is also noticeable that the bird's response is presented in a matter-of-fact way, and it is the interlocutor who raises the question of their likely emotional state (they were 'scared away', 25).

The story therefore could have made a different point, for example along the following lines: *Not only do we destroy ecosystems and leave only tiny polluted spaces for these magnificent creatures to breed in, but when they do manage to nest we violate their privacy, we terrorize them and drive them off. All this for a 5-minute thrill as we show off our new toy by posting a video on Facebook.*

Yet, as the narrative structure analysis shows, this is not really the main takeaway of the story. Explicit evaluation relates only to the Priolo reserve:

> the most <u>important</u> nesting site (28) / the <u>first</u> nesting site in Sicily (29) / quite a <u>good</u> record (29–30) (+ App: Valuation)

The story of the drone attack is therefore incidental; it appears as part of an overall narrative whose purpose is apparently to underline the importance of the Priolo reserve, its unique role in the panorama of flamingo breeding in Sicily.

The contribution of the interlocutor to the story that unfolded should be noted, since it was arguably Cilea's understanding of the inference of the first question that led to the story of the drone being told. The story was not told to underline how insensitive people can be towards breeding flamingos; rather, it should be seen in the context of the speaker's theory that the flamingos who bred successfully at Vendicari came originally from Priolo.

5.4 A flamingo story

The dramatic situation in Priolo was described as follows by a visiting journalist who came to care very much for the area:

> I will write a story to pass on – I am not sure, to whom – a few fragments of truth about what happened in a corner of the world I love, sacrificed to the God of the present[11]

'Sacrificed to the God of the present' is an apt interpretation of events, and regrettably the words could be applied to many outcomes in human/non-human relations in the modern period, worldwide.

The director of the Priolo Saltpans site, who featured in the last section, is a man called Fabio Cilea, a LIPU activist with whom I have had several meetings over the last ten years. He is a significant figure in this section of the book, as Chris Skinner was in the last. Like Skinner, his words may be sifted for perspectives, to be cited as instances of an inherent ecosophical wisdom, with the aim of providing fragments of 'positive discourse', in the terms laid out elsewhere in this book (Section 2.6). Just as Skinner's mission is carried out in a specific locus, dear to him for family reasons, so Cilea's activism regards his own backyard, places he frequented in childhood. Finally, like Skinner, Cilea can be seen as a professional environmentalist, one whose whole life is engaged in torch-bearing, a man in perpetual conflict against human ignorance, a voice frequently raised on behalf of the natural world; an influencer, even a *symbol*. However, though both legitimately occupy the role of 'hero' in the story of this book, there are important differences.

Skinner's approach to environmental discourse is full of self-disclosure; it is based on narratives that mingle the minutely observed actions of non-human social actors with details of his own daily routine. It is possible for the listener to the Countryside Hour to be drawn in by a fascination with the Bombadil-like personality at its centre, to be won over to ecological positions on the basis of a human sympathy, that develops through virtual contact in the intimate medium of a radio broadcast. It is not possible to have similar contact with Cilea, who maintains a media presence only comparatively infrequently, via the more transient resources of Facebook.

In general, Cilea does not tend to discuss his private life with visitors to the reserve. Instead he will provide them with hints on what they should visit, which trails to follow, what they can expect to see at this time of year, as well as technical details about the various species, and especially flamingos, of course. For this reason it may be worth beginning this section with one of Cilea's stories (Table 5.6, below) which we do find an autobiographical element that will provide us with clues as to the nature and origin of his environmental vocation.

As we can see by counting the number of references in the Orientation analysis in Table 5.7, there are two possible candidates for the main focus of the story – the stuffed pink flamingo and Cilea's father. Probably both have a claim

Table 5.6 Cilea Flamingo Story

1	Above the highest of the shelves of one of the many bookshelves in my parents' Roman
2	home there was always – and still is – a stuffed pink flamingo. One of the poor bird's
3	two legs rests with its webbed foot on top of a mound of white plaster, as if resting on
4	silt, while the other is positioned curved under its wings; the pink plumage is still quite
5	vivid though the bird's size is smaller than natural, a phenomenon that often happens
6	when stuffing animals. The result is rather lopsided; the little beast hangs dangerously to
7	one side and there was always a risk that it would plummet from up there, perhaps onto
8	someone's head. Clearly to all of us children this unsteady flamingo always aroused
9	great curiosity and we often asked our father about the origin of the curious bird. Each
10	time the answer was veiled by a certain sadness for the fate of the animal and also by a
11	certain anger towards those who had reduced it to that state. To cut a long story short,
12	it was like this: before the cesspool of rubbish came to ruin Agro Priolese, those lands
13	were wonderful. My dad used to gallop on horseback along the pure white beaches of
14	Priolo and go hunting at the old saltpans. He loved to shoot coots (which my mother
15	prepared for him with olives) and he also shot mallards, which were always as abundant
16	as they were delicious (duck breasts with orange . . .). But that will do. Other species were
17	not shot. They were rare and it was important not to disturb their passage or nesting.
18	One year flamingos arrived, which was amazing for those times. Dad knew them well
19	because he had been several times to see them in the Camargue (when I was 10 years
20	old he took me there too, and on top of little horses we arrived in the flooded valleys to
21	see flamingos and wild bulls), but he had never seen them in Priolo. He could not
22	remember them ever being there. A farmer saw fit to shoot a specimen then bragged all
23	about it for miles around. When my father heard of the misdeed, with something of his
24	ancient strength he seized the bird's body and severely rebuked the careless marksman.
25	Father, in fact, was also a hunter, and yet on that occasion he really suffered, as if the
26	lead from those pellets had pierced him and not the flamingo. So this is the story of how
27	the poor beast came to remain forever in the company of the man who wanted to protect
28	it.

Table 5.7 Cilea Flamingo Story: Narrative Structure

Abstract	-
Orientation	**Who?** My parents (1), my dad (9, 13, 14, 15, 18, 19, 20, 21, 23, 24, 25, 26, 27), a stuffed pink flamingo (2–11, 22, 24, 26, 27, 28), flamingos (18, 19, 21), us children (8, 9), a farmer (22, 23, 25) **When?** Childhood (1–11), before the cesspool of rubbish came to ruin Agro Priolese (12), dad's maturity (13–26), the present (27–28) **What?** a stuffed pink flamingo (2) **Where?** Rome (1), Agro Priolese (12), the beaches of Priolo (13–14), the Camargue (19), Priolo (21)
Complication	the little beast hangs dangerously [...] someone's head (6–9) A farmer thought it would be good to shoot a specimen (22)
Evaluation	-ive Affect: unhappiness: <u>poor</u> bird (2), the <u>poor</u> beast (27) + App: Impact: the <u>curious</u> bird (9) -ive Affect: unhappiness: a certain <u>sadness</u> for the fate of the animal (10) -ive Affect: dissatisfaction: a certain <u>anger</u> (11) -ive App: Quality, intens.: the <u>cesspool of rubbish</u> (12) + J(udgement): propriety: A farmer <u>saw fit</u> (22) –J: propriety: the <u>careless</u> marksman t–J: propriety: *A farmer thought [...] for miles around* (22–23) –J: propriety: the <u>misdeed</u> (23)
Result	he seized the bird's body and [...] rebuked the careless marksman (24–25)
Coda	So this is the story [...] wanted to protect it. (27–28)

to importance. The story is situated at the start of Cilea's book about the reserve of Priolo Saltpans where, as we have seen, flamingos have a central role. Thus, by beginning with this story Cilea identifies the stuffed flamingo of his childhood memories as a kind of symbol for the reserve itself, for flamingos and the natural world generally and for the birth of his own ecological consciousness. But the flamingo is also revealing about the author's relationship with his father, and it is hard not to feel that his own pathway towards a life dedicated to environmental protection might have originated in this anecdote of his father's brave stand against human cruelty and ignorance:

The presence of two complications alerts us to the fact that here there are really two stories. The first regards a dead, stuffed flamingo in Cilea's boyhood home, and the 'complication' may be seen as its unsteady bearing, the possibility that it could fall from its insecure location. Psychologically, in a sense it does 'fall', by provoking curious questions from the children that lead into the second story, of the same beast when it was a live creature. The second complication is more significant, since it involves the animal's death, an act of ignorant violence by a Sicilian farmer.

Sympathy for the bird is evident in the first reference, significantly via a noun denoting a creature ('bird') rather than an artefact (*object, curio, effigy, piece, paperweight, decoration, cast, statuette, model, figure, ornament, thing*, etc.):

'One of the poor bird's two legs' (2–3)

This may seem a trivial point, but such details are considered worth pausing over by pragmatic linguistic analysts for what they may reveal about the speaker/writer's attitude to the object in question. Supposing an inventory of the flat had been compiled by an official for the purpose of selling its contents at auction, the entry might have read:

Item. Curio: Stuffed flamingo. Good condition.

In this short text, a living bird has undergone two transformations; passing first from this life, it then becomes an item of furniture, a commodity on which a monetary value can be placed. The fact that alternative ways of representing the object in question are available justifies the attention linguists pay to these choices – in this context, the term establishes that the author considers it an 'animal', and that something in its story evokes an emotion of sorrow.

Interestingly, though the writer is clearly concerned with the desecration of an immaculate landscape (evident from the verbal choice 'came to ruin'), there is only one – admittedly, *intense* – negative evaluation of the industrial zone:

before the cesspool of rubbish came to ruin Agro Priolese (12)

Again, it is noticeable that this event is represented not as the result of deliberate choices by human social actors, but more like a natural event, an instance of the category of 'naturalization', discussed above (Section 3.4). While this might normally occur in the discourse of powerful social actors with the intention of obscuring responsibility, it features here in Cilea's discourse because he is not concerned, in this moment, with directing blame or critiquing those involved but simply to delineate a temporal watershed in the narrative.

At the heart of the story is the second complicating action:

A farmer saw fit to shoot a specimen then bragged all about it for miles around. (22–23)

Here there is a nested evaluation involving a social actor whose perspective is distinguished from that of the authorial voice, that of the farmer who 'saw fit' to shoot the bird:

> Un contadino *pensò bene* di sparare ad un esemplare

'To see fit' to do something apparently locates the action among a category of ethically acceptable activities, though the overtones of this lexical choice, in both languages, alert the reader to the presence of irony (Ibáñez and Lozano-Palacio 2019). The semantics of 'to see fit' tend to indicate an authorial stance of negative judgement on the behaviour concerned, as in this example, from the British National Corpus:

> We stayed in a cheap boarding-house from which the landlord <u>saw fit</u> to evict us for all the hours of daylight

That the author's meaning is to critique the action can be inferred not just from this lexical choice but from the semantics of the verb that follows: 'to brag' (in Italian, *vantarsi*) generally, if not always, has negative connotations. Moreover, we have already appreciated that there is something tragic, from the author's point of view about this flamingo, and this too is a factor that supports this interpretation. Thus, though there is no explicit condemnation of the farmer's behaviour – he is not referred to as an *immoral/bad/evil/violent/thoughtless*, etc. farmer – in readers' minds, some such associations will be evoked.

It should be noted that the author delineates a fairly subtle ethical framework in the co-text that precedes this episode, via the descriptions of his father's own hunting habits:

> He loved to shoot coots (which my mother prepared for him with olives) and he also shot mallards, which were always as abundant as they were delicious (duck breasts with orange . . .) (14–16)

There is no visible condemnation of his father's action, which in the final analysis appears no different from that of the farmer. Indeed, his father is taking the lives, not just of a single exemplar but of numerous beasts, actions for which the sheer tastiness of the birds is adduced as a kind of justification. The key detail that nullifies potential negative evaluation of such behaviour consists here in the fact that these birds were 'abundant', and this is spelled out in the text that immediately follows:

> Other species were not shot. <u>They were rare</u> and it was important not to disturb their passage or nesting

If a bird is 'rare', this changes the evaluation of the action in question. Cilea is tacitly suggesting an ethical framework in which it is perfectly okay to shoot and eat birds if they are common, but if they are rare then this becomes heinous. Interestingly, this perspective appears to be shared by other modern environmentalists, including Chris Skinner (Ponton 2022b). The detail concerning the importance of not disturbing their passage or nesting should also be weighed: perhaps flamingos, as a global species were not so rare – indeed, the text describes their notable presence in the Camargue. However, their arrival in Agro Priolese suggests that they are in need of new nesting sites, migration routes and so on, and to an environmentalist this is indicative of some crisis in which the species will need extra protection.

So far this analysis has rested on the Labovian framework used elsewhere in the book, but at this point it will be useful to extend this by considering cultural elements. This is a factor largely extraneous to Labov's model, though central in some pragmatic approaches, where the relevant dimension of meaning-transfer relates to a shared body of cultural knowledge among text creators and their readers. An instance of this kind of thing occurs in the following description of his father's actions on hearing of the shooting:

> with something of his <u>ancient</u> strength (23–24)

It is impossible to precisely pin down the reference here, but via the adjective 'ancient' (in the original Italian, '*antico*') the author arguably evokes the vanished world of Greek heroes like Odysseus. At any rate, among the various interpretations that compete for salience (see Section 3.1.3), that is the one that I find most suggestive, especially given the context of the action, which occurs in Magna Graecia itself and evokes a sort of natural paradise, untouched by the hand of modernity. It might be felt that Samson, who recovered his superhuman strength for one final religious gesture, could be a more plausible inference, but this feels like a false trail somehow, given the Greek elements. As the fragment continues, possible allusions to the crucifixion story occur:

> he seized the bird's body (24)

There is no reason provided for why Cilea's father removes the body, so readers can surmise that it was to mark his own displeasure at the deed, to give the bird a decent burial, to deprive the hunter of the spoils and thus ruin his bragging and so on. Especially in a Catholic country like Italy, this may be read as a reference to Joseph of Arimathea, who took the body of Christ from the cross for burial.

Thus, readers are primed for the dramatic finale to the story, in which the writer's father appears to be identified with Christ himself:

he really suffered, as if the lead from those pellets had *pierced him* and not the flamingo (25–26)

The Italian verb *trafiggere* (to pierce) is the typical choice by writers describing scenes of Christ's crucifixion.

As we have seen (Section 4.4.2), the Coda section serves a summing up function; it returns the hearer to everyday life, and underlines the message of the story if it has one, as in this case it does:

So this is the story of how the poor beast came to remain forever in the company of the man who wanted to protect it. (26–28)

Once again, sympathy for the flamingo is evoked by repetition of the evaluative affective adjective 'poor'. But Cilea here makes it clear that the significance of the story also relates to his father, finally explicitly revealed as a man with an environmental calling – he 'wants to protect' nature. Such references help to appreciate the underlying ethical stance outlined in this tale, which could be summarized as follows. It is good to protect the environment, and in this cause courage will be needed, as the environmentalist may have to confront people who are ignorant and may also be armed and dangerous. Sacrifices in terms of one's personal well-being may therefore be required. Though it is permitted to enjoy the pleasures of galloping around the Camargue and eating wild duck, you may end up on a kind of cross, metaphorically 'pierced' by the bullets of a society which does not share your environmental sensibilities.

References to cultural factors, the use authors make of other stories in telling their own, create a phenomenon termed 'intertextuality' (Allen 2021), which complicates texts by enriching the range of meanings that they evoke. At least two other instances of this occur in this story, in references to Coleridge's *Rhyme of the Ancient Mariner* and to one of Italy's key novels *Il Gattopardo* (*The Leopard*). The former hinges on a dramatic 'complication', as an old seaman shoots an albatross, unleashing the vengeance of fearsome natural and supernatural powers. In the poem he is made to wear the bird's corpse until his final repentance, when it slips from his neck into the ocean. Curiously, in Cilea's story it is not the farmer who must suffer; rather, his father appears to be the one condemned to 'bear' a simulacrum of martyred nature, having to keep the unsteady curio forever in his flat. Like the mariner, whose purgatory consists in an endless pilgrimage to spread his holistic message across the face of the Earth, Cilea's father also has to repeat the flamingo's story, to relive his own piercing and sorrow each time his children prompt him to tell it, and ends by passing on to his son an environmental conviction that will determine his career.

In *The Leopard*, a key symbolic role is played by Prince Fabrizio's Great Dane, Bendicò. In the vibrant days of the Prince's splendour in Palermo the creature was a faithful companion, and his stuffed body reminded the family of better days during their decline. Eventually the dusty curio is tossed away without a thought, just like the trappings of Sicilian aristocracy in the more democratic age ushered in by unification. However, as every Italian schoolboy should know, the overall message of the book is that '*Se vogliamo che tutto rimanga com'è, bisogna che tutto cambi*' (everything must change if everything is to stay the same). In this light Bendicò's final disappearance can be viewed. Since, after all the revolutions described in the book, nothing has really changed, this memento of the ancient ruling classes serves no useful purpose – in reality the old bosses are still present, still ruling, though in a less visible fashion.

By analogy, the stuffed flamingo in Cilea's story becomes a sort of nexus of meanings, standing perhaps for the natural world in general, perhaps for environmental sensibility. Its material passage across the generations is suggestive of a father-to-son transmission, the keeping alive of environmental idealism from one generation to the next.

5.5 The glass half full

In this section we hear Cilea discuss various topics; the role of the reserve and its local impact, some global future predictions and some issues specific to the local context. Perhaps, of all the mini-texts presented in the book, this is the one that least conforms to the expectations that the notion of 'story' might stimulate. However, though it is a diffuse stretch of narrative without an apparent unity, as we will see it does have a coherent narrative structure that aligns it with the other texts studied.

The title of the section, 'the glass half full', is taken from a phrase used by Cilea (line 25) to signal his optimism about the future. Like other texts studied then, this final narrative (Table 5.8, below) is an instance of positive discourse, though how convincing Cilea's solutions are, to the problems he presents, will perhaps be questioned:

Table 5.8 Glass Half Full

1	Yes, I can also give you a fact that is important to me, even a little shocking to me in
2	some ways, but we started in around 2010, with around 6,000 visitors. In 2015, with
3	the first nesting of the Flamingo in Sicily, we started we went from these 6,000 annual
4	visitors to 9,000 people. These numbers have increased year by year up to a number of
5	12,000 visitors in 2017. So, in 2017, from January to February we had 12,000 visitors.
6	In 2018, based on September calculations, we had 14,000 visitors, that is even before
7	closing the year we already had far higher numbers, and this is because the reserve has
8	become a fundamental reality for this territory. One thing that many in Priolo say
9	about me is that I've changed the way the word Priolo is used. While before, as we
10	said at the beginning, when Priolo Gargallo was talked about this was always only in a
11	negative sense because the industries, the pollution, the problems that existed which, I
12	repeat, still exist, were talked about. But today people are enthusiastic because they
13	see Priolo Gargallo on the national television news, in the newspapers, in the national
14	newspapers, even on the front pages, for example of Corriere della Sera. Talking about
15	it positively, talking about and seeing the reality of the nesting of Flamingos, Sea
16	Turtles, the revaluation that has been done, so somehow the reserve has had an effect
17	there. It is obvious that the predominant image is still that one, but as we said just
18	now, you need time to be able to recover this territory. The industrial pole, as it is
19	currently understood, that is the refining of crude oil, pollution of large areas, will not
20	survive for long. A series of – of course, not thanks to the reserve, for heaven's sake -
21	but a series of conditions at an international level will lead to us having to change our
22	habits, we will abandon petrol and diesel cars, and so move more and more towards
23	electric cars. We will give up our need of large spaces for production, we will forget
24	the need to continuously consume land for useless projects. [. . .]
25	If we always want to see the glass half full, let's try to see the presence of industry in a
26	positive sense, as I told you. For the record this is an idea of mine that I discuss with
27	my brother Sergio, who I often share ideas with, where the industrial pole today could
28	in some way provide a positive future perspective. Where the dismantling of industrial
29	structures could return significant portions of territory to the legitimate uses of the
30	population, could guarantee a healthy redevelopment of the territory, and this won't
31	be able to happen in those areas where overbuilding has happened for purposes of
32	tourism, where hotels have been built, and villas built practically in the sea. You won't
34	be able to recover those places. It will be very difficult to recover those elements, and
35	at this point enter the enlightened politician, the one who will plan the future of the
36	territory – he comes back for the umpteenth time. Enlightenment in this case means
37	to see, after twenty, thirty years, as the industrial pole no longer needs to produce on
38	large spaces, large surfaces, to give the possibility to some areas to be converted into
39	industrial structures, but for others into structures for the territory. I mean, into
40	something for the area. So that's something that I hope can happen.

As can be seen from a glance at the Who? section in the Orientation column in Table 5.9, the social actors in this text are numerous, including some non-human actors (flamingos and sea turtles) and some human figures who have so far not featured, the general public and a hypothetical 'enlightened' politician:

Table 5.9 Glass Half Full: Narrative Structure

Abstract	-
Orientation	**Who?** I, me (1, 9, 26–27, 40) / We (2, 3, 5, 6, 7, 1–24) / The flamingo (3, 15) / The sea turtle (15) / Visitors (2–8) / People in Priolo (8, 12, 14–15) / Sergio (27) / The enlightened politician (35) **When?** 2015–2018 (2–6), Before (9–12), Today (12–16, 27), The future (19–24, 28–40) **What?** The future of the industrial area **Where?** The reserve (1–8), Priolo Gargallo (10–40)
Complication	The predominant image is still that one (17)
Evaluation	+ App: Valuation: a fact that is <u>important</u> (1) + Aff: inclination: even a little <u>shocking</u> (1) + App: Valuation: a <u>fundamental</u> reality (8) t + J: propriety: *I've changed the way of using the word Priolo* (9) + Aff: satisfaction: people are <u>enthusiastic</u> (12) -ive App: Valuation: <u>useless</u> projects (24) + App: Valuation: a <u>positive</u> future perspective (28) + App: Valuation: <u>significant</u> portions of territory (29) + App: Valuation: <u>legitimate</u> uses of the population (29–30) + App: Valuation: a <u>healthy</u> redevelopment of the territory (30) t -ive J: propriety: *overbuilding has happened [. . .] in the sea* (31–32) + J: capacity/propriety: the <u>enlightened</u> politician (35) + Aff something that <u>I hope</u> can happen (40)
Result	The creation of 'structures for the territory' (39)
Coda	So that's something that I hope can happen (40)

Let us explore the representation of social actors in a little more detail, beginning with the narrator himself, who appears to claim a central role in the story as a whole:

many in Priolo say [. . .] that <u>I've changed</u> the way the word Priolo is used (9)

As the reserve's director, it is understandable that he regards the data concerning the increasing number of visitors as 'important' (1), though not quite clear why he sees this phenomenon as 'shocking' (1). This seems rather exaggerated: in essence, numbers have doubled since the flamingos began to breed. Given what has been said about their flagship status, and what Cilea goes on to say himself about the levels of media coverage afforded the reserve after 2015, this is only what one would expect; indeed, an average of around forty visitors a day throughout the year might seem quite low for such a spectacular site.

What is relevant is the narrator's perspective, and a general sense of his optimistic outlook can be observed even here, in his emotional way of representing these statistics. The reserve's success in the field of flamingo breeding is not just an ecological matter but, as lines 8–16 make plain, has helped to rebrand the image of Priolo Gargallo. The townspeople are clearly pleasantly conscious that their town is being talked about in a positive sense in national media (12–16), and pass on to him their enthusiastic congratulations (9). The positive vibes that result from this first part of the story continue in the remainder, with Cilea's 'glass half full' descriptions of a global movement towards environmentally friendly fuel, and the local implications of these trends. Interestingly, his views on the latter are represented as situated in discussions with his 'brother Sergio'; in other words, they occur within the speaker's family context. This precision serves to dissociate them from those held by Cilea in his institutional role, that of a prominent environmentalist with a role to play in the local social mosaics and webs of political relations.

In effect, his argument is quite controversial. In essence, he defends the industrial plants because the zones they occupy have a potential for complete environmental recovery – they can be dismantled completely, their polluted lands cleansed and made available for what he calls 'structures for the territory' (39), by which he presumably means environmentally friendly and sustainable resources such as parks, beaches, a larger nature reserve. In this restorative potential they differ entirely from many other constructions around Siracusa which will never be removed or revalued in any way. The picture he paints of 'tourism facilities, hotels and villas built practically in the sea' (32) refers to Sicily's post-war history of rampant coastal cementification, where inadequate enforcement of planning laws, among other factors, has been held responsible for these developments. Though less pernicious and toxic than the industrial sites, he suggests, these hotels and villas have left a mark on the landscape that will never be removed.[12]

Cilea outlines these attractive future scenarios in evaluative language that features positive evaluation of 'things'; using, that is, the 'appreciation' category. Martin and White (2005) distinguish between references to actual things or states, which are termed 'realis' and references to future, imaginary, hypothetical, abstract or otherwise unreal objects, called 'irrealis', and it is noticeable that Cilea's references are all of this latter type:

+ App: Valuation: a <u>positive</u> future perspective (28), irrealis
+ App: Valuation: <u>significant</u> portions of territory (29), irrealis
+ App: Valuation: <u>legitimate</u> uses of the population (29–30), irrealis

The contingent, uncertain nature of these outcomes is underlined by his use of epistemic modality (see Section 5.3); the modal verb 'could' is used three times in connection with these future possibilities (27, 29, 30), as in the following instance:

the industrial pole today <u>could</u> in some way provide a positive future perspective (27–28)

A remarkable statement indeed, for the director of a nature reserve situated on the doorstep of this behemoth, this symbol of environmental devastation. As he proceeds, however, his certainty concerning these outcomes is frequently undermined; for example, we notice a sort of clash between the epistemic semantics of 'could' and the verbal choice 'guarantee' when he says that:

the dismantling of industrial structures [. . .] <u>could guarantee</u> a <u>healthy</u> (+ App: Valuation, irrealis) redevelopment of the territory (30)

In other words, Cilea is not fully committed to the truth value of his rosy predictions – they might be realized, they might not, and this is consistent with the nature of future predictions in general. As Allan and Jaszczolt (2012: 441) say, 'the reason for a generalizing assumption about an intrinsic link between future time and epistemic modality is that future states of affairs are by nature uncertain'. However, it is noticeable that Cilea uses a different modal to refer to the outcomes associated with processes of tourist cementification:

this <u>won't</u> be able to happen in those areas where overbuilding has happened for purposes of tourism, where hotels have been built, and villas built practically in the sea. You <u>won't</u> be able to recover those places. It <u>will</u> be very difficult to recover those elements (30–34)

The modal 'will/will not' is expressive not of absolute certainty, but does express the speaker's attitude to the likelihood of a future outcome,[13] and contrasts with the case of 'could', which acknowledges an element of possibility.[14] Here, Cilea is certain that hotels and villas constructed 'practically in the sea' will not be recovered, though it is noticeable that in his final thought on the topic – for which he still uses the modal 'will' – he does concede that recovery is not impossible (it will be 'very difficult'). Again, his use of the modal underlines his certainty towards the proposition he utters (he is certain that it will be very difficult).

In the last text cited, above, it is noticeable that Cilea permits the inference of a negative judgement on the social actors involved in the unbridled developments that occurred for the purposes of tourism:

t -ive J: propriety: overbuilding has happened [. . .] in the sea (31–32)

Even here, however, he is not explicitly involved in pointing a finger: the 'overbuilding' is represented as an impersonal process, as something that 'has happened' rather than as something that specific people have 'done'. Even milder is his representation of the industrial pole itself:

> While before, as we said at the beginning, when Priolo Gargallo was talked about this was always only in a negative sense because the industries, the pollution, the problems that existed which, I repeat, still exist, were talked about. (9–12)

Once again we notice the absence of the note of condemnation or any kind of evaluation of human behaviour. Instead the impersonal phrase 'the problems that existed which, I repeat, still exist' is used; a phrase that would be appropriate to characterize natural processes with harmful consequences for humans such as volcanic eruptions, earthquakes, flooding.[15]

Curiously, the only explicit judgement of human behaviour in the entire text is that reserved for a figure who appears towards the end, and belongs to a class of social actor – politicians – that we might have expected Cilea, on the whole, to condemn. Instead his judgement is extremely positive, though since it refers to the realm of future interventions, it is also *irrealis*:

> the <u>enlightened</u> politician (35); + J: capacity/propriety, *irrealis*

This is doubly coded (capacity/propriety) since it is unsure if the reference intends to praise the politician's abilities, for example their far-sightedness – which would refer to the semantic domain of *capacity* – or their moral probity, the tendency to do the right thing, which is the domain of *propriety*. In such a reference the two are superimposed, conflated. It is noticeable that Cilea's language as he describes this person reflects his own certainty regarding this future outcome:

> at this point enter the enlightened politician, the one who will plan the future of the territory – he comes back for the umpteenth time (34–36)

The theatrical metaphor ('at this point enter') with its use of the present tense helps to characterize the politician's appearance as a future certainty – something that is scheduled to happen, that is planned, that is part of a script. Cilea does not use conditional formulae, which would give quite a different flavour, such as: *what we would need, the situation would require, if only we could find, what wouldn't we give for (an enlightened politician)?* Again, the modal 'will' helps to characterize the action in question – the future planning of the territory – as a certainty, as something that *will* happen. Moreover, the reference concludes, the politician's appearance is something that is an often repeated event; again, the present tense underlines the speaker's certainty that it will occur.

The politician is an unlikely hero, especially if we recall what was said in an earlier section about the responsibility of the political classes for the environmental disasters that have taken place in the area (see Section 5.1). It is noticeable that, following these positive beginnings, Cilea's characterization of the actual future of the area is extremely modest, not to say vague:

> to give the possibility to some areas to be converted into industrial structures, but for others into structures for the territory (38–39)

This is not a vision of unrestrained biodiversity, the return of the 'wonderful lands' where one could 'gallop on horseback along the pure white beaches of Priolo and go hunting at the old saltpans' (see Section 5.4). Indeed, it gives discursive recognition to the fact that at least part of the reconversion will be to 'industrial structures', without any mention of their environmental impact. He does not, for example, specify that they will be 'environmentally friendly/sustainable/ low-tech/ industrial structures'. The vague phrase 'structures for the territory', then, must enfold Cilea's visions for the post-industrial future of the area. As mentioned above, we can only 'presume' that these may regard sustainable tourism, nature trails, the promotion of natural features such as woods, rivers, increasing biodiversity, greater accessibility to cleaner coastal areas.

The sense that Cilea's glass is, as he tells us, half full pervades the text. It is present in his positive descriptions of increasing public use of the reserve. Interestingly, the same presumption that 'more is better' that has been critiqued in environmental CDA (see Section 1.2) seems to apply here as well. This is not to say, by the way, that more visitors to a nature reserve can ever be a bad thing. Rather, it is to draw attention once more to this pervasive mindset, which apparently also applies in an ecological context. It is not hard to deconstruct the necessarily positive nature of such an increase: for example, by asking, if the new visitors have only been drawn in by the flamingos' 'pink miracle', the flagship species and its possibly transient, media-driven fame, then how genuine will be their sympathetic interest in environmentalism? Can such superficial interest ever result in the development of deep ecological attitudes? and so on.

As we have seen, Cilea's optimism is also linked to the positive feedback he receives from the local communities. Having grown up in the area and, as we saw in the last section, with strong family traditions and connections of all kinds, it is obvious that positive local attitudes towards the reserve, and to himself as its director, will be keenly felt. It also apparently derives from his understanding of global trends in the fuel industry, as he talks confidently of 'conditions at an international level', of the abandonment of petrol and diesel in favour of electric cars (21–24).

His optimism also concerns the nature of the political process, since from an objective point of view, it is on this sphere that any positive future outcomes depend.

This is a future narrative, a story of what could be, if the speaker's hopes (40) are realized. Since Cilea's vision is a positive one, it is legitimate to approach the text as a sample of positive discourse, in the spirit of positive discourse analysis (see Section 2.6). However, old habits die hard, and as I have indicated at stages of the above analysis, there is a certain tension in the text that derives from a sense that Cilea's positive outlook could be out of synch with the facts of the real world. Can we be sure, for example, that when we no longer need to refine crude oil into usable petrol and gas, we will 'give up our need of large spaces for production', and 'forget the need to continuously consume land for useless projects' (21–23)? For one thing, the discourse of electric cars is yet to convincingly address the question of where the electricity is to come from, and presumably 'large spaces' could be needed for this. Undoubtedly, the environmental impact of giant wind farms, solar or hydro energy plants will be less toxic than that of fossil fuels, but it will not be negligible, and if it is to be minimized, far-sighted political choices will be required. Cilea's trust that it is possible to find 'enlightened' politicians to direct these processes is perhaps the most surprising element of all, especially in the current context where faith in politicians' goodness – in terms of capacity or propriety – has seldom been lower, and this is not just true for Italy.

This is one man's vision, his 'hope'. We can imagine that, apart from the circumstances he has adduced in the text for having a half full glass, he also has received many other signals that are not included; personal experiences of changes that have taken place at the site, meetings, discussions, study, readings and so on, all feeding into an overall sense that things have improved at Priolo, they are improving and will continue to improve in future. No doubt these life experiences also include 'umpteen' meetings and conversations with 'enlightened' politicians. As the director of the reserve, he is also in the best position to assess the contribution of the flamingos of Priolo to an awakening of true environmental awareness in the area.

6

Conclusion

6.1 Boiling planet

By way of moving the discourse away from the case studies in the last sections towards a more ample frame of reference, a text I encountered recently concentrates many of the themes that have been addressed in the book, especially language and its intimate, multiple connections with the pressing ecological issues of our time.

By contrast with the narratives selected for the case study segments, the text is not exactly a specimen of positive discourse, something that 'inspires, encourages, heartens, discourse we like, that cheers us along' (Martin 1999: 51–2, see Section 2.6). Rather, it seems at first sight a piece of polemical writing which questions scientific orthodoxy on climate change and thus, since I generally accept the scientific consensus on these matters, it runs counter to my own views. In such a case, when a text goes against the grain of a linguist's cherished beliefs or principles, their mind will wander in the direction of Critical Discourse Analysis. Here, for example it seems, after reading the first few paragraphs, that the writer (a) does not believe that climate change is real, (b) believes that prominent politicians are wildly exaggerating its dangers, and (c) that a complicit global media repeats their pronouncements uncritically, thus creating a state of emergency bordering on panic. The text begins:

> And just like that we've entered a new epoch. 'The era of global warming has ended, the era of global boiling has arrived', decreed UN chief António Guterres last week. It's hard to know what's worse: the hubris and arrogance of this globalist official who imagines he has the right to declare the start of an entire new age, or the servile compliance of the media elites who lapped up his deranged edict about the coming heat death of Earth. 'Era of global boiling has arrived and it is terrifying', said the front page of the Guardian, as if Guterres's word was gospel, his every utterance a divine truth. We urgently need to throw the waters of reason on this delirious talk of a 'boiling' planet.[1]

From the outset, the views of Guterres are undermined by high octane condemnation ('hubris' and 'arrogance', 'deranged', 'delirious', etc.); however, from a deep ecological point of view, urgency about the escalating crisis could appear as an appropriate reaction from a high-profile public figure such as the secretary-general of the United Nations. The text thus appears to be written from an anti-ecological perspective. After all industrialization, growthism, mass extinctions, pollution, the unchecked CO_2 emissions that accompany the logic of global capitalism – the familiar 'problem' features of modern times that were presented in the first part of this book – all these appear to confirm the hypothesis of Anthropocenic, human-driven climate change. Guterres would seem to be guilty of nothing more than proclaiming the situation in a rather melodramatic phrase; to pillory him as this text does seems to align the writer with positions of climate change denial.

The text's headline, which appears above a dramatic photo of a man gazing at countless fires that blaze across a devastated landscape, proclaims a message that is sufficient to ruffle the feathers of any eco-sensitive reader:

It's time to stand up to the eco-fearmongering of our medieval elites

The headline's use of framing is worth unpacking from a pragmatic perspective (Table 6.1). It consists in a blend of several nested frames that may be teased out singly as follows:

Table 6.1 Global Boiling Headline and Framing

Text Element	Frame	Pragmatic Meaning
It's time to stand up to	Social resistance	Unspecified elite social forces are spreading fear about the state of the climate, and it is vital that we resist this
Eco-fearmongering	Rumour spreading	
Medieval elites	Feudal system	

The social vision(s) that underlie the headline's frames can be further explored. For example, the use of a 'medieval' frame to characterize modern social relations is suggestive of a power division between the haves (one strongly salient hypothesis here is that these consist of the usual suspects – CEOs of multinationals, financiers, politicians, media moguls, royals, celebrities, etc.) and the have-nots, that is, the vast masses of ordinary people. Indeed, the frame arguably looks towards conspiracy theories in which an even more restrictive, anonymous global elite today stand in the same relation to the masses as feudal kings did in their day. Only by 'standing up to' these invisible conspirators will readers demonstrate that there is a difference between a modern democracy and an ancient medieval society. Precisely what is meant by 'To stand up to' in this context is unclear; perhaps the writer wants readers to resist the dominant narrative by not engaging in differentiated rubbish collection, not cutting down on the use of plastic bags in supermarkets and so on. To engage in 'eco-fearmongering', meanwhile, is to spread rumours concerning the state of the climate and the ecosystem in general, with the aim of creating a state of panic. But if such rumours are false or true appears a relevant question here, and I shall return to this aspect of the matter later.

Collectively, the frames depict a world of social relations in which a tiny group of extremely powerful social actors dictate how the masses behave and use media to create a state of fear – in this case, of climate disaster – so that the latter will be easier to control. Despite the text's problematic stance on the environment, I do have sufficient sympathy with the assumptions that underlie such a view of Western social organization to include it, after all, alongside other texts studied under the PDA umbrella. The notion that 'we' are responsible for the fate of the planet has been persuasively insinuated into public discourse over recent decades and though, as we saw in Greta's accusations (Section 2.7) powerful social actors are occasionally held to account, media usually lay the blame squarely at the door of Joe Public. It is not hard to find texts online that underline this point: the following, for example, obtained by a Google search for 'who is to blame for climate change?' is quite typical:

> 'We are all both culpable and not', Fasenfest observed. People who can afford and use air conditioning during hot weather, or continue to eat beef even though it exacerbates climate change, all contribute to a system that is destroying the planet. As Fasenfest observed, most people have no practical alternatives to participating in this system on a day-to-day basis; they can make lifestyle alterations which make teensy dents in the greater problem, but that is about it. If you are fortunate enough to live in a society that prospers under capitalism (relatively speaking), the chances are that you fall into the category of major climate perpetrator in one way or another.[2]

In most Western societies, people of all social strata are included in the categories indicated here, that is people who can afford to use air conditioning and eat beef. In these, and in numerous other ways, they 'participate in the system on a day-to-day basis'. Though the author concedes that they can do little to improve the situation, at the end of the day, ordinary people are called 'major climate perpetrators', and thus receive the judgement Martin and White's system metes out to criminals and the grossly immoral (-ive Judgement: propriety). Meanwhile, the people who not only could do more than make 'teensy dents' in the system but actually reform it so that it becomes environmentally friendly rather than harmful are not mentioned at all. Indeed, their activities are naturalized via a nominalized reference to 'this *system*'.[3]

This kind of discourse is so familiar that nowadays the idea that 'climate change is everyone's fault' is uncontroversial, a trope repeated or implied so often in media that, returning to the boiling planet text, we have no difficulty processing the writer's allusions in the following:

> World entering 'era of global boiling', cried the Independent, and we 'know who is responsible'. No prizes for guessing who that is. It's you, me and the rest of our pesky species.

The pronouns 'You' and 'me' here, I would suggest, delineate an in-group that consists of ordinary people. The powerful, elite social actors listed above – CEOs of multinationals, financiers, politicians and so on – however much they also use air conditioning and eat beef – are not included, but are implicitly viewed as the out-group. In other words, the text is developing an argument that is not so much about denying that climate change is happening; rather, it is denouncing processes that obfuscate responsibility for it. In its stance against such inferences, from my perspective, the boiling planet text is on the side of the angels.

The following analysis focuses mainly on the text's judgements of social actors, with the aim of exploring its construction of in- and out-groups, and appreciating the rhetorical and linguistic devices used to persuade readers of the writer's view. The data are collected in two tables, one for the in-group and a much larger one for the out-group, since it is in this direction that the writer directs their vitriol (Table 6.2):

Table 6.2 In-group Judgement Evaluation

	Reference	Who Is Appraised?	Appraisal
1	we 'know who is <u>responsible</u>'. No prizes for guessing who that is. It's you, me and the rest of our pesky species	You, me, our species	-ive J: propriety
2	SBS in Australia advised us to 'Reduce meat intake', 'Stop driving cars' and 'Cut down on flights'	Us	t+J: propriety, irrealis

There are only a few judgement references: the first, a *realis* case, that is one that applies to a case of actual, rather than hypothetical behaviour, has already been dealt with. The writer attributes to Guterres – and the media channels that repeat his words – the view that the social practices of ordinary people are responsible for climate change, behaviour meriting severe condemnation. The other case refers to hypothetical responses – if the public respond appropriately to Guterres's message by, for instance, reducing their meat intake, then they will merit praise.

However, though there are few cases of evaluation of human behaviour, there is a great deal of use made of the semantic field of Affect, that is the emotional realm, especially of fear which, in the author's view, exclusively involves the in-group. To be clear, the out-group of elite social actors, almost by definition, are not involved in such references. If they did feel 'terror' at an approaching climate Armageddon then they would do something about it. The following instances (Table 6.3) concern the likely responses of members of the in-group to the ongoing events:

Table 6.3 In-group Affect Evaluation

1.	Era of global boiling has arrived and it is <u>terrifying</u> (-ive Aff: dissatisfaction, fear)
2.	*families running from the flames [and] workers collapsing in scorching heat* (t-ive Aff: dissatisfaction, fear, irrealis);
3.	*it is just the beginning* (t-ive Aff: dissatisfaction, fear, irrealis);
4.	*World entering 'era of global boiling', cried the Independent* (t-ive Aff: dissatisfaction, fear, irrealis);
5.	the green politics of <u>fear</u>. It's the latest addition to the already fat dictionary of <u>eco-dread</u>. (-ive Aff: dissatisfaction, fear);
6.	*This is why we've gone from climate change to climate crisis to climate emergency. And it's why we're now going from global warming to global boiling.* (t-ive Aff: dissatisfaction, fear, irrealis);
7.	Language is used to <u>terrorise</u> the masses (-ive Aff: dissatisfaction, fear, irrealis);
8.	*the end really is nigh* (t-ive Aff: dissatisfaction, fear, irrealis);
9.	convey to the public an <u>increasingly urgent threat</u> (-ive Aff: dissatisfaction, fear, intens.);
10.	they want to coerce us *into the realm of doom* (t-ive Aff: dissatisfaction, fear, irrealis);
11.	climate chaos, climate disaster, even climate apocalypse (t-ive Aff: dissatisfaction, fear, irrealis);
12.	<u>scary</u> words and <u>warnings</u> of a <u>hellish</u> future (-ive Aff: dissatisfaction, fear, irrealis)

Thus, from the point of view of the in-group, the dominant response indicated by the text is one of fear. In most cases this is conveyed by the author himself (5, 6, 7, 8, 9, 10, 11, 12) who suggests that 'this (fear) is how they (elite social actors and complicit media) *want* you to feel'. In other cases, the words come from Guterres (1, 2, 3) and/or from newspapers (1, 4).

Judgement of the out-group, as expected, is more frequent and also more intense (Table 6.4):

Table 6.4 Out-group Judgement Evaluation

	Reference	Who Is Appraised?	Appraisal
1	what's worse: the <u>hubris</u> and <u>arrogance</u> of this globalist official	Guterres	-ive J: propriety
2	the <u>servile</u> compliance of the media elites *who lapped up*	Media (elites)	-ive J: tenacity
3	his <u>deranged</u> edict	Guterres	-ive J: normality
4	*said the front page of the Guardian [...] his every utterance a divine truth*	The Guardian	-ive J: tenacity
5	*Guterres issued his neo-papal bull*	Guterres	t-ive J: propriety
6	doing his best impersonation of a 1st-century millenarian <u>crackpot</u>.	Guterres	-ive J: normality
7	The <u>obsequious</u> speed with which the media [...] was extraordinary.	Media	-ive J: tenacity
8	They behaved less like reporters than like the <u>slavish</u> scribes	Media	-ive J: tenacity
9	this secular god and his <u>delusional</u> visions	Guterres	-ive J: normality
10	'Planet is boiling', one headline <u>breezily</u> declared	Media	-ive J: veracity
11	Guterres's fearful phrase, his <u>propagandistic</u> line	Guterres	-ive J: veracity
12	no doubt drawn up with the aid of <u>spin doctors</u>	Spin doctors/ Guterres	-ive J: veracity
13	*media outlets started lecturing readers*	Media	t-ive J: propriety
14	Even <u>self-styled</u> radicals	Radical media	-ive J: veracity
15	*made themselves mouthpieces of the UN's medieval sermonising*	Radical media	t-ive J: propriety
16	*you should not use a phrase like 'global boiling'*	Guterres	t-ive J: veracity
17	*one professor of climate physics rebuked Guterres*	Guterres	t-ive J: veracity
18	*gleefully described by our green elites*	Green elites	t-ive J: veracity
19	There are no <u>propaganda</u> points [...] in fearmongering over cold weather.	Guterres and his 'apostles'	-ive J: veracity
20	The <u>catastrophism</u> of climate change in particular is <u>puffed up</u> on pretty much a weekly basis.	Media	t-ive J: veracity
21	the <u>cranky</u> elites	Elite social actors	-ive J: normality
22	*Extinction Rebellion protested outside the offices of the New York Times [...] the panic-inducing 'climate emergency'*	Extinction Rebellion	t-ive J: veracity

(Continued)

Table 6.4 (Continued)

	Reference	Who Is Appraised?	Appraisal
23	They're trying to <u>manipulate</u> us.	They	-ive J: propriety
24	they want to <u>coerce us</u> into the realm of doom	They	
25	it is also an insult to truth, reason and us	Guterres	-ive J: propriety
26	That such a <u>fact-lite, post-scientific, hysterical</u> phrase has been used by the UN	the UN, the activist set and the media elites	-ive J: veracity, intens.
27	this <u>arrogant</u> crusade of <u>emotional manipulation</u>	Guterres, media	-ive J: propriety

Even without the rest of the text, from a brief perusal of Table 6.4 one could gain a fairly accurate idea of the content it covers as well as, crucially, the author's stance towards the material. This is not nuanced, nor does it attempt any kind of rhetorical balance or classical approach to argumentation. The writer claims that he will use rational arguments:

> We urgently need to throw <u>the waters of reason</u> on this delirious talk of a 'boiling' planet.

However, as even a glance at Table 6.4. will show, the temperature of the piece is as hot as the planet described by Guterres, with an abundance of insults for everyone. The dominant rhetorical strategy seems to be ad hominem, and the chief target is Guterres (1, 3, 5, 6, 9, 11, 12, 16, 17, 19, 25, 27). Not only is he the recipient of the multiple insults we have already covered, but he is also undermined more subtly, as in the following:

> this *globalist official* who imagines he has the right to declare the start of an entire new age

The adjective 'globalist' aligns Guterres with a discredited group of elite social actors (i.e. the invisible promoters of international capitalism), and he is further mocked for supposed delusions of grandeur.

In another key frame in the text, Guterres appears as a Messiah:

> as if Guterres's word was <u>gospel</u>, his every utterance <u>a divine truth</u>

The references to religious language are numerous, and collectively develop a cosmic, religious frame in which climate change orthodoxy appears as an article of faith, and Guterres is cast as a Christ, a 'secular god', a pope and so on (Table 6.5):

Table 6.5 Boiling Planet, Religious Terms

Guterres's word was gospel, his every utterance a divine truth.
Guterres issued his neo-papal bull
a 1st-century millenarian crackpot
It all brings to mind the Book of Job
Leviathan's back, only we call him climate change now.
Guterres's commandment
the slavish scribes of this secular god
already being christened as fact
make sacrifices to appease nature's angry gods.
the UN's medieval sermonising
Guterres and his apostles
the end really is nigh
apocalyptic superlatives
the grammar of Armageddon
its demands for sacrifice in everyday life
climate apocalypse
a hellish future
this arrogant crusade

By these linguistic means, the text accesses both pagan and Christian cultural scripts (Wierzbicka 1994; Wierzbicka 2002), or reservoirs of meaning associated with the terms in question that are specific, in this case, to Anglo culture. The frame plays on readers' faith, or lack of it, in a scattergun fashion, attempting to align readers' sympathies with the writer's position towards the material. The text works to situate climate change within a largely discredited worldview, crucially linked to the Middle Ages (it mentions 'medieval elites', 'medieval sermonising'). Moreover, Britain as a Christian country is largely Protestant, so a reference like 'neo-papal bull' alienates readers from Guterres by associating him with the distant, Latin, Catholic tradition. Biblical references, especially ones that relate either to the Old Testament or the eschatological perspectives of the Book of Revelation, are liberally sprinkled through the text: *gospel, divine, Leviathan, commandment, scribes, sacrifices, apostles, the end is nigh, the apocalypse, Armageddon, hell.*

The text performs its persuasive work largely via the emotional force of this frame, which is considerable both for practising believers and for those with a rational, modern outlook but with a vestigial attachment to traditional beliefs and practices. The climate change hypothesis is mapped onto the faith in God that was a ubiquitous feature of medieval Christendom – it has become official orthodoxy, a religious dogma to be blindly accepted. Faith in the mediated pronouncements of elite figures replaces faith in God, while the all-powerful social and discursive structures of the medieval church are today replaced by those of the media, who play the role of willing 'apostles' to Guterres's Christ.

Paradoxically, at the same time as the text consciously adopts a specific persuasive linguistic strategy, it also warns of the importance of the role of language, of an 'arrogant crusade of emotional manipulation' by 'media elites' who 'terrorise the masses' by using 'scary words and warnings', and 'catastrophic language', because 'fretful terminology can help to convey to the public an increasingly urgent threat'.

Indeed, as the writer claims, 'the meaning of words is important', and the role of language and its social implications is at the heart of the Boiling Planet text. The writer's anger at Guterres is not motivated by social considerations such as his complicity with powerful corporate elites, for example, but mainly by linguistic ones. Like George Orwell, he is fully aware of the enslaving potentialities of language, and resists what he sees as the 'threat inflation' in the media's hyperbolic metaphor formation:

> This is why we've gone from climate change to climate crisis to climate emergency. And it's why we're now going from global warming to global boiling.

He also mentions a circumstance that shows how culturally aware climate activists are ready to campaign over such linguistic matters:

> Extinction Rebellion protested outside the offices of the New York Times to put pressure on it to dump the passive phrase 'climate change' in preference for the panic-inducing 'climate emergency'.

It seems, then, that for some people, the language used to represent events can be as important as the events themselves. It is curious, to say the least, that the linguistic strategies of the UN should coincide with those of an ostensibly anti-establishment, activist group like Extinction Rebellion.

To conclude, we should focus a little on the substance of the debate, on the 'facts' of the climate change hypothesis and on whether or not we believe the planet is boiling. Here is the text's position:

> Can't we have just a little critical thinking on the idea of 'global boiling'? The first thing a rational mind ought to note is that boiling is when liquid turns into vapour. Sorry to be pedantic, but I think the meaning of words is important. Does anyone really believe our planet is now so fantastically hot that lakes and rivers and seas will shortly start to evaporate? If you don't – and you shouldn't, because it's baloney – then you should not use a phrase like 'global boiling'.

It all depends what you mean by 'shortly'. Perhaps most of us would agree with the writer that lakes, rivers and seas will not evaporate tomorrow. But whether we would be equally confident that they will still be here in fifty years' time, or a hundred – both extremely 'short' periods of time measured in ages of the Earth – is not such a sure thing. This is not the place to assess the merits of the climate change hypothesis but, since it is widely accepted among the scientific community, it cannot be simply set aside by attacking a Straw Man, and the use of a characteristically colourful insult ('baloney') for the opponent's position. Critical thinking on the climate change hypothesis would mean to engage with the facts, or produce new ones that encourage more favourable climate predictions.

In conclusion, the 'positive discourse analysis' element here relates to the fact that the writer's anger is directed against powerful elites who control media discourse, and displace blame for climate change onto ordinary people; however, from a purely ecological point of view, it could be necessary to critique the facticity of his environmental positions.

6.2 In retrospect

In this section the intention is to draw the threads of the book together, to compare the two case studies and to offer some reflections on their significance both in terms of a broadly ecological perspective and from an Ecolinguistic point of view. The two contexts, High Ash Farm in Norfolk and Priolo Saltpans in Sicily, have certain features in common. Both are projects touched by the philosophies of Deep Ecology which, as we have seen, recognize the right of the natural world to exist and allow its importance for its own sake, not necessarily because it has instrumental value for us. Both men struggle for these values against powerful manifestations of industrial capitalism. For Chris Skinner, the context is the UK, the home of the industrial revolution and a place where the 'green and pleasant land' is in the process of being replaced by grimmer realities of plastic, glass and cement. On recordings of his early morning walks he sometimes comments on the noise from the bypass that encroaches on the dawn chorus. At times, he reports on the deaths of badger or deer at the roadside, struck down by motorists in a hurry, and laments the shrinking spaces available for wildlife in the modern world. As we saw, moreover, his vision of sustainable eco-farming is at odds with the dominant currents of thought and practice in this sector, and he faces hostility from his peers in the farming profession, who view biodiversity in quite a different light, and who carry on a 'war' on all wildlife that has negative effects on a balance sheet.

For Fabio Cilea, the aim of promoting biodiversity, and not just the health of flamingos, is equally important. In Priolo Saltpans, the main opposition to this was shown to be the petrochemical industries and refineries that are contiguous with the reserve although, as we saw, Cilea has a pragmatic, conciliatory attitude to his messy neighbours and, indeed, their collaboration was key in the reserve's success. Oil has tremendous symbolic importance in the current global climate debate because its use at all levels of the industrial capitalist complex has such a potential to harm the environment. Even though Cilea may not be seen as an anti-petrol activist, then, for the visitor to Priolo it is natural to view the reserve as a case of fragile nature, flourishing in the midst of industrial desolation, an authentic 'oasis among the smokestacks'.

From an ecological perspective, the question is what future animals, plants, birds, insects and other non-human actors might have in our world, since their survival depends on the frail support of minority activists who oppose the great currents of industrial development. Without a committed naturalist at the helm, High Ash Farm would simply have been another small farm like dozens around Norwich. If Cilea moves on from the reserve, if LIPU withdraw their support, the marshes at Priolo could dry up or succumb to the pressures of their toxic surroundings.

One characteristic of stories, of narratives in general, that has been brought out in the examples provided is that there is assumed to be a reason for their telling – that they matter in some way, and that the teller expects their hearer to share this assumption. As we saw in the discussion of relevance theory, we do not produce random verbiage that has no meaning (not knowingly, at least), nor do we expect our interlocutors to do this. Many everyday human stories feature accounts of something that happened to the narrator in a specific time and place, with certain context features, accompanying emotional responses, some signals that guide the listener in understanding how the narrator wishes the tale to be heard (are they looking for sympathy, advice, congratulations?, etc.). Underlying this 'sharing experiences' narrative genre is the assumption that our fellow humans will be interested in these tales because whatever happens to one member of the human species may happen to another. A tale concerning a house burglary will put a listener on guard about potential dangers to their property, a story about an offer at a store may help the listener get a bargain for themselves and so on. Or, there may be no specific added value to the story, but there may be a more functional or phatic way of accounting for its significance. In the case of a joke, for instance, the purpose of the narrative is to create laughter, to share a moment of lightness and thereby improve social relations with that person. Often there seems to be no particular 'point' to narrative, but people talk simply for the sake of talking, as silence can be a dispreferred state in which to pass time together.

In the case of many stories that we looked at in the earlier parts of the book, it is noticeable that they concern non-human social actors such as turtles, foxes, badgers, moles, trees, woods, the Spring, starlings, ants, woodpeckers, carrion crows, pheasants and, of course, flamingos. In some cases the stories had some direct relevance for the human world; in other words, the substance of the story, its pragmatic purpose, was no different from the human–human cases just outlined. For example, in the Country Diary story, the writer tells us:

> I sit there, feeling the balm of long-awaited spring sunshine on my face.

For her, 'Spring' is important, but the pragmatic sense of this part of the tale could be paraphrased as *'get out and sit somewhere with the Spring sunshine on your face, relax and just be with Nature – it's an amazing feeling!'* Skinner's story about the ants, as we saw, also contained an explicit appeal, that *'Since ants are so fascinating, think twice before you reach for the ant spray when you find them in your house!'*

However, there were also stories in which what was important has little or no bearing on the relationship of the natural world with the human, but regards the creature itself. For example, Cilea describes the flamingos' crèche behaviour (Section 5.3), a story which refers entirely to the flamingos and their social organization. Skinner's anecdote about the ants' rescue of a fellow worker trapped in honey was wholly concerned with understanding ant behaviour and had no real connection, to speak of, with human realities. Here, the narrators flout the narrative presumptions mentioned of 'normal' verbal interaction, and it is quite impossible for such stories to be categorized as the kind of 'person to person' story we have just discussed. If a stranger, or even an acquaintance, began telling us stories about the doings of non-human social actors like spiders or ants they would be considered mad, or eccentric at best – at least, if there were no discernible 'point' to the story, that is no conceivable way that the tale could be related to the human world.[4] Yet, as we have seen, both Skinner and to a lesser extent, Cilea, are quite willing to tell stories about non-human social actors, because they make a different kind of presumption, one that is in line with deep ecological thinking, and could be expressed as follows: *The natural world is important in its own terms and is a legitimate subject for human interest.* They expect that their listeners will also share this presumption. Skinner knows his audience: after some thirty years broadcasting, interacting with listeners, answering their questions, showing visitors around the farm, he is aware of their ecological sympathies which, indeed, his radio programme will have had a role in forming. However, if he tried to tell his ant anecdotes to an audience full of the kind of person who does reach for the ant spray when they find ants in the house, he would struggle to hold their interest, at the very least.

Once this point has been appreciated, it becomes possible to understand Skinner's narrative style, which at times appears rather rambling or unfocused. If, instead of asking ourselves *'what relevance does this tale have to my concerns as a human being?'* we wonder *'what else has Skinner got to reveal about the fascinating non-human world and its doings?'*, then the potential stories become infinite. Skinner hardly has time to offer an evaluation of a story he has just concluded before he is moving off at a tangent to start another:

> They're really social little insects and of course they're great food. If you love things like green woodpeckers, the largest of our three species of native woodpecker, and they absolutely love the ants and gobble them up with their long sticky tongues which they probe down into the ant colonies. They can't do that in my porch because they're in amongst the cacti.

'They're really social little insects' was the final evaluation of Skinner's long tale about the ants, the porch, the honey and so on. That was the point – to underline the 'social' nature of ants, that they move together, act together, think together – and will drop the task they are engaged in to help a comrade in difficulty: *Ants are great, so don't just reach for the ant spray*! However, he suddenly remembers that ants are also 'great food', a remark which would risk alienating listeners who relate everything to the human realm. No, he is not talking about humans at all, but the ants are 'great food' for the green woodpecker! And so it goes on.

6.3 The simpler way

The large-scale issues dealt with in this book that relate among other things to oil pollution, industrial damage, toxic communities, global warming, growthism, capitalism and anti-ecological farming methods will not disappear any time soon. Their resolution will involve macro processes at the level of global politics, and it is beyond the scope of this book to do more than has been done already, that is to show how such practices impinge on the environment, how they have shaped a world in which our relationships with the natural world are characterized by indifference, if not actual hostility. We have seen how narratives are everywhere. At a macro level, they crystallize attitudes and determine power lines, giving shape to the invisible railway tracks along which, in Eliot's words, 'the world moves in appetency on its metalled ways'.[5] As individual consumers our desires for more, better, cheaper consumer goods feed the monster; all we can do in a private way to help the situation is to 'want less'.

In the realm of Economics, such subversive ideas have been raised by Serge Latouche and others in the de-growthism movement (Cohen 2010). New stories to rival the mantra that 'more is better' occasionally emerge, as happened in 1973 with the publication of E. F. Schumacher's classic *Small is Beautiful*, which argued for small-scale, bottom-up solutions to day-to-day problems, intermediate technology and closer ties with nature. More recently, the notion of a 'Simpler Way' has harnessed dissatisfaction with the capitalist system and the de-growth ideology to depict a radical reorganization of society that, its proponents argue, will be driven by necessity as the climate crisis worsens. Unlike other schemes for social reform such as classical Marxism, for example, this approach gives full weight to the importance of cultural change and popular assent. The Simpler Way also proposes that the shock of major lifestyle change, particularly in terms of greatly reduced living standards, will be amply compensated for by gains in individual happiness and well-being. The citations that follow are all from Trainer (2012):

> The present economy is literally driven by the quest to get richer; this motive is what gets options searched for, risks taken, construction and development

underway, etc. The most obvious alternative is for these actions to be motivated by a collective effort to work out what society needs, and organise to produce and develop those things. However this involves an utterly different world view and driving mechanism. (593)

The above changes could not be made unless there was also a profound cultural change, involving nothing less than the complete abandonment of any concern with gain. For more than two hundred years Western society has been focused on the quest to get richer, to accumulate wealth and property. This is what drives all economic activity, including the innovation and developmental firms undertake [sic], and the behaviour of individuals and firms in the market, and it is the supreme principle of national policy. (Ibid.)

Trainer underlines the extent to which the necessary mindset would rely on major changes in culture and societal values taking place, with the gradual development of a more collective mentality:

It would be difficult to exaggerate the magnitude of this cultural transition from the mentality that is typical in consumer society and that has been dominant in Western culture for a long time. (Ibid.)

a sustainable and just society all could enjoy has to be defined primarily in terms of frugality, micro-scale localism, 'subsistence', self-sufficiency and non-material life satisfactions, at the household, neighbourhood and town levels. (594)

Obviously this vision could not possibly work unless there had been a huge change in values. It requires a world view which is basically collectivist, cooperative and concerned to nurture other individuals and the community. (597)

Yet even today as we saw above (Section 2.8), there are elements of modern Western societies that do emphasize community over individualism. These are not just 'alternative' or minority schemes but, in the case of something like the modern allotment movement, can represent mainstream attempts to combine ecological knowledge and practices with community values in the interests of collective and individual well-being (Breuste 2010). Interestingly, references to the natural world are few and far between in Trainer's paper; the environment would of course benefit from the absence of heavy industry from the following scenario, but is referred to via a vague term, 'a beautiful landscape':

the Simpler Way vision is its emphasis on the alternative sources of life satisfaction that would be enabled, including security (e.g., from unemployment, economic depression, poverty and 'exclusion'), a relaxed pace, a nurturing community, participation in community self-government, growing and making and creating things, being respected for work that makes a valued contribution, living in a beautiful landscape and a leisure-rich environment, having access to artists and craftsmen, enjoying a rich and varied cultural life including festivals and celebrations and having much time to devote to personal development – and having the peace of mind that comes from knowing that you are not part of the global problem. The claim here is that we could easily ensure a far higher quality of life than is now experienced in consumer society. (Ibid.)

Trainer suggests that most leftists and even greens who casually argue against the capitalist system do not realize how radical would be the social changes in first world societies that would accompany a de-growth revolution, how great the collapse of material living standards. It is not just a matter of a more equitable re-distribution of profits; rather, the unsustainable character of capitalist-industrial production will necessitate a transition to the kind of community-based social structures described in the last citation and for this, he argues, the change must come not from social elites but from the people:

the basic block to progress, is not the corporations or the capitalist class. They have their power because people in general grant it to them. The problem group, the key to transition, is people in general. (Ibid. 597)

Whether or not we buy into such a vision of a future without capitalism, the takeaway from Trainer's article is the notion that such changes can only come from the bottom up, and so we should work on education, encouraging the emergence of currents that respect the principles on which such a new society would be based. For their part, ecolinguists would mostly agree with these perspectives, especially those who follow Halliday and his problematization of the lexico-grammar of growth (Section 2.1). In the Simpler Way's programme, they would probably wish for a greater emphasis on relations with the natural world and on deep ecological principles generally.

6.4 Saving the ant

The last section explored a macro-narrative, an alternative to the dominant stories that have given shape to the modern world. In this final section, the emphasis returns to micro-narratives and an individual dimension since in the last analysis, when asking ourselves what we can do in the current global crisis, the answer of Voltaire still has relevance: *il faut cultiver notre jardin*.[6] This year a friend asked if I could translate a poem from Italian to English for an art exhibition catalogue. I was struck by the resonance of the text with the themes of this book and asked him if he would mind if it appeared here:

> Ants by Liborio Palmeri
>
> If we have to die,
> There's still time to think about it.
>
> We'll still make wishes
> And, as stars are falling,
> Savour the fragrant inflorescence
> Of a Spring breeze.
>
> We won't stand around
> While seeds turn into flowers,
> Drooling over salad days;
> But rapidly restrain
> Such thoughts
> Under a black cloud's rain.
>
> If we have to die, no hurry,
> Still time to think about it;
> And Time will take snaps of us –
> Flashing away as the night falls.
>
> Dressed for the occasion.
> No fear of the drop;
> On oblivion's doorstep
> The panic's in check;
> If we have to die, yes! –
> There's still time to think about all of that
>
> But now, let me save
> this ant on my neck

The poem is not explicitly ecological, and it is not clear that 'if we have to die' refers exclusively – or indeed, at all – to the climate crisis and the doom scenario, according to which we are all heading for a fatal apocalypse. Still, the text seems to fit such a narrative. The narrator is concerned with mortality, but not too concerned about it, since he says there's 'no hurry', and emphasizes – three times – that 'there's still time to think about it'. There is a feeling of deckchairs being moved around the Titanic as the writer makes wishes on falling stars, sniffs the Spring breeze, first indulges in nostalgic thoughts and then represses them, poses for photos, takes time to dress properly and so on. However, there is a general sense of increasing urgency throughout the poem, of time running out. From the pleasurable associations of the first verses – reminiscences of youth, romantic fancies (catch a falling star and put it in your pocket), the fragrance of Spring – the final stanza moves to an 'occasion' for which it is necessary to 'dress' – in our culture these are generally weddings, funerals, ceremonial occasions. Would one dress for one's own execution? That is the direction the lexis takes us: 'fear of the drop', 'oblivion's doorstep', 'panic', we 'have to die'. It is noticeable that the refrain now appears in a longer form than before, as if the narrator wishes to drag every microsecond out of the time it will take to pronounce, to delay the inevitable: *There's still time to think about all of that.* The human condition. Time 'taking snaps of us' at various points – here we are being born, graduating, getting married, laughing randomly, making up numbers at dull events; here we are with grey hair, wrinkled, old. Going, going.

What makes the poem memorable is the close. Even as the narrator concludes this mock heroic meditation on his own inevitable demise, his attention is distracted by a tickling sensation, and – instead of brushing it away, squashing it with a careless hand or 'reaching for the ant spray' – he saves the ant.

In their different ways, both Chris Skinner and Fabio Cilea, the heroes of the tales narrated in this book, have spent their lives 'saving the ant'. Perhaps, to express the poem's simple message in Ecolinguistic, or Deep Ecological terms, it could represent a first step in the birth of an ecological consciousness, an essential beginning in the achievement of a more holistic and healthy relationship with the natural world.

As a final word, a personal story. Some years ago, soon after we arrived in Sicily, my wife and I lived in an old town house with an orchard. We came across a struggling fledgling in the garden one day. We had no idea what species it was but picked it up and took it inside, where we tried to get it to drink milk, eat breadcrumbs, whatever. We racked our brains about how to help it. It seemed possessed of a suicidal instinct, as whenever we let it go it would thrash around and hobble to the edge of the table where it would have dropped to the floor if unrestrained. Long story short, the next day the poor thing was dead. I picked it up and tossed it over the wall into a neighbour's garden. Some time later I was telling an old Sicilian countryman the story. He explained that the bird was no doubt a swallow, that these birds cannot fly unless they start from a high position and that if you come across one struggling on the ground, the thing to do is just pick them up and fling them into the sky. Nature will do the rest. This was terrible to hear, and we both felt a lot of remorse for our ignorance. Time passed and one afternoon in the swallow season we were driving down our Baroque town's High Street and I spotted the same kind of fledgling struggling on the road in front of us. Without thinking I stopped the car, held up my hand to the drivers behind. I picked up the bird and tossed it aloft. Indeed, it fluttered away and disappeared, like a miracle.

We are faced on all sides by reports of climate crisis, of an approaching disaster which we feel powerless to avert. Perhaps it is true that we can do little, unless we are born with the dynamism and certainty that fuel Greta's activism. But we can all try to improve our relations with the natural world; we can all 'save the ant'.

Notes

Chapter 1

1. The 'natural world' is an unfashionable term but will mainly be used throughout the book in preference to more trendy options. The 'non-human world', via the negative prefix, appears to stigmatize all that is not human, the 'more than human world' is too much of a mouthful, while the 'extra human world' appears to have a different meaning in Anthropology.
2. David Suzuki retires from 'the Nature of Things': https://www.youtube.com/watch?v=Q6Np5aR73rI, retrieved 30.08.2023.
3. See, for example, the discussion of what Brabazon calls 'Claustropolitanism' (Brabazon 2021).
4. *Harvard Business Review*. Online at: https://hbr.org/2013/10/this-isnt-capitalism-its-growthism-and-its-bad-for-us, retrieved 30.08.2023.
5. See, for example, a recent high-profile environmental stand-off between Elon Musk and defenders of the smooth snakes and sand lizards threatened by his project in Germany. *Guardian*, https://www.theguardian.com/technology/2021/jan/05/elon-musk-new-tesla-gigafactory-germany, last visit 13.01.2021.
6. In a later section (2.3) I present other examples similar to Halliday's 'my watch *says*', and discuss the notion that such linguistic formulae, by attributing human characteristics to an inanimate object, could represent distant echoes of a sort of animism long absent from the cultural register of the English language.
7. 'Politics and the English Language': http://www.orwell.ru/library/essays/politics/english/e_polit, last access 25/09/2018.
8. Ibid.
9. Ibid.
10. *Guardian* online: https://www.theguardian.com/us-news/2021/jan/07/donald-trump-final-13-days-security-threat-politicians-activists-warn, retrieved 27.02.2023.
11. 'Phenomenon' is another word prescribed by Orwell's list of examples of pretentious diction. The rules, as Orwell himself admits, are almost impossible to follow.

12. *The Guardian* explores the question at: https://www.theguardian.com/science/2019/aug/15/why-its-time-to-stop-worrying-about-the-decline-of-the-english-language, retrieved 27.02.2023.
13. https://www.urbandictionary.com/, last visit 06/01/2021.
14. This refers to an episode in an Indiana Jones movie, in which Jones managed to escape a nuclear explosion by hiding in a fridge. It signals an absurd situation.
15. *Guardian* online: https://www.abc.net.au/news/2018-08-15/fraser-anning-history-of-the-nazi-phrase-final-solution/10122812, last visit 13.01.2021. See Browning 2004.
16. There was some suggestion, at the time, that what was meant by this phrase was not conventional but more sinister weapons such as anthrax, nerve gas. However, it is not clear that the Western powers are without such weapons, nor that they would have greater destructive potential than the atom bomb, for example, which the United States has in abundance.
17. British National Corpus: online at https://www.merriam-webster.com/dictionary/collateral%20damage, retrieved 4.01.2023.
18. *Moscow Times*. Online at: https://www.themoscowtimes.com/2022/02/26/russia-bans-media-outlets-from-using-words-war-invasion-a76605, retrieved 03.02.2023.

Chapter 2

1. Legislation.gov.uk. Online at: https://www.legislation.gov.uk/eut/teu/article/3#:~:text=The%20Union%20shall%20offer%20its,3., retrieved 07.02.2023.
2. There could be linguistic traces even in English of such animistic thinking, in certain constructions that are perhaps rarer today than they were at one time. For instance, I remember my grandfather watching me as a child blowing up a bicycle tyre, and saying something like 'That *wants* a bit more air', as if the desire were centred in the tyre itself. Or consider the well-known 'intentional future' (*to be going to*), which can also be used to indicate the likely outcomes of observed sets of physical conditions. A standard example of this in ELT textbooks is: 'Look at that black cloud. It's going to rain.' Here a sort of primitive consciousness, which includes the dimension of intentionality, appears to be grammatically attributed to the inanimate rain cloud; these grammatical forms have their origins in remote time periods when it may not not have been absurd to speak thus of apparently inanimate phenomena.
3. YouTube: online at https://www.youtube.com/watch?v=ozgcKw4MyvY, retrieved 8.02.2023.
4. Examples of the metaphors collected from just one of these categories: a cold fish – person who is unfriendly or negative in emotions; an old trout – old, ugly woman;

jellyfish – cowardly person; shark – dishonest person; loan shark – rapacious money lender; queer fish – strange person; come the raw prawn – try to deceive by pretending ignorance; urchin – small, rough child. Goatly comments: 'The negative emotional slant of these metaphors reinforces the ideology of human superiority and disdain for animals, making it very difficult for us to conceive of animals and humans as having equal rights to exist, or for animals to be worth our sympathy.'

5   The notion of 'naturalization' is a familiar one in CDA and refers to processes whereby contingent phenomena, behaviour, opinions and so on are made to appear part of the fabric of reality itself, rather than as what they in fact are, that is human constructs, supported by human efforts. Barthes (2006), in an often cited example of a young negro soldier saluting the French flag, together with other examples, was one of the first to describe these effects. According to him, by strategic use of such images 'French imperiality achieves the natural state' (Barthes, ibid.: 129). In quite the same way, the Marlboro man adverts portray a pack of cigarettes alongside a cowboy hat, saddle, lassoo, spurs, pistol, jeans and so on as fundamental parts of what it means to be a cowboy.

6   EU Parliament. Online at: https://www.europarl.europa.eu/doceo/document/TC1-COD-2012-0366_EN.pdf?redirect, retrieved 09.02.2023.

7   Vox. Online at: https://www.vox.com/down-to-earth/2022/9/29/23373427/amazon-rainforest-brazil-jair-bolsonaro-lula-deforestation#:~:text=%E2%80%9CWe%20had%20reduced%20deforestation%20in,turning%20point%20for%20the%20Amazon., retrieved 10.02.2023.

8   *Guardian*. Online at https://www.theguardian.com/world/2019/jul/19/jair-bolsonaro-brazil-amazon-rainforest-deforestation, retrieved 10.02.2023.

9   Shell Global. Online at https://www.shell.com/sustainability/our-approach/sustainability-at-shell.html, retrieved 09.02.2023.

10 Online at: https://www.vox.com/down-to-earth/23168326/polarbears-sea-ice-glaciers-extinction-greenland, retrieved 12/10/2023. For copyright reasons the image may not be shown.

11 In the same essay, which looks back from a future vantage point on the origins of CDA, Kress recommends a change of emphasis from 'deconstructive activity, to productive activity', outlining the beginnings of a kind of PDA (ibid.: 15–16).

12 CondéNast Traveller. Online at https://www.cntraveller.in/story/full-text-greta-thunberg-speech-how-dare-you-un-climate-action-summit/, retrieved 20.02.2023.

13 The story of DDT is told in Chapter 1, Rachel Carson, American Experience. Online at: https://www.youtube.com/watch?v=SeJNRaE11A0, retrieved 22.02.2023.

14 The authors conclude: 'If organic agriculture is (. . .) to stay truer to its original ideas and include a holistic understanding of ecosystem and human health and more

sustainable (soil) management practices, organic regulations should include more environmental best practices in their process standards.'
15 Global Alliance on Health and Pollution: online at https://gahp.net/, last visit 23.09.2021. Global Green Growth Institute: https://www.greengrowthknowledge.org/, last visit 23.09.2021.

Chapter 3

1 Aesop's fables. Online at: https://www.litscape.com/author/Aesop/The_Hawk_and_the_Nightingale.html, retrieved 08.03.2023.
2 The device of relating human realities through the actions and words of animal protagonists, or anthropomorphism, could be seen as a means of increasing the persuasive impact of these stories. The meanings are 'naturalized' (see Section 2.4) in terms of our analytical approach: they come across as truths, as the 'way things are', part of the fabric of a holistic natural framework.
3 See also Visual capitalist. Online at: https://www.visualcapitalist.com/cp/visualized-the-largest-online-gambling-markets/, retrieved 9.03.2023.
4 BBC Countryside Hour, More Overseas Correspondence. 3.11.2020. online at: https://www.bbc.co.uk/programmes/p02tfhrt/episodes/downloads, retrieved 7.03.2023.
5 Grice theorized that conversational exchanges respect what he called the 'Cooperative Principle': 'Make your conversational contribution such as is required, at the stage at which it occurs, by the accepted purpose or direction of the talk exchange in which you are engaged' (Grice 1975: 45). He further suggested four 'maxims of conversation' (Grice 1975: 45–6), which provided early pragmatics with important interpretative keys and ground rules for understanding what is going on in conversation:

Quality: Try to make your contribution one that is true.

1. Do not say what you believe to be false.
2. Do not say that for which you lack adequate evidence.

Quantity:

1. Make your contribution as informative as is required (for the current purposes of the exchange).
2. Do not make your contribution more informative than is required.

Relation (or Relevance): Be relevant.

Manner: Be perspicuous.

1. Avoid obscurity of expression.
2. Avoid ambiguity.
3. Be brief (avoid unnecessary prolixity).
4. Be orderly.

6 It could therefore be wondered whether these ecosophical attitudes are typical of the BBC, and to an extent, this must be true. Similar values are also found in its nature documentaries, for example those of Sir David Attenborough or Chris Packham. As a national broadcaster however, the BBC is a broad church and also produces programmes such as Top Gear, of questionable environmental credentials. It has been accused of a lack of coverage of issues such as the climate crisis. See *Guardian*. Climate Crisis https://www.theguardian.com/environment/2022/jul/27/bbc-criticised-over-climate-question-in-tory-leadership-debate, retrieved 21.03.2023.

7 British National Corpus: https://www.english-corpora.org/bnc/, retrieved 21.03.2023.

8 Getting up close with WILD Giant sea turtles on the beach: https://www.youtube.com/watch?v=jkyci6AhKdo, retrieved 21.03.2023.

9 For some years following the publication of Martin and White's definitive book on AF, similar points were debated at great length in an online forum which, indeed, could still be active. The solution to this quandry is indicated in the table by a double-code −/+, which leaves the question in doubt, but this is not one recommended by Martin and White, as far as I know. Such debatable interpretations underline the complexity of semantics and show the difficulties of applying epistemological categories to naturally occuring samples of language.

10 Ads of the world. https://www.adsoftheworld.com/campaigns/retail-therapy-00793869-f7e9-4781-a780-2a632f9644ba, retrieved 18.04.2023.

11 British National Corpus: https://www.english-corpora.org/bnc/, retrieved 18.04.2023.

12 British National Corpus: https://www.english-corpora.org/bnc/, retrieved 18.04.2023.

13 Covestro. Online at: https://report.covestro.com/annual-report-2022/management-report/report-on-future-perspectives-and-on-opportunities-and-risks/report-on-future-perspectives/economic-outlook.html, retrieved 18.04.2023.

Chapter 4

1. Many farmers view moles as vermin and have them destroyed. BBC Manchester, https://www.bbc.co.uk/manchester/content/articles/2008/11/12/121108_molecatcher_feature.shtml, last visit 20.04.2023.
2. 'To cull' comes from a Latin verb 'colligere' meaning 'to collect' or 'gather', and refers to processes of selectivity in animal husbandry. Thus, it is not synonymous with 'to kill', but has only phonic similarity. In practice, in the case of badgers, for example, the two verbs do correspond, since it is not that some, 'healthy' badgers are selected for survival. Rather the process appears to be a case of systematic slaughter, which would support mention of Orwellian language in this context.
(Badger Trust, https://www.badgertrust.org.uk/cull, retrieved 20.04.2023.)
3. BBC Manchester, ibid.
4. See Gov.UK: https://www.gov.uk/countryside-stewardship-grants/winter-bird-food-ab9, retrieved 21.04.2023.
5. Winter's paper is an early example of work that identified textual relations 'beyond the clause'; in this case a rhetorical pattern of problem/solution, an extremely common pattern, found in texts where the description of a certain problem creates an expectation that what follows can be 'read' as the solution.
6. Equinews. Online at: https://ker.com/equinews/color-horse-hay-mean/#:~:text=Without%20question%2C%20the%20most%20desirable,vitamin%20A%2C%20and%20vitamin%20E, retrieved 28.04.2023.
7. In the organic farming debate we find an instance of the tension that exists between rational, scientific faith in 'progress' and the kind of holistic, deep-ecological thinking that was discussed at the book's outset (Section 1.1). DeGregori views genetic modification as a practical solution to the world's food supply problems, and mocks beliefs that 'pure' food 'confers some special kind of virtue both on those who produce it and those who consume it' (DeGregori 2004: xvi). He writes, of opposition to scientific farming methods:

> 'This opposition, often based on irrational fear, is as old as the science that it counters and I follow its development through the nineteenth and twentieth centuries in a kind of a double helix as I contrast advances in science, medicine, and agriculture with the oppositional beliefs – homeopathy and "organic" agriculture – that continue to the present. I find the thread of continuity that runs through these various antiscience views to be a belief in an unmeasurable, essentially unknowable vital force, or vitalism' (DeGregori ibid.: viii). Again, in the context of Berlin's perspectives on Enlightenment rationalism cited above, what he terms 'agrivitalism' is explicitly characterised as 'contrary to nineteenth- and twentieth- century science'. (ibid.: 52)

8. GovUK. Online at https://www.gov.uk/guidance/countryside-stewardship-get-funding-to-protect-and-improve-the-land-you-manage#about-countryside-stewardship, retrieved 9.05.2023.
9. State of Nature Report 2016. Online at: https://www.rspb.org.uk/globalassets/downloads/documents/conservation-projects/state-of-nature/state-of-nature-uk-report-2016.pdf, retrieved 16.05.2023.
10. The reference *objectifies* the ants in the sense that, like a puzzle, they stimulate the observer's curiosity: however, this point would require lengthier treatment than is possible here.
11. Darwin was closely interested in the question of animal morality and maintained a varied correspondence on the topic with other thinkers of the time. See Darwin Correspondence Project. Moral Nature, online at: (4), last accessed 09/06/2023.
12. Skinner's choice of words here is worth exploring, as he characterizes the supposed moral blamelessness that attaches to egg-eating: 'that's probably quite alright' (15). The inference to be drawn from his use of the adverb 'probably' is that he is aware that there are some, perhaps among the listeners, who will not be willing to accept bald statements such as: *and we see nothing wrong with that*, or *and it's perfectly fine for humans to eat eggs*. For example, vegans would contest the statement, and there are likely to be some with such views among listeners to the Countryside Hour. Nevertheless, Skinner's overall argument loses nothing because of these considerations, since he is not arguing that both crows and humans are doing something ethically neutral or positive by eating eggs. Rather, his point is that, if a majority of humans think that it's okay to eat eggs – and they demonstrably do, on an industrial scale – then it is hypocritical to attach any blame whatsoever to crows for doing the same thing.

Chapter 5

1. The processes involved are documented in texts such as Peggio et al. (1960), Butera (1981), Adorno (2007).
2. Sacrifice. Online at: https://www.visapourlimage.com/en/festival/exhibitions/sacrifice, retrieved 11/07/2023.
3. I am indebted to Emilio Cicciarella for the following rendition in local dialect: '*Miegghju morri ppi "ntumuri ca no"'morri ppi fami*'.
4. I was explaining all this to an Israeli friend on a visit, who simply commented: 'I suppose you want to put them all in the Middle-East!'
5. The phrase occurs in his well-known poem 'Easter 1916'.
6. Interviewed by the author. Original Italian text: Il Fenicottero però, è un animale molto ingombrante, molto importante per la valorizzazione di un territorio, ma

che se lasciato libero di fare quello che vuole, occupa ogni spazio possibile ed immaginabile. Dando la possibilità ad altri animali di poter vivere in quel contesto di nidificare, soprattutto in quel contesto, allora, in quello che è. L'ambito della gestione attiva. Stiamo iniziando a studiare delle alternative per favorire. Anche le altre specie interessanti per la conservazione, come possono essere il fraticello, il Fratino, il Cavaliere d'Italia, la Vocetta.

7 The phenomenon is discussed and recorded in a video from Priolo Saltpans: https://www.youtube.com/watch?app=desktop&v=Urh97k_gjtc, retrieved 11/07/2023.

8 Original Italian text:

Speaker 1: Come, secondo te, come si organizzano, come comunicano fra di loro? Cioè, non è che puoi dire che questo è istinto o sì eh?

Speaker 2: Ma è probabile sì, gli animali hanno l'istinto e sempre sanno quello che devono fare. Come si organizzano, chi decide cosa, questo non te lo so dire, non so neanche se si sa nell'ambito degli studi dei comportamenti degli animali, se ci sono delle... Precise, però, sta di fatto chè una struttura decisamente ben organizzata, cioè nel senso che riescono i tedeschi.

Speaker 1: Questa mi interessa, conoscendo che fanno questa organizzazione senza il linguaggio. Ecco loro fanno dei rumori, o cosa?

Speaker 2: Vabbè, non hanno la parola, ma hanno dei loro modo, loro modi di comunicare come succede spesso nel mondo animale, ogni gruppo animale ha il suo modo per poter trasferire l'informazione. Se prendi l'esempio delle formiche, insomma, è un mondo incredibilmente affascinante, fatto di socialità, fatto di gruppi organizzati e di una comunicazione chimica che riesce sempre ad indicare la situazione del del momento.

9 The idea that animals do prodigious things such as navigate halfway around the world to return to the precise point from which they set out months before, by 'instinct', is unsatisfactory. The word is an Orwellian generality that means everything and nothing; its use implies that we simply do not yet understand how something is done. Developments and discoveries in ethology tend to deconstruct the notion of instinct, substituting for it more precise knowledge of the complex mechanisms involved in such processes. As Lehrmann (1953: 359) concludes, in his critique of Konrad Lorenz's theories of instinct and 'innate' types of knowledge: 'Any instinct theory which regards "instinct" as immanent, preformed, inherited, or based on specific neural structures is bound to divert the investigation of behavior development from fundamental analysis and the study of developmental problems. Any such theory of "instinct" inevitably tends to short-circuit the scientist's investigation of intraorganic and organism-environment developmental relationships which underlie the development of "instinctive" behavior.' I call it 'demeaning' because the term underlines a familiar human/non-human

distinction which situates wo/man at the top of a hierarchy of being, endowed with fundamentally different psycho-genetic structures of consciousness from those of animals. Humans are supposedly directed by the promptings of reason, while animals, in this account, are simply conditioned by 'instinct'. This mental habitus underlies the historical abuse of non-humans by humans, as has been shown in numerous ecolinguistic studies, including some of the case studies in the current book.

10 Regrettably, nothing has been said so far about this key feature of narrative. It is normally regarded as the speaker's deployment of linguistic resources that indicate their certainty or otherwise of the truth of what is asserted, via lexical formulae (*it is/it's not an established fact,*), adverbs (X *certainly/definitely/probably* happened) or the use of modal verbs (*could/may/might*, etc.). See, for example, Hyland (1998), Palmer (2001), Wood (2001).

11 Original Italian text: Scriverò una storia per consegnare, non so a chi, pochi frammenti di verità su quel che è accaduto su un angolo di mondo che amavo ed è stato sacrificato al dio del presente. It is a citation from Salemi, Rosellina 2020. *Il Nome di Marina*. Cairo.

12 Schneider and Schneider (2006) movingly describe these processes, especially in the Western part of Sicily, in townscapes like Palermo and Agrigento. However, these 'scars of runaway building unrestrained by planning' (ibid.: 66) are all too common across the whole island.

13 Thibault (2004: 192), for example, says of a certain use of the modal *will*, that it 'indicates that the speaker is certain that the still hypothetical (future) situation specified by this proposition will come into being'.

14 Biber et al. (1999: 493) on the modal 'could' comment that it 'usually marks logical possibility in conversation, expressing a greater degree of uncertainty or tentatitiveness'.

15 A 'naturalized' phenomenon is something that is 'seen as something that has always been, was "meant to be", or cannot be altered' (Litosseliti and Sunderland 2002: 19). For a critical perspective on this linguistic device, see Reisigl and Wodak (2000).

Chapter 6

1 Spiked. Global boiling? Don't be ridiculous. Brendan O'Neill, 31 July 2023. Online at: https://www.spiked-online.com/2023/07/31/global-boiling-dont-be-ridiculous/, retrieved 03.08.2023.

2 Salon. Online at: https://www.salon.com/2021/10/23/how-the-1-is-tricking-you-into-thinking-climate-change-is-your-fault/, retrieved 03.08.2023.

3 See Section 3.v. Once again, the point is that once we start to think of social structures as a 'system' then they assume the impersonal qualities of natural elements like the weather, gravity, the cycle of seasons. It is curious that those with only a 'teensy' share of responsibility for the situation are represented as 'major climate perpetrators', while those who are in fact responsible escape without the reprimand they truly deserve. They slip through the net of social sanction altogether because a 'system' appears to be part of 'the way things are'.

4 This pragmatic account helps explain humour like that of Peter Cook and John Cleese, in the 'Interesting Facts' sketch, where Cook bores a man on a park bench with details about the grasshopper, which may be biologically accurate ('The interesting fact about the grasshopper is its disproportionate leaping ability due to its powerful hind legs') but, as they are apropos of nothing in the situation, are received as the ramblings of an eccentric. Secret Policeman: https://www.youtube.com/watch?v=Gn08cA5zNAI, retrieved 31.08.2023.

5 Four Quartets, Burnt Norton. https://www.poetryverse.com/ts-eliot-poems/four-quartets-burnt-norton, retrieved 01.09.2023.

6 Vive la culture: https://www.vivelaculture.com/il-faut-cultiver-son-jardin/, retrieved 01.09.2023.

Appendix

La formica, original Italian text (reproduced with permission from Liborio Palmeri)

Se ci sarà da morire,
penseremo anche a quello . . .

. . . non guarderemo
se é dolce il vento di nuova fioritura
a primavera,
né staremo a guardare le stelle cadenti
con tutti i loro desideri . . .

. . . non aspetteremo piante dai semi
e non diremo: 'era meglio ieri',
ma calpesteremo in corsa
i nostri pensieri
sotto la pioggia dalla nube nera . . .

Se ci sarà da morire, beh . . .
ci penseremo . . . !
e lasceremo al tempo
di scattarci qualche foto
sotto i flashes della sua sera.

Pronti all'appuntamento,
sul precipizio in piedi,
fieri dinanzi al vuoto,
senza perdere il controllo,
se ci sarà da morire, sì . . .
. . . penseremo anche a quello . . .

intanto metto in salvo
la formica
sul mio collo.

Bibliography

Adorno, Salvatore. 2007. Imprenditori e impresa a Siracusa in età contemporanea. In Gaetano Calabrese (ed.), *Gli archivi d'impresa in Sicilia, FrancoAngeli*, 43–57. Milan: FrancoAngeli.
Alexander, Richard. 2009. *Framing Discourse on the Environment: A Critical Discourse Approach*. New York: Routledge.
Allan, K. and Jaszczolt, K. M. eds., 2012. *The Cambridge Handbook of Pragmatics*. Cambridge: Cambridge University Press.
Allen, G. 2021. *Intertextuality*. London and New York: Routledge.
Arendt, Florian, and Jörg Matthes. 2016. Nature Documentaries, Connectedness to Nature, and Pro-Environmental Behavior. *Environmental Communication* 10(4): 453–72. https://doi.org/10.1080/17524032.2014.993415.
Aristotle, and Robert C. Bartlett. 2019. *Aristotle's Art of Rhetoric*. Chicago: The University Of Chicago Press.
Atwater, Deborah F. 2007. Senator Barack Obama; The Rhetoric of Hope and the American Dream. *Journal of Black Studies* 38(2): 121–29.
Austin, John L. 1975. *How to Do Things with Words*. 2d ed. Oxford [Eng.]: Clarendon Press.
Ayala, F. J. 2010. Colloquium Paper: The Difference of Being Human: Morality. Proceedings of the National Academy of Sciences of the United States of America. May 11; 107(Suppl 2): 9015–22.
Baker, Sandra E., and David W. Macdonald. 2000. Foxes and Foxhunting on Farms in Wiltshire: A Case Study. *Journal of Rural Studies* 16(2): 185–201.
Balasubramanian, S. K. 1994. Beyond Advertising and Publicity: Hybrid Messages and Public Policy Issues. *Journal of Advertising* 23(4): 29–46.
Ball-Rokeach, Sandra, Milton Rokeach, and Joel W. Grube. 1984. *The Great American Values Test: Influencing Behavior and Belief Through Television*. New York; London: Free Press ; Collier Macmillan.
Bartlett, Tom. 2012. *Hybrid Voices and Collaborative Change. Contextualising Positive Discourse Analysis*. New York: Routledge.
Barthes, Roland. 2006. *Mythologies*. 47. [print.]. New York: Hill and Wang.
Bartlett, Tom. 2017. Positive Discourse Analysis. In J. Richardson, and J. Flowerdew (eds.), *The Routledge Handbook of Critical Discourse Studies*, 133–147. London: Routledge.
Benton, T. G., J. A. Vickery, and J. D. Wilson. 2003. Farmland Biodiversity: Is Habitat Heterogeneity the Key? *Trends in Ecology & Evolution* 18(4): 182–8.

Boardman, J., M. L. Shepheard, E. Walker, and I. D. Foster. 2009. Soil Erosion and Risk-Assessment for on-and Off-farm Impacts: A Test Case Using the Midhurst Area, West Sussex, UK. *Journal of Environmental Management* 90(8): 2578–88.

Brockwell, S., T. Gara, S. Colley, and S. Cane. 1989. The History and Archaeology of Ooldea Soak and Mission. *Australian Archaeology* 28: 55–78.

Browning, C. (ed.). 2004. *The Origins of the Final Solution: The Evolution of Nazi Jewish Policy*. London: William Heinemann.

Butera, Salvatore (ed.). 1981. *Regionalismo siciliano e problema del Mezzogiorno*. Varese: Giuffre` Editore.

Bybee, Joan. 2010. *Language, Usage and Cognition*. Cambridge: Cambridge University Press.

Benadusi, Mara. 2018a. Macerie Che Parlano: Spazi Eterotipici Del Tardo-Industrialismo. In Marco Navarra (ed.), Metamorfosi. Architettura e Territori Tardo-Industriali. Il Dipolo Siracusa-Augusta, 167–73. LetteraVentidue.

Benadusi, Mara. 2018b. Oil in Sicily: Petrocapitalist Imaginaries in the Shadow of Old Smokestacks. *Economic Anthropology* 5(1): 45–58. https://doi.org/10.1002/sea2.12101.

Benadusi, Mara. 2019. Sicilian Futures in the Making. *Nature and Culture* 14(1): 79–104. https://doi.org/10.3167/nc.2019.140105.

Berlin, Isaiah, and Henry Hardy. 2013. *Three Critics of the Enlightenment: Vico, Hamann, Herder*. 2nd ed. Princeton: Princeton University Press.

Biber, Douglas, and Bethany Gray. 2016. Grammatical Complexity in Academic English: Linguistic Change in Writing (Studies in English Language). Cambridge: Cambridge University Press.

Billig, M. 2008. The Language of Critical Discourse Analysis: The Case of Nominalization. *Discourse & Society* 19(6): 783–800. https://doi.org/10.1177/0957926508095894.

Brabazon, Tara. 2021. Claustropolitanism, Capitalism and Covid: Un/Popular Culture at the End of the World. *International Journal of Social Sciences & Educational Studies* 8(1). https://doi.org/10.23918/ijsses.v8i1p1.

Breuste, Jürgen H. 2010. Allotment Gardens as Part of Urban Green Infrastructure: Actual Trends and Perspectives in Central Europe. *Urban Biodiversity and Design* 25: 463–75.

Caimotto, Maria Cristina. 2020. *Discourses of Cycling, Road Users and Sustainability An Ecolinguistic Investigation*. London: Palgrave MacMillan.

Cameron, Deborah. 1995. *Verbal Hygiene*. Abingdon and New York: Routledge.

Cancro, Robert. 1969. Automation: The Second Emancipation Proclamation. *American Journal of Psychotherapy* 23(4): 657–66. https://doi.org/10.1176/appi.psychotherapy.1969.23.4.657.

Caracciolo, M. 2020. Flocking Together: Collective Animal Minds in Contemporary Fiction. Modern Language Association of America. March 135(2): 239–53.

Carson, Rachel. 1962. *Silent Spring*. Boston: Houghton Mifflin.

Cassidy, Angela. 2012. Vermin, Victims and Disease: UK Framings of Badgers In and Beyond the Bovine TB Controversy: Vermin, Victims and Disease. *Sociologia Ruralis* 52(2): 192–214. https://doi.org/10.1111/j.1467-9523.2012.00562.x.

Chaffee, S., Z. Pan, and G. Chu. 1997. Western Media in China: Audience and Influence. *Mass Communication Review* 24(3/4): 19–39.

Charlesworth, Annemarie, and Stanton A. Glantz. 2005. Smoking in the Movies Increases Adolescent Smoking: A Review. *Pediatrics* 116(6): 1516–28. https://doi.org/10.1542/peds.2005-0141.

Chilton, Paul A. 2004. Analysing Political Discourse: Theory and Practice. London ; New York: Routledge.

Chouliaraki, Lilie and Norman Fairclough. 1999. *Discourse in Late Modernity: Rethinking Critical Discourse Analysis*. Edinburgh: Edinburgh University Press.

Cilea, Fabio (ed.). 2009. *Riserva naturale Saline di Priolo: Un'Oasi fra le ciminiere*. Siracusa: Arnaldo Lombardi Editori.

Cloudsley, Tim. 1990. Romanticism and the Industrial Revolution in Britain. *History of European Ideas* 12(5): 611–35. https://doi.org/10.1016/0191-6599(90)90175-E.

Cohen, Maurie J. 2010. Unsustainable Consumption and the New Political Economy of Growth. In Karin M. Ekström, and Kay Glans (eds.), *Beyond the Consumption Bubble*, 174–90. London: Taylor & Francis.

Cohen, Ted. 1973. Illocutions and Perlocutions. *Foundations of Language* 9(4): 492–503.

Conover, M. R., and D. J. Decker. 1991. Wildlife Damage to Crops: Perceptions of Agricultural and Wildlife Professionals in 1957 and 1987. *Wildlife Society Bulletin* 19(1): 46–52.

Conway, G. R., and J. N.Pretty. 1991. *Unwelcome Harvest: Agriculture and Pollution*. London: Earthscan.

Cook, John. 2020. Deconstructing Climate Science Denial. In Holmes, D. and Richardson, L. M. (eds.), *Edward Elgar Research Handbook in Communicating Climate Change*. Cheltenham: Edward Elgar, 62–78.

Cortazzi, Martin. 1994. Narrative Analysis. *Language Teaching* 27(3): 157–70. https://doi.org/10.1017/S0261444800007801.

Croney, Candace. 2010. Words Matter: Implications of Semantics and Imagery in Framing Animal-Welfare Issues. *Journal of Veterinary Medical Education* 37(1): 101–6. https://doi.org/10.3138/jvme.37.1.101.

Damer, T. Edward. 2012. Attacking Faulty Reasoning. 7th ed. Cengage Learning.

de Beaugrande, Robert. 1991. Language and the Facilitation of Authority: The Discourse of Noam Chomsky. *Journal of Advanced Composition* 11(2): 425–42.

De Beaugrande, Robert. 2004. Critical Discourse Analysis from the Perspective of Ecologism. *Critical Discourse Studies* 1(1): 113–45.

DeGregori, T. R. 2004. *Origins of the Organic Agriculture Debate*. Iowa State Press.

Diamant, Emna, and Andrew Waterhouse. 2010. Gardening and Belonging: Reflections on How Social and Therapeutic Horticulture May Facilitate Health, Wellbeing and Inclusion. *British Journal of Occupational Therapy* 73(2): 84–8. https://doi.org/10.4276/030802210X12658062793924.

Diehl, Kristin, Gal Zauberman, and Alixandra Barasch. 2016. How Taking Photos Increases Enjoyment of Experiences. *Journal of Personality and Social Psychology* 111(2): 119.

Downs, Sara H, Alison Prosser, Adam Ashton, Stuart Ashfield, Lucy A. Brunton, Adam Brouwer, Paul Upton, Andrew Robertson, Christl A Donnelly, and Jessica E Parry. 2019. Assessing Effects from Four Years of Industry-Led Badger Culling in England on the Incidence of Bovine Tuberculosis in Cattle, 2013–2017. *Scientific Reports* 9(1): 14666. https://doi.org/10.1038/s41598-019-49957-6.

Dryzek, John. 2013. *The Politics of the Earth: Environmental Discourses*. Oxford: Oxford University Press.

Dudley, Michael Kioni. 2004. Traditional Native Hawaiian Environmental Philosophy. In Roger S. Gottlieb (ed.), *This Sacred Earth: Religion, Nature, Environment*. 2nd ed. New York: Routledge, 111–116.

Dunnage, Jonathan. 2022. Sicilian Bandits and the Italian State: Narratives About Crime and (in)Security in the Post-War Italian Press, 1948–1950. *Cultural and Social History* 19(2): 185–202.

Eckstein, David, Vera Künzel, and Laura Schäfer. 2021. Global Climate Risk Index. https://www.germanwatch.org/en/19777. Retrieved 7 March 2023.

Eder, Klaus. 1990. The Rise of Counter-Culture Movements Against Modernity: Nature as a New Field of Class Struggle. *Theory, Culture & Society* 7(4): 21–47. https://doi.org/10.1177/026327690007004002.

Edlin, H. L. 1952. *The Changing Wild Life of Britain*. London: Batsford.

Edwards, Lynne Y. 2005. Victims, Villains, and Vixens: Teen Girls and Internet Crime. In Sharon R. Mazzarella (ed.), *Girl Wide Web: Girls, the Internet and the Negotiation of Identity*, 13–30. New York: Peter Lang.

Entman, Robert M. 1993. Framing: Toward Clarification of a Fractured Paradigm. *Journal of Communication* 43(4): 51–8.

Faimau, Gabriel. 2020. Towards a Theoretical Understanding of the Selfie: A Descriptive Review. *Sociology Compass* 14(12): 1–12. https://doi.org/10.1111/soc4.12840.

Fairclough, Norman. 2003. *Analysing Discourse: Textual Analysis for Social Research*. London: Routledge.

Fairclough, Norman. 2015 (1989). *Language and Power*. 3rd ed. London; New York: Routledge, Taylor &Francis Group.

Fairclough, Norman. 2015. *Language and Power*. 3rd ed. London ; New York: Routledge, Taylor & Francis Group.

Fairlie, Simon. 2010. *Meat: A Benign Extravagance*. White River Junction: Chelsea Green Pub.

FAO. 1999. *Organic Agriculture, Food and Agriculture*. Rome: Organization of the United Nations.

Feber, R. E., E. J. Asteraki, and L. G. Firbank. 2006. Can Farming and Wildlife Coexist? In David Macdonald, and Katrina Service (eds.), *Key Topics in Conservation Biology*, 239–53. Malden and Oxford: Blackwell.

Feltham, H., K. Park, J. Minderman, and D. Goulson. 2015. Experimental Evidence that Wildflower Strips increase Pollinator Visits to Crops. *Ecology and Evolution* 5(16): 3523–30.

Ferretti, Francesco, and Ines Adornetti. 2021. Persuasive Conversation as a New Form of Communication in Homo Sapiens. *Philosophical Transactions of the Royal Society of London. Series B, Biological Sciences* 376(1824): 20200196. https://doi.org/10.1098/rstb.2020.0196.

Fiddes, Nick. 2004. *Meat: A Natural Symbol*. London: Routledge.

Fill, Alwin. 2001. Language and Ecology: Ecolinguistic Perspectives for 2000 and Beyond. *AILA Review* 14: 60–75.

Fill, Alwin. 2015. Language Creates Relations Between Humans and Animals: Animal Stereotypes, Linguistic Anthropocentrism and Anthropomorphism. In Reingard Spannring, Reinhard Heuberger, Gabriela Kompatscher, Andreas Oberprantacher, Karin Schachinger, and Alejandro Boucabeille (eds.), *Tiere - Texte - Transformationen: Kritische Perspektiven der Human-Animal Studies*, 179–92. Bielefeld: Transcript Verlag.

Fill, Alwin, and Peter Mühlhäusler. 2001. *The Ecolinguistics Reader: Language, Ecology, and Environment*. London: Continuum.

Fill, Alwin, and Hermine Penz (eds.). 2018. *The Routledge Handbook of Ecolinguistics*. New York: Routledge.

Forte, Diego. 2020. Ecolinguistics: The Battlefield for the New Class Struggle. *Language & Ecology*. https://www.Ecolinguistics-association.org/Journal. Retrieved 7 March 2023.

Fowler, H. W. 2009. In David Crystal (ed.) *Dictionary of Modern English Usage*. Oxford: Oxford University Press.

Fowler, R., B. Hodge, G. Kress, and T. Trew. 1979. *Language and Control*. London: Routledge and Kegan Paul.

Fürsich, Elfriede. 2003. Between Credibility and Commodification: Nonfiction Entertainment as a Global Media Genre. *International Journal of Cultural Studies* 6(2): 131–53.

Gardelle, Laure, and Sandrine Sorlin (eds.). 2015. *The Pragmatics of Personal Pronouns*, Vol. 171. John Benjamins Publishing Company.

Geertz, Clifford. 2008. Thick Description: Toward an Interpretive Theory of Culture. In Tim Oakes, and Patricia Lynn Price (eds.), *The Cultural Geography Reader (ebook)*, 29–49.London and New York: Routledge.

Gellers, Joshua C. 2015. Greening Critical Discourse Analysis. *Critical Discourse Studies* 12(4): 482–93.

Genus, A., M. Iskandarova, and C. Warburton Brown. 2021. Institutional Entrepreneurship and Permaculture: A Practice Theory Perspective. *Business Strategy and the Environment* 30(3): 1454–67.

Georgakopoulou, Alexandra. 2007. *Small Stories, Interaction and Identities*, Vol. 8. Amsterdam: John Benjamins.

Gilman, Sander L., and Xun Zhou (eds.). 2004. *Smoke: A Global History of Smoking*. London: Reaktion Books.

Glenn Cathy, B. 2004. Constructing Consumables and Consent: A Critical Analysis of Factory Farm Industry Discourse. *Journal of Communication Inquiry* 28(1): 63–81.

Goatly, Andrew. 1996. Green Grammar and Grammatical Metaphor, or Language and the Myth of Power, or Metaphors We Die By. *Journal of Pragmatics* 25(4): April, 537–60.

Goatly, Andrew. 2006. Humans, Animals, and Metaphors. *Society and Animals* 14(1): 15–37.

Goatly, Andrew. 2017. The Poems of Edward Thomas: A Case Study in Ecostylistics. In John Douthwaite, Daniela Virdis, and Elisabetta Zurru (eds.), *The Stylistics of Landscapes, the Landscapes of Stylistics* (Linguistic approaches to literature), Vol. 28, 95–122. Amsterdam: John Benjamins.

Goatly, Andrew. 2018. Lexicogrammar and Ecolinguistics. In Alwyn Fill, and Hermine Penz (eds.), *The Routledge handbook of Ecolinguistics*, 227–49. New York and Abingdon: Routledge.

Goffman, Erving. 1974. *Frame Analysis: An Essay on the Organization of Experience*. New York: Harper & Row.

Goffman, Erving. 1986. *Frame Analysis: An Essay on the Organization of Experience*. Boston: Northeastern University Press.

Gottlieb, Roger S. (ed.). 2004. *This Sacred Earth: Religion, Nature, Environment*. 2nd ed. New York: Routledge.

Goulding, K. W. T. 2016. Soil Acidification and the Importance of Liming Agricultural Soils with Particular Reference to the United Kingdom. *Soil Use and Management* 32(3): 390–9.

Graham, Hilary. 2012. Smoking, Stigma and Social Class. *Journal of Social Policy* 41(1): 83–99. https://doi.org/10.1017/S004727941100033X.

Green, R. E., A. Balmford, P. R. Crane, G. M. Mace, J. D. Reynolds, and R. K. Turner. 2005. A Framework for Improved Monitoring of Biodiversity: Responses to the World Summit on Sustainable Development. *Conservation Biology* 19(1): 56–65.

Green, Melanie, Helena Bilandzic, Kaitlin Fitzgerald, and Elaine Paravati. 2020. Narrative Effects. In Mary Beth Oliver, Arthur A. Raney, and Jennings Bryant (eds.), *Media Effects: Advances in Theory and Research*. 4th ed. 130–46. New York and London: Routledge.

Gregory, R. D., and J. H. Marchant. 1996. Population Trends of Jays, Magpies, Jackdaws and Carrion Crows in the United Kingdom. *Bird Study* 43(1): 28–37.

Grice, H. P. 1975. Logic and conversation. In P. Cole and J. Morgan (eds.) (1975) *Syntax and Semantics 3: Speech Acts*, 41–58. New York: Academic Press.

Grice, H. P. 1978. Further notes on logic and conversation. In P. Cole (ed.) (1975) *Syntax and Semantics 9: Pragmatics*. 113–28. New York: Academic Press.

Greer, J., and K. Bruno. 1996. *Greenwash: The Reality Behind Corporate Environmentalism*. Third World Network.

Grosso, Jean-Luc E., Sherry S. Grosso, Teresa L. Smith, and Vincent J. Grosso. 2015. Consumerism and the Portrayal of Cars in Russian Media: Marketing Implications. *International Journal of Business, Marketing, and Decision Sciences* 8(1): 32–42.

Halliday, M. A. K. 1992. New Ways of Analysing Meaning: The Challenge to Applied Linguistics. In M. Pütz (ed.), *Thirty Years of Linguistic Evolution*, 59. Amsterdam: John Benjamins.

Halliday, M. A. K. 2004. *An Introduction to Functional Grammar*. 3rd ed. London: Edward Arnold.
Halliday, M. A. K. 2006. The Language of Science: Volume 5 (Collected Works of M. A. K. Halliday). 1st ed. London: Continuum.
Halliday, M. A. K. 2010. *On Language and Linguistics*. Continuum.
Hamilton, Patrick. 2014. Welcome to the Anthropocene. In Diana Dalbotten, Gillian Roehrig, and Patrick Hamilton (eds.), *Future Earth—Advancing Civic Understanding of the Anthropocene*, 1–9. Washington, DC: Wiley.
Hansen, Birgitte, Hugo Fjelsted Alrøe, and Erik Steen Kristensen. 2001. Approaches to Assess the Environmental Impact of Organic Farming with Particular Regard to Denmark. *Agriculture, Ecosystems & Environment* 83(1–2): 11–26. https://doi.org/10.1016/S0167-8809(00)00257-7.
Hao, Jing. 2018. Reconsidering "Cause Inside the Clause" in Scientific Discourse – from a Discourse Semantic Perspective in Systemic Functional Linguistics. *Text & Talk* 38(5): 525–50. https://doi.org/10.1515/text-2018-0013.
Haque, Umair. Harvard Business Review. https://hbr.org/2013/10/this-isnt-capitalism-its-growthism-and-its-bad-for-us. Retrieved 14 January 2021.
Hassink, Jan, Willem Hulsink, and John Grin. 2014. Farming with Care: The Evolution of Care Farming in the Netherlands. *NJAS: Wageningen Journal of Life Sciences* 68(1): 1–11. https://doi.org/10.1016/j.njas.2013.11.001.
Haugen, Einar. 2001[1972]. The Ecology of Language. In Alwin Fill, and Peter Mühlhäusler (eds.), *The Ecolinguistics Reader: Language, Ecology and Environment*, 57–66. London: Continuum.
Haugen, Einar. 1971. The Ecology of Language. Linguistic Reporter.
Haute, Émilie van (ed.). 2019. *Green Parties in Europe. First Issued in Paperback*. London; New York: Routledge.
Heckman, Joseph. 2006. A History of Organic Farming: Transitions from Sir Albert Howard's War in the Soil to USDA National Organic Program. *Renewable Agriculture and Food Systems* 21(3): 143–50.
Heuberger, Reinhard. 2007. Language and Ideology: A Brief Survey of Anthropocentrism and Speciesism in English. In Alwin Fill, and Hermine Penz (eds.), *Sustaining Language: Essays in Applied Ecolinguistics*. Münster: Lit Verlag, 107 –124.
Howarth, William. 2017. Reading Thoreau at 200. *The American Scholar* 86(3): 44–53. https://theamericanscholar.org/reading-thoreau-at-200/. Retrieved 7 March 2023.
Hunston, Susan, and Geoff Thompson. 2003. Beyond Exchange: Appraisal Systems in English. Editors' Introduction. In Susan Hunston, and Geoff Thompson (eds.), *Evaluation in Text: Authorial Stance and the Construction of Discourse*, 1–26. Oxford and New York: Oxford University Press.
Hyland, Ken. 1998. Boosting, Hedging and the Negotiation of Academic Knowledge. *Text* 18(3): 349–82.
Ibáñez, Francisco José Ruiz de Mendoza, and Inés Lozano-Palacio. 2019. A Cognitive-Linguistic Approach to Complexity in Irony: Dissecting the Ironic Echo. Metaphor and Symbol 34(2): 127–38. https://doi.org/10.1080/10926488.2019.1611714.

Jacob, Jeffrey. 1997. *New Pioneers: The Back-to-the-Land Movement and the Search for a Sustainable Future*. University Park: Pennsylvania State University Press.

Jessop, Bob. 1992. Fordism and Post- Fordism: A Critical Reformulation. In Allen J. Scott, and Michael Storper (eds.), *Pathways to Industrialization and Regional Development*, 46–69. London: Routledge.

Joyce, Jenny, and Alison Warren. 2016. A Case Study Exploring the Influence of a Gardening Therapy Group on Well-Being. *Occupational Therapy in Mental Health* 32(2): 203–15. https://doi.org/10.1080/0164212X.2015.1111184.

Kayam, Orly. 2017. The Readability and Simplicity of Donald Trump's Language. *Political Studies Review* 16(1): 73–88.

Kecskes, Istvan. 2014. *Intercultural Pragmatics*. Oxford: Oxford University Press.

Kecskes, Istvan. 2016. A Dialogic Approach to Pragmatics. *Russian Journal of Linguistics* 20(4): 26–42.

Keulartz, Jozef. 2007. Using Metaphors in Restoring Nature. *Nature & Culture* 2(1): 27–48. https://doi.org/10.3167/nc.2007.020103.

Khan, Md Zulfequar Ahmad. 2012. Climate Change: Cause & Effect. *Journal of Environment and Earth Science* 2(4): 48–53.

Kjeldsen, Jens E. 2017. *Rhetorical Audience Studies and Reception of Rhetoric: Exploring Audiences Empirically* (Rhetoric, Politics and Society). 1st ed. 2018. Cham: Palgrave Macmillan.

Kohn, Eduardo. 2013. *How Forests Think: Toward an Anthropology Beyond the Human*. Berkeley: University of California Press.

Krebs, J. R., J. D. Wilson, R. B. Bradbury, and G. M. Siriwardena. 1999. The Second Silent Spring? *Nature* 400: 611–12.

Kress, G. 1996. Representational Resources and the Production of Subjectivity: Questions for the Theoretical Development of Critical Discourse Analysis in a Multicultural Society. In C. R. Caldas-Coulthard and M. Coulthard (eds.), *Texts and Practices: Readings in Critical Discourse Analysis*, 24–40. London: Routledge.

Kress, G., and B. Hodge. 1979. *Language as Ideology*. London: Routledge and Kegan Paul.

Kress, G., and T. Van Leeuwen. 2020. *Reading Images: The Grammar of Visual Design*. 3rd ed. London ; New York: Routledge.

Kukla, André. 2013. *Social Constructivism and the Philosophy of Science*. New York: Routledge.

Labov, William. 1972. The Transformation of Experience in Narrative Syntax. In W. Labov (ed.), *Language in the inner city: Studies in the Black English Vernacular*, 354–96. Philadelphia: University of Pennsylvania Press.

Lakoff, George. 2010. Why It Matters How We Frame the Environment. *Environmental Communication* 4(1): 70–81. https://doi.org/10.1080/17524030903529749.

Lakoff, George, and Mark Johnson. 2003. *Metaphors We Live By*. Chicago: University of Chicago Press.

Larson, Brendon. 2011. *Metaphors for Environmental Sustainability: Redefining Our Relationship with Nature*. New Haven: Yale University Press.

Lawless, R. M., W. A. Buttemer, L. B. Astheimer, and K. R. Kerry. 2001. The Influence of Thermoregulatory Demand on Contact Crèching Behaviour in Adélie Penguin Chicks. *Journal of Thermal Biology* 26(6): 555–62.

Lazareva, Ekaterina. 2018. The Futurist Concept of 'Man Extended by Machines'. In G. Berghaus, D. Pietropaolo, and B. Sica (eds.), *International Yearbook of Futurism Studies*, 213–31. De Gruyter.

Lehrman, Daniel S. 1953. A Critique of Konrad Lorenz's Theory of Instinctive Behavior. *The Quarterly Review of Biology* 28(4): 337–63.

Lin, C. A. 2001. Cultural Values Reflected in Chinese and American Television Advertising. *Journal of Advertising* 30(4): 83–94.

Litosseliti, L., and J. Sunderland (eds.). 2002. *Gender Identity and Discourse Analysis*, Vol. 2. Amsterdam: John Benjamins.

Loland, Sigmund. 2021. The Poetics of Everyday Movement: Human Movement Ecology and Urban Walking. *Journal of the Philosophy of Sport* 48(2): 219–34. https://doi.org/10.1080/00948705.2021.1915148.

Lorenz, Konrad, and Marjorie Kerr Wilson. 2002. *King Solomon's Ring: New Light on Animal Ways*. London ; New York: Routledge.

Lovelock, James E., and Lynn Margulis. 1974. Atmospheric Homeostasis by and for the Biosphere: The Gaia Hypothesis. *Tellus A: Dynamic Meteorology and Oceanography* 26(1–2): 2. https://doi.org/10.3402/tellusa.v26i1-2.9731.

Lutz, W. 1997. *The New Doublespeak: Why No One Knows What Anyone's Saying Anymore*. New York: Harper Collins.

Macdonald, David W., and R. Feber (eds.). 2015. *Wildlife Conservation on Farmland*. 1st ed. Oxford : New York: Oxford University Press.

Macy, J., and C. Johnstone. 2012. *Active Hope: How to Face the Mess We're in Without Going Crazy*. Novato: New World Library.

Martin, J. R. 1999. Grace: The Logogenesis of Freedom. *Discourse Studies* 1(1): 29–56. https://doi.org/10.1177/1461445699001001003.

Martin, J. R. 2004. Positive Discourse Analysis: Solidarity and Change. *Canarian Journal of English Studies* 49: 179–202.

Martin, J. R., and D. Rose. 2003. *Working with Discourse: Meaning Beyond the Clause*. London ; New York: Continuum.

Martin, J. R., and P. R. R. White. 2005. *The Language of Evaluation: Appraisal in English*. Basingstoke: Palgrave Macmillan.

McKay, Calum J., Carolin Sommer-Trembo, and Marcelo R. Sánchez-Villagra. 2022. The Portrayal of Animal Interactions in Nature Documentaries by David Attenborough and Bernhard Grzimek. *Evolution: Education and Outreach* 15(1): 15. https://doi.org/10.1186/s12052-022-00171-5.

Mead, Margaret. 1932. An Investigation of the Thought of Primitive Children, with Special Reference to Animism. *The Journal of the Royal Anthropological Institute of Great Britain and Ireland* 62: 173. https://doi.org/10.2307/2843884.

Meisner, Mark, and Bruno Takahashi. 2013. The Nature of Time: How the Covers of the World's Most Widely Read Weekly News Magazine Visualize Environmental Affairs. *Environmental Communication: A Journal of Nature and Culture* 7(2): 255–76. https://doi.org/10.1080/17524032.2013.772908.

Midgley, Mary. 2011. *The Myths We Live By*. New York: Routledge.

Milstein, Tema. 2007. Human Communication's Effects on Relationships with Animals. In M. Bekoff (ed.), *Encyclopedia of Human-Animal Relationships: A Global Exploration of Our Connections with Animals*, 1044–54. Westport: Greenwood Publishing Group.

Milstein, Tema. 2012. Banging on the Divide: Cultural Reflection and Refraction at the Zoo. In E. Plec (ed.), *Perspectives on Human-Animal Interaction: International Communication*, 162–81. London: Routledge.

Mills, B. 2015. Towards a Theory of Documentary Representation for Animals. *Screen* 56(1): 102–7. https://doi.org/10.1093/screen/hjv013.

Mitchell, L. 2012. Nonhumans and the Ideology of Purpose. *Anthrozoos: A Multidisciplinary Journal of the Interactions of People & Animals* 25(4): 491–502.

Mitchell, L. 2013. Farming: Animals or Machines? *Southern African Linguistics and Applied Language Studies* 31(3): 299–309. https://doi.org/10.2989/16073614.2013.837606.

Montevecchi, William A. 1976. Egg Size and the Egg Predatory Behaviour of Crows. *Behaviour* 57(3/4): 307–20.

Moe, Nelson J. 2002. The View from Vesuvius: Italian Culture and the Southern Question. 1st ed. Berkeley, CA: University of California Press.

Moral Nature | Darwin Correspondence Project [Internet]. [cited 2023 Jun 9]. https://www.darwinproject.ac.uk/learning/universities/darwin-and-human-nature/moral-nature.

Morris, T., P. V. Sundareshwar, C. T. Nietch, B. Kjerfve, and D. R. Cahoon. 2002. Responses of Coastal Wetlands to Rising Sea Level. *Ecology* 83(10): 2869–77.

Morton, L. W., J. Hobbs, and J. G. Arbuckle. 2013. Shifts in Farmer Uncertainty Over Time About Sustainable Farming Practices and Modern Farming's Reliance on Commercial Fertilizers, Insecticides, and Herbicides. *Journal of Soil and Water Conservation* 68(1): 1–12. https://doi.org/10.2489/jswc.68.1.1.

Mudu, P., B. Terracini, and M. Martuzzi. 2014. *Human Health in Areas with Industrial Contamination*. World Health Organization. Regional Office for Europe.

Munro, J. 1977. Crèche Formation in the Common Eider. *The Auk* 94(4): 759–71. https://doi.org/10.2307/4085272.

Musschenga, A. W. 2016. Moral Animals and Moral Responsibility. Ateliers. February 29; 10(2): 38–59.

Naess, Arne. 1973. The Shallow and the Deep, Long-Range Ecology Movement: A Summary. *Inquiry* 16(1–4): 95–100. https://doi.org/10.1080/00201747308601682.

Nature Conservancy Council. 1984. *Nature Conservation in Great Britain*. Peterborough: NCC.

Newell, Jay, Charles T. Salmon, and Susan Chang. 2006. The Hidden History of Product Placement. *Journal of Broadcasting & Electronic Media* 50(4): 575–94. https://doi.org/10.1207/s15506878jobem5004_1.

Nielsen, C., A. A. Agrawal, and A. E. Hajek. 2010. Ants Defend Aphids Against Lethal Disease. Biology Letters April 23; 6(2): 205–8.

Oddo, John. 2011. War Legitimation Discourse: Representing 'Us' and 'Them" in Four US Presidential Addresses. *Discourse & Society* 22(3): 287–314.

Oerlemans, Onno. 2002. *Romanticism and the Materiality of Nature*. Toronto; Buffalo: University of Toronto Press.

Ogaji, Joy. 2005. Sustainable Agriculture in the UK. *Environment, Development and Sustainability* 7(2): 253–70. https://doi.org/10.1007/s10668-005-7315-1.

Okri, B. 1996. *Birds of Heaven*. London: Phoenix.

Oktar, Lütfiye. 2001. The Ideological Organization of Representational Processes in the Presentation of Us and Them. *Discourse and Society* 12(3): 313–46.

Oliver, Mary Beth, Arthur A. Raney, and Jennings Bryant (eds.). 2019. *Media Effects*. 4th ed. New York: Routledge.

Omer, A., U. Pascual, and N. Russell. 2008. Biodiversity Conservation and Productivity in Intensive Agricultural Systems. In Andreas Kontoleon, Unai Pascual, and Melinda Smale (eds.), *Agrobiodiversity Conservation and Economic Development*, 137–60. London: Routledge.

O'Neill, Sean P. 2015. Sapir–Whorf Hypothesis. *The International Encyclopedia of Language and Social Interaction*: 1–10.

Oreskes, Naomi. 2004. The Scientific Consensus on Climate Change. *Science* 306(5702): 1686–86.

Orford, Jim. 2003. *Gambling and Problem Gambling in Britain: Hove, East Sussex*. New York: Brunner-Routledge.

Paek, Hye-Jin, and Zhongdang Pan. 2004. Spreading Global Consumerism: Effects of Mass Media and Advertising on Consumerist Values in China. *Mass Communication and Society* 7(4): 491–515. https://doi.org/10.1207/s15327825mcs0704_7.

Palmer, F. R. 2001. *Mood and Modality*. Cambridge: Cambridge University Press. https://doi.org/10.1017/CBO9781139167178.

Partington, Alan. 2004. Utterly Content in Each Other's Company. International Journal of Corpus Linguistics 9(1): 131–56. https://doi.org/10.1075/ijcl.9.1.07par.

Peggio, Eugenio, Mario Mazzarino, and Valentino Parlato. 1960. *Industrializzazione e sottosviluppo. Il progresso tecnologico in una provincia meridionale*. Torino: Einaudi.

Peters, Robert, and Joan Darling. 1985. The Greenhouse Effect and Nature Reserves. *BioScience* 35(11): 707–17.

Peterson Del Mar, David. 2014. *Environmentalism*. London and New York: Routledge.

Polkinghorne, D. E. 1988. *Narrative Knowing and the Human Sciences*. Albany: State University of New York Press.

Ponton, Douglas Mark. 2007. An End to Fox-Hunting: A Study of Consensus-Building in Parliamentary Rhetoric. In L. Jottini, G. Del Lungo, and J. Douthwaite (eds.), *Cityscapes: Islands of the Self*, 293–309. Cagliari: CUEC.

Ponton, Douglas Mark. 2014. Global Warming and the Role of Language in Social Transformation. *Language and Text* 2: 76–90.
Ponton, Douglas Mark. 2017. Persuasive Farce. Dialogical Pragmatics in the Novels of P.G. Wodehouse. University of Salento. https://doi.org/10.1285/i22390359v23p195.
Ponton, Douglas Mark. 2022a. *Ecolinguistics and Positive Discourse Analysis: Convergent Pathways*. MediAzioni A36-A54 Pages. https://doi.org/10.6092/ISSN.1974-4382/15506.
Ponton, Douglas Mark. 2022b. Shades of Green: Aspects of Dialogicity in Environmental Discourse. *International Review of Pragmatics* 14(2): 145–68. https://doi.org/10.1163/18773109-01402001.
Ponton, Douglas Mark. 2022c. Narratives of Industrial Damage and Natural Recovery: An Ecolinguistic Perspective. *Text & Talk* 42(4) (26 July): 475–97. https://doi.org/10.1515/text-2020-0079.
Ponton, Douglas Mark. 2023. Tourism and Natural Imaginary in Sicily: An Ecolinguistic Perspective. *Journal of World Languages*. https://doi.org/10.1515/jwl-2023-0008.
Ponton, Douglas Mark, and Dilyara Davletshina. 2022. Poems in Lockdown: Cultural Aspects of English and Russian "Coroneologisms". *Topics in Linguistics* 23: 24–38.
Ponton, Douglas Mark, and Małgorzata Sokół. 2022. Environmental Issues in the Anthropocene: Ecolinguistic Perspectives Across Media and Genres. *Text & Talk* 42(4): 445–51. https://doi.org/10.1515/text-2022-0040.
Praet, Istvan. 2014. *Animism and the Question of Life*. New York: Routledge.
Pretty, Jules. 2000. Towards Sustainable Food and Farming Systems in Industrialised Countries. *International Journal of Agricultural Resources, Governance and Ecology* 1(1): 77–94.
Prince, Gerald Joseph. 1973. *A Grammar of Stories*. The Hague: Mouton.
Prince, Gerald Joseph. 1982. *Narratology: The Form and Function of Narrative*. The Hague: Mouton.
Pusey, A. E., and C. Packer. 1994. Non-Offspring Nursing in Social Carnivores: Minimizing the Costs. *Behavioral Ecology* 5(4): 362–74. https://doi.org/10.1093/beheco/5.4.362.
Redondo, Ignacio, and Jorge Bernal. 2016. Product Placement Versus Conventional Advertising: The Impact on Brand Choice of Integrating Promotional Stimuli into Movies. *Journal of Promotion Management* 22(6): 773–91. https://doi.org/10.1080/10496491.2016.1214205.
Richardson, A. 2013. Becoming an Animal: Darwin and the Evolution of Sympathy. After darwin: Animals, Emotions, and the Mind. *BRILL*: 112–35.
Ricoeur, P. 1984. *Time and Narrative, 1, 2, 3*. Chicago: University of Chicago Press.
Ripple, W. J., C. Wolf, T. M. Newsome, M. Hoffmann, A. J. Wirsing, and D. J. McCauley. 2017. Extinction Risk Is Most Acute for the World's Largest and Smallest Vertebrates. *Proceedings of the National Academy of Sciences* 114(40): 10678–83.
Robinson, Jake M., Nick Gellie, Danielle MacCarthy, Jacob G. Mills, Kim O'Donnell, and Nicole Redvers. 2021. Traditional Ecological Knowledge in Restoration Ecology:

A Call to Listen Deeply, to Engage with, and Respect Indigenous Voices. *Restoration Ecology* 29(4). https://doi.org/10.1111/rec.13381.

Ross, D. 2019. Consciousness, Language, and the Possibility of Non-Human Personhood: Reflections on Elephants. *Journal of Consciousness Studies* 26(4): 227–51.

Rothenberg, David. 2005. *Why Birds Sing: A Journey into the Mystery of Birdsong*. New York: Basic Books.

Russell, Cristel. 2009. *Advertainment: Fusing Advertising and Entertainment*. William Davidson Institute: University of Michigan.

Salazar, Noel B. 2012. Tourism Imaginaries: A Conceptual Approach. *Annals of Tourism Research* 39(2): 863–82.

Saunders, Glen R., Matthew N. Gentle, and Christopher R. Dickman. 2010. The Impacts and Management of Foxes Vulpes Vulpes in Australia: Impact and Management of Foxes in Australia. *Mammal Review* 40(3): 181–211. https://doi.org/10.1111/j.1365-2907.2010.00159.x.

Schneider, J., and P. Schneider. 2006. Sicily: Reflections on Forty Years of Change. *Journal of Modern Italian Studies* 11(1): 61–83.

Schumacher, Ernst F. 1973. *Small is Beautiful: Economics as If People Mattered*. New York: Harper Collins.

Searle, John R. 1964. How to Derive 'Ought' From 'Is'. *The Philosophical Review* 73(1): 43. https://doi.org/10.2307/2183201.

Serpell, J. A. 1999. Sheep in Wolves' Clothing? Attitudes to Animals Among Farmers and Scientists. In F. L. Dolins (ed.), *Attitudes to Animals: Views in Animal Welfare*, 26–37. Cambridge: Cambridge University Press.

Seufert, Verena, Navin Ramankutty, and Tabea Mayerhofer. 2017. What Is This Thing Called Organic? – How Organic Farming Is Codified in Regulations. *Food Policy* 68: 10–20. https://doi.org/10.1016/j.foodpol.2016.12.009.

Sheail, John. 1995. Nature Protection, Ecologists and the Farming Context: A U.K. Historical Context. *Journal of Rural Studies* 11(1): 79–88. https://doi.org/10.1016/0743-0167(94)00038-B.

Shmelev, Stanislav E. 2012. *Ecological Economics: Sustainability in Practice*. Dordrecht, London and New York: Springer.

Soeder, Daniel J. 2020. *Fracking and the Environment: A Scientific Assessment of the Environmental Risks from hydraulic Fracturing and Fossil Fuels*. Springer Nature.

Sontag, S. 1973. *On Photography*. New York: Farrar, Straus & Giroux.

Sperber, Dan, and Deirdre Wilson. 1986. *Relevance: Communication and Cognition*. Oxford: Blackwell.

Steffen, Will, Crutzen Paul, and John McNeill. 2007. The Anthropocene: Are Humans Now Overwhelming the Great Forces of Nature? *AMBIO: A Journal of the Human Environment* 36(8): 614–21.

Steffen, W., A. Sanderson, P. D. Tyson, et al. 2004. *Global Change and the Earth System: A Planet Under Pressure*. The IBBP Book Series. Berlin, Heidelberg, New York: Springer Verlag.

Steffen, Will, et al. 2011. The Anthropocene: Conceptual and Historical Perspectives. *Philosophical Transactions of the Royal Society A: Mathematical, Physical and Engineering Sciences* 369(1938): 842–67.

Steffen, Will, Wendy Broadgate, Lisa Deutsch, Owen Gaffney, and Cornelia Ludwig. 2015. The Trajectory of the Anthropocene: The Great Acceleration. *The Anthropocene Review* 2(1): 81–98.

Stibbe, Arran. 2003. As Charming as a Pig: The Discursive Construction of the Relationship Between Pigs and Humans. *Society and Animals* 11(4): 375–92.

Stibbe, Arran. 2005. Chance Encounters: Ecology and Haiku-Inspired Photography. Stibbe, Arran, "Chance Encounters: Ecology and Haiku-Inspired Photography," The Haiku Foundation Digital Library. https://www.thehaikufoundation.org/omeka/items/show/6071. Accessed 6 March 2023.

Stibbe, Arran. 2007. Haiku and Beyond: Language, Ecology, and Reconnection with the Natural World. *Anthrozoös* 20(2): 101–12. https://doi.org/10.2752/175303707X207891.

Stibbe, Arran. 2012. *Animals Erased: Discourse, Ecology, and Reconnection with the Natural World*. Middletown: Wesleyan University Press.

Stibbe, Arran. 2014. An Ecolinguistic Approach to Critical Discourse Studies. *Critical Discourse Studies* 11(1): 117–28.

Stibbe, Arran. 2015. *Ecolinguistics: Language, Ecology and the Stories We Live By*. London; New York: Routledge, Taylor & Francis Group.

Stibbe, Arran. 2017. Positive Discourse Analysis: Re-thinking Human Ecological Relationships. In Alwyn Fill, and Hermine Penz (eds.), *The Routledge Handbook of Ecolinguistics*, 165–79. London: Routledge.

Stibbe, Arran. 2021. Ecolinguistics as a Transdisciplinary Movement and a Way of Life. In Burkette Allison, and Tamara Warhol (eds.), *Crossing Borders, Making Connections: Interdisciplinarity in Linguistics*, 71–88. Boston: Mouton.

Stringer, Martin D. 1999. Rethinking Animism: Thoughts from the Infancy of Our Discipline. *The Journal of the Royal Anthropological Institute* 5(4): 541. https://doi.org/10.2307/2661147.

Suzuki, Toshitaka N. 2016. Semantic Communication in Birds: Evidence from Field Research Over the Past Two Decades. *Ecological Research* 31(3): 307–19. https://doi.org/10.1007/s11284-016-1339-x.

Tawney, R. H. 1961. *Religion and the Rise of Capitalism; a Historical Study*. Harmondsworth: Penguin Books.

Taylor, Dorceta. 2014. *Toxic Communities: Environmental Racism, Industrial Pollution, and Residential Mobility*. New York & London: New York University Press.

Thibault, P. 2004. *Agency and Consciousness in Discourse: Self-Other Dynamics as a Complex System*. London and New York: Continuum.

Thompson, Tok. 2019. Listening to the Elder Brothers: Animals, Agents, and Posthumanism in Native Versus Non-Native American Myths and Worldviews. *Folklore: Electronic Journal of Folklore* 77: 159–80. https://doi.org/10.7592/FEJF2019.77.thompson.

Tillyard, Eustace Mandeville Wetenhall. 1960. *The Elizabethan World Picture: A Study of the Idea of Order in the Age of Shakespeare, Donne and Milton*. New York: Random House.

Timmons Roberts, J. 2001. Global Inequality and Climate Change. *Society & Natural Resources* 14(6): 501–9.

Tinbergen, Nikolaas. 1989. *The Study of Instinct*. Oxford: Clarendon Press.

Toohey, Peter. 1996. *Epic Lessons: An Introduction to Ancient Didactic Poetry*. London and New York: Routledge.

Trainer, Ted. 2012. De-growth: Do You Realise What It Means? *Futures* 44(6): 590–99.

Trautmann, N. M., K. S. Porter, and R. J. Wagenet. 2015. *Modern Agriculture: Its Effects on the Environment*. Ithaca: Cornell Cooperative Extension, Pesticide Safety Education Program.

Trewavas, Anthony. 2004. A Critical Assessment of Organic Farming-and-Food Assertions with Particular Respect to the UK and the Potential Environmental Benefits of No-Till Agriculture. *Crop Protection* 23(9): 757–81.

Trimboli, S. 2004. *Industrializzazione ed evoluzione del movimento sindacale nel comprensorio di Milazzo [Industrialization and development of the trade union movement in the area of Milazzo]*. Milazzo: Il Punto (in Italian).

Tudorache, Daniela, and Luminița Leocadia Sàrbu. 2013. World Promotion of Organic Farming. *Economic Engineering in Agriculture and Rural Development* 13(4): 291–94.

Uscinski, Joseph E., and Santiago Olivella. 2017. The Conditional Effect of Conspiracy Thinking on Attitudes Toward Climate Change. *Research & Politics* 4(4): 2053168017743105.

Usubiaga-Liaño, A., G. M. Mace, and P. Ekins. 2019. Limits to Agricultural Land for Retaining Acceptable Levels of Local Biodiversity. *Natural Sustainability* 2: 491–98.

Väliverronen, E. 1998. Biodiversity and the Power of Metaphor in Environmental Discourse. *Science Studies* 11(1): 19–34.

Van Dijk, T. A. 1997. Cognitive Context Models and Discourse. In M. Stamenov (ed.), *Language Structure, Discourse and the Access to Consciousness*, 189–226. Amsterdam: John Benjamins.

Van Dijk, T. A. 2001. Critical Discourse Analysis. https://semiotics.nured.uowm.gr/pdfs/Critical_discourse_analysis_TEUN_A_VAN_DIJK.pdf. Retrieved 21 March 2023.

Van Leeuwen, Theo. 1996. The Representation of Social Actors. In M. Coulthard, and C. R. Caldas-Coulthard (eds.), *Texts and Practices: Readings in Critical Discourse Analysis*, 32–70. London and New York: Routledge.

Varah, A., H. Jones, J. Smith, and S. G. Potts. 2013. Enhanced Biodiversity and Pollination in UK Agroforestry Systems. *Journal of the Science of Food and Agriculture* 93(9): 2073–5.

Vasta, Nicoletta. 2005. Profits and Principles: Is There a Choice? The Multimodal Construction of SHELL's Commitment to Corporate Social Responsibility and the

Environment in and Across Advertising Texts. In G. Cortese, and A. Duszak (eds.), *Identity, Community, Discourse: English in Intercultural Settings*, 429–52. Bern: Peter Lang.

Verhagen, F. 2008. Worldviews and Metaphors in the Human-Nature Relationship: An Ecolinguistic Exploration Through the Ages. *Language & Ecology*. www.ecoling.net/articles. Retrieved 20 February 2023.

Virtanen, Tuija, and Helena Halmari. 2005. Persuasion across Genres: Emerging Perspectives. In Helena Halmari, and Tuija Virtanen (eds.), *Persuasion Across Genres: A Linguistic Approach*, 130, 3–24. Pragmatics & Beyond New Series. Amsterdam: John Benjamins Publishing Company. https://doi.org/10.1075/pbns.130.03vir.

Wang, Yunyun, and Guangwei Hu. 2023. Shell Noun Phrases in Scientific Writing: A Diachronic Corpus-Based Study on Research Articles in Chemical Engineering. English for Specific Purposes 71(July): 178–90. https://doi.org/10.1016/j.esp.2023.05.001.

Waugh, Linda R., Theresa Catalano, Khaled Al Masaeed, Tom Hong Do, and Paul G. Renigar. 2016. Critical Discourse Analysis: Definition, Approaches, Relation to Pragmatics, Critique, and Trends. In Alessandro Capone, and Jacob L. Mey (eds.), *Interdisciplinary Studies in Pragmatics, Culture and Society*, 71–137. Heidelberg, New York, Dordrecht and London: Springer.

Wei, R., and Z. Pan. 1999. Mass Media and Consumerist Values in the People's Republic of China. *International Journal of Public Opinion Research* 11(1): 75–96.

White, Cameron, John L. Oliffe, and Joan L. Bottorff. 2012. From the Physician to the Marlboro Man: Masculinity, Health, and Cigarette Advertising in America, 1946–1964. *Men and Masculinities* 15(5): 526–47. https://doi.org/10.1177/1097184X12461917.

Widdowson, H. G. 2004. *Text, Context, Pretext: Critical Issues in Discourse Analysis*. Malden: Blackwell Pub.

Wierzbicka, A. 1994. Cultural Scripts: A Semantic Approach to Cultural Analysis and Cross-Cultural Communication. *Pragmatics and Language Learning* 5: 1–24.

Wierzbicka, A. 2002. Russian Cultural Scripts: The Theory of Cultural Scripts and Its Applications. *Ethos* 30(4): 401–32.

Williams, Raymond. 1975. *The Country and the City*. Oxford: Oxford University Press.

Williams, D. R., M. Clark, G. M. Buchanan, et al. 2021. Proactive Conservation to Prevent Habitat Losses to Agricultural Expansion. *Nature Sustainsbility* 4: 314–22.

Wilson, Deirdre, and Dan Sperber. 2015. Outline of Relevance Theory. *HERMES - Journal of Language and Communication in Business* 3(5): 35. https://doi.org/10.7146/hjlcb.v3i5.21436.

Winter, Eugene O. 1977. A Clause-Relational Approach to English Texts: A Study of Some Predictive Lexical Items in Written Discourse. *Instructional Science* 6(1): 1–92.

Withers, Paul J. A., Colin Neal, Helen P. Jarvie, and Donnacha G. Doody. 2014. Agriculture and Eutrophication: Where Do We Go from Here? *Sustainability* 6, no. 9: 5853–75.

Wood, Alistair. 2001. International Scientific English: The Language of Research Scientists Around the World. In *Research Perspectives on English for Academic Purposes*, 71–83. Cambridge University Press. https://doi.org/10.1017/CBO9781139524766.008.

Wong-Parodi, Gabrielle, and Irina Feygina. 2021. Engaging People on Climate Change: The Role of Emotional Responses. *Environmental Communication* 15(5): 571–93.

Woodcock, Ben A., Nicholas J. B. Isaac, James M. Bullock, David B. Roy, David G. Garthwaite, Andrew Crowe, and Richard F. Pywell. 2016. Impacts of Neonicotinoid Use on Long-Term Population Changes in Wild Bees in England. *Nature Commununication* 7. https://doi.org/10.1038/ncomms12459.

Zhang, Xiaochen. 2011. Communicating Coffee Culture Through the Big Screen: Starbucks in American Movies. *Comparative American Studies An International Journal* 9(1): 68–84. https://doi.org/10.1179/147757011X12983070064953.

Zhou, Wenjuan. 2022. Ecolinguistics: A Half-Century Overview. *Journal of World Languages* 7(3): 461–86. https://doi.org/10.1515/jwl-2021-0022.

Zemanek, Evi. 2022. Between Fragility and Resilience: Ambivalent Images of Nature in Popular Documentaries with David Attenborough. *The Anthropocene Review* 9(2): 139–60. https://doi.org/10.1177/20530196221093477.

Index

advertising 24, 59, 60
Aesop 44, 45, 156
agriculture 2, 37–40, 67, 68, 73–5, 78, 99, 155
animals 7, 16, 18–22, 25, 28, 39–42, 52, 54, 56, 67, 68, 77, 84, 85, 93, 97, 110, 113, 114, 119, 143, 155, 160
Anthropocene/ic 17, 35, 134
ants 1, 44, 65, 66, 80–90, 96, 97, 113, 144–6, 149, 159
Appraisal 55–7, 83, 84, 136, 138, 139
Aristotle 22, 43, 92
Attenborough, Sir David 67, 77, 97, 157

BBC, the 1, 2, 46, 50, 53, 65, 97, 156–8
Benadusi, Mara 101, 104–6, 109, 110
Berlin, Isaiah 6
biodiversity xii, 26, 39, 63, 66–8, 73–6, 95, 109, 131, 143
biosphere 17, 34, 35, 68, 73, 94, 110
butterflies 1, 5, 66
buzzards 1, 51, 66

capitalism 3, 4, 17, 61, 66, 134, 135, 139, 143, 146, 148
Carson, Rachel 5, 37, 39, 155
Catania 2, 99, 101
Chris Skinner 1, 65, 77, 80, 96, 112, 118, 123
climate change 25, 30, 35, 36, 54, 133, 135–8, 140–2
Countryside Hour 1, 46, 50, 65, 77, 78, 80, 81, 83, 84, 86–8, 94, 118, 156, 159
critical discourse analysis (CDA) 8–10, 13, 30–3, 40, 58, 61, 103, 131, 132

Darwin, Charles 85, 159
discourse analysis 50
  positive xii, 29–31, 132, 142
drone 111, 114–18

Ecology 15, 25, 30, 58, 73
  Deep ecology 17, 19, 142
  Shallow ecology 17, 19
economic growth 1, 32, 33, 57, 61, 62, 105
ecosophy xii, 34, 63, 72, 96
ecosystems xi–xiii, 1, 2, 22, 23, 26, 32, 33, 37, 67, 74, 76, 105, 117
Enel 105–10
evaluation 3, 46, 47, 51–7, 70, 71, 78–81, 83–8, 91, 103, 104, 107–9, 115, 117, 120–2, 127, 128, 130, 136–8, 145

Fabio Cilea xii, 105, 110, 111, 114, 118, 143, 150
flagship species xiii, 110, 131
flamingos xiii, 2, 105–11, 113–20, 123, 126, 127, 131, 132, 143, 144
foxes 39–41, 43, 66, 67, 144
framing 51, 53, 60–2, 79, 80, 82, 86, 88, 107, 108, 134

Greta Thunberg 32, 34, 35
growthism xii, xiii, 4, 15, 32, 134, 146, 154

habitats 2, 5, 29, 67, 74–7, 106
Halliday, M. A. K. 6, 7, 15–17, 29, 62, 148
Hawaiian 18, 19, 28, 54, 96
health 6, 8, 17, 24, 25, 37–9, 42, 63, 75, 100, 101, 143, 156
High Ash Farm xi, xii, 1–3, 65, 66, 68, 69, 71–3, 78, 80, 90, 91, 96, 142, 143
human existence 1, 36, 43

ideology 6, 15, 22, 26, 58, 146, 155
industrial activity 1, 5, 57
instinct 86, 113, 150, 160, 161

Konrad Lorenz 20, 160

Labov, William   46, 47, 52, 57, 81, 87, 108

Martin, James   31, 32, 40, 53, 55, 133
  and White, Peter   55–7, 71, 81, 83, 84, 93–5, 128, 135, 157
meat   20, 21, 67, 136, 137
metaphor   8, 10, 13, 15, 16, 21–3, 43, 48, 53, 86, 130, 155
modernity   3, 9, 11, 60, 97, 123

Naess, Arne   17, 27, 97
narrative   43–6, 50, 53, 58, 60, 69, 71, 72, 78, 80, 81, 85–7, 89, 91, 92, 107, 108, 117, 120, 121, 125, 127, 132, 135, 144, 145, 148, 149, 161
natural world   2, 3, 5–7, 9, 15, 17, 19, 20, 23, 25, 27, 29, 36, 51, 52, 60, 63, 67, 73, 75, 83, 86, 118, 120, 125, 142, 145, 147, 153
  relations with   1, 58, 66, 82, 94, 97, 144, 146, 148, 150, 151
nature reserve   xii, 2, 105, 108–10

orientation   57, 70, 81, 84, 92, 114, 119, 126
Orwell, George   8–11, 13, 14, 141, 153
Orwellian   11, 13, 41, 67, 158, 160

Packham, Chris   67, 97, 157
planet   16, 133, 135, 136, 138–42
poetry   6, 8, 19, 27, 28, 40, 43–5
politician   13, 14, 126, 127, 130
pragmatics   48–50, 53, 56, 115, 156

Priolo Gargallo   2, 100, 101, 106, 108, 109, 126–8, 130
Priolo Saltpans   xi–xiii, 2, 65, 99, 105–6, 109, 111, 114–5, 117–8, 120, 142, 143, 160

Relevance Theory   49, 50, 53, 143
religion   4, 17, 25

Sicily   xi, xiii, 2, 65, 99, 100, 105, 114–17, 126, 142, 150, 161
Silent Spring   5, 37
Siracusa   2, 105, 128
skylark   69, 70, 72
species loss   3, 5, 33, 35
Sperber, Dan   49, 50, 89
Stibbe, Arran   7, 8, 19, 21–3, 27, 32, 57, 58, 60–3
stories   18, 32, 43, 45, 47, 50, 52, 58, 59, 80, 99, 110, 115, 119, 120, 124, 143–6, 148, 156
  stories we live by   xii, 7, 58, 60, 63, 98
sustainable farming   xii, 66

tourism   36, 100, 126, 128, 129, 131
toxic   xiii, 2, 17, 35, 67, 101, 107, 128, 132, 143, 146
turtles   28, 54–7, 126, 144, 157

Wilson, Deirdre   49, 50, 89
wisdom   xiii, 6, 22, 44, 45, 52, 118
Wordsworth, William   27, 28, 97

www.ingramcontent.com/pod-product-compliance
Lightning Source LLC
Chambersburg PA
CBHW070724020526
44116CB00031B/1745